Fundamentals of Digital Forensics

Joakim Kävrestad

Fundamentals of Digital Forensics

Theory, Methods, and Real-Life Applications

Second Edition

Joakim Kävrestad
School of Informatics
University of Skövde
Skövde, Sweden

ISBN 978-3-030-38953-6 ISBN 978-3-030-38954-3 (eBook)
https://doi.org/10.1007/978-3-030-38954-3

This Springer imprint is published by the registered company Springer Nature Switzerland AG.
The registered company address is: Gewerbestrasse 11, 6330 Cham, Switzerland

Preface

Overview and Audience

Fundamentals of Digital Forensics: Theory, Methods, and Real-Life Applications presents and discusses the fundamental building blocks of computer forensics in a practical and accessible manner. Building on *Guide to Digital Forensics: A Concise and Practical Introduction*, it presents a theoretical background discussing forensic methods, artifacts, and constraints primarily relating to computer forensic examinations in the context of crime investigations. Furthermore, it discusses artifacts and methodologies, in a practical manner, that introduce forensic tools commonly used in forensic examinations in law enforcement as well as in the corporate sector.

This book was written to fulfill a need for a book that introduces forensic methodology and sound forensic thinking combined with hands-on examples for common tasks in a computer forensic examination. The author of *Fundamentals of Digital Forensics* has several years of experience as a computer forensic examiner with the Swedish Police and is certified as an AccessData examiner. He currently works as a university-level lecturer and researcher in the domain and as a forensic consultant. To further ensure that the content provided in this book is relevant and accurate in the real world, the book has been developed in close relation with the Skövde Office of the Swedish Police in general and with Jan-Åke Pettersson in particular, for which the author is extremely thankful. *Fundamentals of Digital Forensics* is intended for students that are looking for an introduction to computer forensics and can also be used as a collection of instructions for practitioners. The aim is to describe and explain the steps taken during a forensic examination with the intent of making the reader aware of the constraints and considerations that apply during a forensic examination in law enforcement and in the private sector. Upon reading this book, the reader should have a proper overview of the field of digital forensics and be able as well as motivated to start the journey of becoming a computer forensic expert!

Following the first edition of this book, this second edition has been updated with more material covering incident response practices and tasks. It has also been partly rewritten following student feedback, and on that note, a special thanks to Marcus Birath for the much appreciated proofreading!

Motivation and Features

This is a book written for the sole reason that when I wanted to hold a course on digital forensics, I could not find a textbook that seemed to fulfill my requirements. What I needed a book to cover was the following:

- Sound forensic thinking and methodology
- A discussion on what computer forensics can assist with
- Hands-on examples

My answer to my own needs was, well, to write my own book. It has become obvious to me that writing a book that fulfills those demands is not a very easy task. The main problem lies within making proper hands-on examples. For that reason, I decided to put emphasis on what digital forensics is at its very core, and to make this piece of literature relevant worldwide, I have tried to omit everything that only seems relevant in a certain legislation. That being said, this is the book for you if you want to get an introduction to what computer forensics is and what it can and cannot do. It did feel good to use some sort of well-known forensic software for the examples in this book. Since forensic software can be quite expensive, I decided to use two options interchangeably. The first collection of tools are the proprietary AccessData Forensic Toolkit, which was chosen for the sole reason that AccessData provided the ability to get certified, free of charge, at the time of writing. Using the predecessor of this book in teaching shows that this book can in fact be used to prepare for the AccessData certification test. Further, this book uses a collection of various open source or otherwise free tools that can accomplish the same as the proprietary AccessData tools.

This book begins with setting the stage for forensics examinations by discussing the theoretical foundation that the author regards as relevant and important for the area. This section will introduce the reader to the areas of computer forensics and forensic methodology as well as will discuss on how to find and interpret certain artifacts in a Windows environment. The book will then take a more practical turn and discuss hows and whys about some key forensic concepts. Finally, the book will provide a section with information on how to find and interpret several artifacts. It should at this point be noticed that the book does not, by far, cover every single case, question, or artifact. Practical examples are rather here to serve as demonstrations of how to implement a forensically sound way of examining digital evidence and use forensic tools. Throughout the book, you will find real-world examples applicable in a real-world setting.

Since most computers targeted for a forensic examination are running some version of Windows, the examples and demonstrations in this book are presented in a Windows environment. Being the most recent version of Windows, Windows

10 was used. However, the information should to a very large extent be applicable for the previous version of Windows.

In this second volume, more content describing digital forensics in the corporate secure has been added, introducing incident response work in a reasonable manner. Furthermore, the chapters on memory analysis have been greatly rewritten to include more practices and tools.

Also, most chapters in this book come with a “Questions and Tasks” section. Some are questions with a right or wrong answer, and some are of more exploratory nature. Whatever the case, answers or discussions are found in Appendix A—Solutions. Complementing the book, there are video lectures covering most of the book content in YouTube: https://www.youtube.com/playlist?list=PLEjQDf4Fr75pBnu8WArpeZTKC9-LrYDTl.

Happy reading!

Skövde, Sweden Joakim Kävrestad

Contents

Part IV Memory Forensics

Part I
Theory

Now that the book has kept you interested this far, it is time to discuss what digital forensics actually is. This will be done in a very theoretical manner, but I have tried to keep it short. This part begins with an overview of what digital forensics and cybercrime is, before discussing some ethical aspects of forensic examinations and crime prevention in the digital world. Then, some computer theory that is necessary for a forensic examiner to be familiar with will be presented. The part ends with a chapter that introduces how to find and interpret forensic artifacts that the author deems to be common and important.

What Is Digital Forensics?

1

So then, what is digital forensics? Well, the simplest explanation could be that it is the examination of digital storage and digital environments in order to determine what has happened. "What has happened" in this context could be whether or not a crime was committed, whether or not someone remote controlled a certain computer, when a picture was taken, or if a computer was subject to intrusion. That being said, it can be basically anything.

However, looking at the target of some actual forensic investigations, it is evident that saying "What has happened" is not covering the entire field of computer forensics since forensic examiners also look into what is currently happening. There have, for instance, been several cases in Sweden and globally were forensic examiners monitored network traffic in order to capture data that was later used to identify sexual predators. There are also situations when forensic examiners, during house searches, record what is currently happening on a computer. The case of using digital forensics to monitor activity in real time may be even more apparent in the corporate world where it is common to examine intrusion attempts and malware behaviors as it is happening.

Looking to the scientific community, Reith et al. (2002) described digital forensics in the following way:

> Digital forensics is a relatively new science. Derived as a synonym for computer forensics, its definition has expanded to include the forensics of all digital technology, whereas computer forensics is defined as "the collection of techniques and tools used to find evidence in a computer"

Today, this definition seems a bit old, but it does hold a few key aspects. To begin with, it describes that computer forensics is a collection of techniques and tools. While those are defiantly two important aspects, this definition does not fit my personal beliefs as it kind of omits the methodology and mind-set that, for me, is the foundation of digital forensics. However, it does capture that digital forensics

J. Kävrestad, *Fundamentals of Digital Forensics*,
https://doi.org/10.1007/978-3-030-38954-3_1

extends to all digital technology, and that is an important aspect as today, important evidence may be found in everything from thumb drives to computers or the cloud.

A more recent description is found on www.forensiccontrol.com (2017):

> Computer forensics is the practice of collecting, analyzing and reporting on digital data in a way that is legally admissible. It can be used in the detection and prevention of crime and in any dispute where evidence is stored digitally. Computer forensics follows a similar process to other forensic disciplines, and faces similar issues.

What is noticeable in this description is that it determines the tasks involved during a forensic investigation: collecting, analyzing, and reporting. It also describes that computer forensics is comparable to other forensic disciplines, and that does suggest that methods used and conclusions drawn during a computer forensic investigation should face the same scrutiny as an analysis of a fingerprint or DNA test. The rest of the section will discuss each of these, beginning with establishing a model that could be used to describe a digital forensic examination.

1.1 A Forensic Examination

As we just established, the foundation of digital forensics is that it is the practice of collecting, analyzing, and reporting on digital data. It does, for sure, also impose that there is some data that we target for examination and a reason for the examination. It does also impose that, unless we do the examination for the fun of it, there is someone that we should report back to. I have collected those aspects and formed the very abstract model shown in Fig. 1.1 that attempts to summarize the named aspects in a graphical way.

Figure 1.1 reflects the discussed processes and the inputs or outputs that should be present in each process. From top to bottom, *Collect* should be the process of collecting digital evidence. I would also say that in this process you do target a person or a data source, which would commonly be a device.

Having a person as a target would be the normal state in a criminal investigation where you have someone that is suspected of a crime. You would then, after getting a search warrant, start searching for devices that belong to the suspect. In a corporate setting, it could be more common to target a device rather than a person, and it would all depend on the reason for doing the investigation.

In this process, it is important to mention that in order to collect the correct data, you need a proper order. The order in this case would include the target person or devices to collect data from, but it should also include the reason for the investigation, at least on an abstract level. This is because you would look for vastly different data sources if you are investigating a suspected malware attack of a child abuse case. It is also important to know if you should prepare to collect information from volatile data sources such as memory circuits or if you only need to care about static media such as hard drives. Another technical consideration is if you should expect encrypted data or not. While there will be a more detailed technical discussion on data collection later in this book, in Chap. 3, it is important to mention that you need

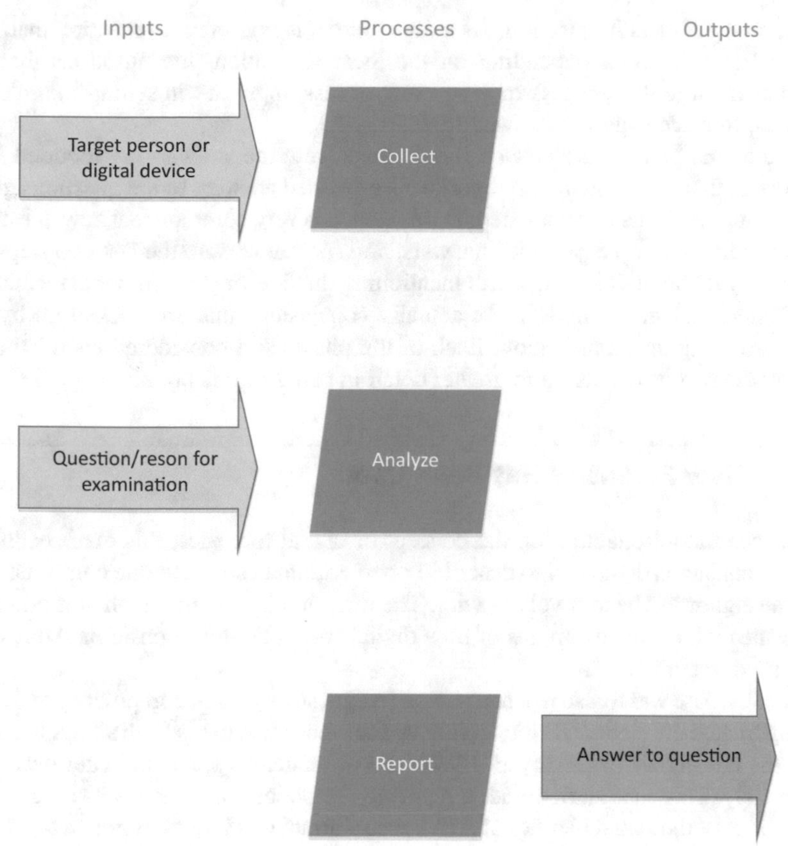

Fig. 1.1 Overview of forensic processes

to come prepared. The preparation steps should help you determine what to expect and should at least include figuring out the reason for the forensic examination and a background check on the person from whom you are collecting data.

The process of *Analyzing* data is more concerned with finding out what has happened in a digital environment or what was done using a digital device. In a corporate environment, a forensic expert would normally be quite free to conduct whatever examinations she wants, guided of course by agreements. However, with a precise question, the examination will without doubt be more efficient. It is worth mentioning that the input to this phase is commonly found in a discussion between the person ordering the examination and the forensic expert. Also, it is common that new questions and follow-up questions will arise during the investigation. As one example, during an investigation of a computer during a drug case, the initial request was to find out if the computer had been involved in any activities related to selling drugs online. The investigation clearly showed that it had been, but a large portion of the evidence was found in folders shared among several computers. In this case, a follow-up question was to determine who, more than the computer owner, had access to the folders in question. As a final note, it is important to mention that, in a criminal investigation, depending on the local legislation, the questions that are taken as input to this process may be more or less important in setting the rules of what the forensic expert is allowed to do.

In the final process, *Reporting*, the findings from the analysis are reported. The purpose of this step is mainly to report well-grounded answers to the questions given to the examiner in the previous step. In this step, it is very common that new questions will arise in light of the provided answers, and for that reason, the last two steps are commonly iterative. It is also worth mentioning that it is of great importance that the conclusions drawn in this step are actually conclusions that are backed up by the findings during the examination. Each of the phases and considerations relating to each phase will be discussed in greater detail in part 2 of this book.

1.2 How Forensics Has Been Used

To deepen the introduction on the concept of digital forensics, this final section of the first chapter is dedicated to describing two criminal cases and one corporate case that the author has been involved with. The intention is to continue the introduction to the area with some examples of how digital forensics and forensic methods have been used in reality.

The first case was a case where a person (A) got suspected of computer intrusion by having tricked the victim (B) into giving up the credentials to his Web site. A had then used the credentials to modify B's Web site in malicious ways and later destroy it completely. This case started with a report to the police, and since B has very good indications of the actual identity of A, a house warrant was issued, A got arrested, and his computers got seized. In this case, the forensic examination was done by the author of this book. What is interesting about this case is that the police investigators did not know anything about computer crimes and the forensic examiner had to assume the role of co-investigator. In the first interrogations with A, it became evident that A had been in contact with B using chat clients. As such, the first forensic task was to map the communication between A and B by searching for usernames related to B. The result of this process was that it became evident that A had contacted B and said that he was a Web designer who offered to aid B with his Web site. After some communication, A managed to trick B into giving away the credentials to said Web site.

The second step in the forensic examination was to actually find evidence of A being involved in the malicious modifications to B's Web site. In this case, searching for URLs and HTML code related to B's Web site revealed that there were modified versions of B's Web site located on A's computer. Moreover, one of the modifications to B's site involved including pictures with sexual content on the Web site. By using forensic tools to search for identical pictures, it was revealed that the pictures did not only reside on A's computer but was also taken with A's iPhone, resulting in A being convicted of computer intrusion.

Another criminal case where the forensic involvement was much smaller but played an important role was in a murder case where the suspect had shot a person. There were some pieces of evidence pointing to the suspect, but he was given alibi by his girlfriend who said that he was at home at the time of the crime. Home in this case was about 90 min away from the murder site, by car. In this case, the suspect's telephone was examined, and the IMEI number of the phone was identified. It was then possible to get records displaying what IMEI numbers had been connected to the mobile towers in close proximity to the murder site at the time of the murder. Turning out, the suspect's phone was connected to a mobile tower very close to the murder site, at the time when he said that he was at home. This was a key piece of evidence that led to the suspect being sentenced to lifetime in prison for murder.

A final example from the corporate sector was a case when an employee of a company was suspected of placing a Trojan horse in the company network. The employment had been terminated, and the suspicion was that the employee had placed a Trojan horse to get back at the company for sacking him. The Trojan horse was detected and analyzed by the company's IT department, and it was evident that it was configured to send information to an IP address located close to where the former employee lived. Since search warrants and tracing IP addresses are off limits for companies, other actions had to be taken. After careful examination of how the Trojan horse got inserted into the network, it seems as if it had been copied from a USB stick. It was also possible to determine the unique identifier for the USB stick.

A USB device that was issued by the company and used by the employee was examined, and the unique identifier was the same as for the USB stick that was used to distribute the malware. When the employee was confronted with the evidence, he admitted to having injected the Trojan horse, and a civil lawsuit was filed.

1.3 Questions and Tasks

Here are the questions for the first chapter, and for these questions, you may benefit from answering them in a group discussion!

1. Consider in what types of criminal investigations that computer forensic experts may be involved and in what way.
2. Consider when a computer forensic expert may be needed in a corporate environment.
3. Brainstorm on what types of devices may be interesting to a computer forensic expert.
4. To whom are the findings of a computer forensic examination of interest?

References

Forensic Control (2017) Beginners guide to computer forensics. Available online: https://forensiccontrol.com/resources/beginners-guide-computer-forensics/ (Fetched: 2017–07-06)

Reith M, Carr C, Gunsch G (2002) An examination of digital forensic models. Int J Digit Evid 1 (3):1–12

2 Ethics and Integrity

As you will come to understand during this book, any forensic examination is essentially about digging around in the data on some digital device that belongs to somebody. Seeing as how we spend more and more time online using various devices, a person's whole life can exist in their device. Thus, any forensic examination is a breach of privacy. This privacy breach is commonly motivated by the need of solving crimes or investigating computer-related incidents, and perhaps rightfully so. However, while we need to conduct forensic examinations in many situations, we shall do so while understanding how what we do affect the people concerned. In a short sentence, forensic examinations should be carried out with integrity in mind and following reasonable ethical guidelines. This chapter provides a short discussion on ethical considerations in regard to digital forensics and highlights some contemporary examples where crime prevention and integrity are in direct conflict. The chapter concludes with suggestions for ethical guidelines derived from ethics in research and the forensics community.

While it is easy, and quite common, to adopt a "suit yourself" approach to the integrity of suspects, that mind-set is very narrow and problematic in reality. As a very important and first rule of thumb, almost any democratic country adopts an "innocent until proven guilty" approach in their legal systems. As such, anyone that is being investigated should be treated as an innocent up to the point when a verdict is expressed in court. It is therefore important to maintain the integrity of any suspect during the course of an investigation. There have been numerous examples throughout the world where, for instance, the name of a suspect has been disclosed to the public, even if the suspect was later declared innocent. At several such occasions, the consequences for the suspect have been dire; there are examples of suspects even being killed. Moving away from the suspects, one should also understand that a criminal investigation is commonly extended to cover not only devices owned by the suspects but also devices belonging to others. Depending on the nature of the case, devices owned by relatives and friends to the suspects or even witnesses that happened to be in the wrong place at the wrong time may have their devices seized. Those devices can hold anything from social media account, chat with loved ones,

J. Kävrestad, *Fundamentals of Digital Forensics*,
https://doi.org/10.1007/978-3-030-38954-3_2

medical history, or pictures of all sorts. Having that material looked at by someone unknown is a huge breach of privacy and should not be taken lightly by the forensic examiners.

We have been discussing ethics of digital forensics as a topic of importance in criminal investigations. It is, of course, equally important in corporate forensics. In a corporate environment, it is more common to employ forensic techniques to examine a computer intrusion or perhaps a corporate espionage. That does not change the fact that the devices that are being examined will be devices that are used by someone and very likely to contain personal data. A company may or may not employ policies against personal use of company resources. However, even if such a policy is in place, one can assume to find personal information originating from social media, online banking, or whatever. Very well, to summarize, any forensic examination is by definition a breach of someone's privacy. While that breach is sometimes necessary, it should not be taken lightly by forensic examiner. The rest of this chapter will exemplify how different societies see the trade-off between crime prevention capabilities and integrity and conclude with a discussion on ethical guidelines.

2.1 Tracing Online Users

The first example is concerned with tracing online users or rather the ability of law enforcements to track the user of an IP address. A little bit simplified, computers use addresses whenever communicating online, and those are called IP addresses. Any device that communicates online must have a unique IP address, and it is often possible to learn the IP address behind an action online, such as an e-mail, online purchase, or chat message. Thus, a very common entry point for the police is an IP address tied to a suspected crime, and if the police can find the user of the IP address, it is a good start on the road toward solving the crime. All good so far, however there is a caveat. Internet is to a very large extent built on IPv4 addressing that can provide a bit over four billion addresses, but there are more devices than that. Since every device needs a unique address, that is cause for a problem. The problems are solved using various techniques called NAT (Network Address Translation) that essentially lets several users use the same IP address and effectively setting the uniqueness out of play and limiting the police's ability to track the user behind an IP address.

One way of managing the issue can be to force all Internet service providers (ISP) to keep track of the actual user behind an IP address. In technical terms, log when the shared IP address is used and by who. If that is done, the police can simply ask the ISP who used the IP address at a particular point in time, and case is closed. This approach was previously used in Sweden but was declared invalid by the European court in 2016 (The European Court 2016). To back the tape a bit, the Swedish approach was to force ISP's to store the information needed for tracing IP addresses for 6 months. The information that was stored included information about what user that used an IP address and at what time. The reasoning behind the court's ruling was that storing information about every uses was a breach of integrity that could not be motivated with the benefits for law enforcement. What is true and correct is not a discussion to be held in this book, so this example will end here.

2.2 Key Disclosure Law(s)

Encryption, further described in REFTEXT, is the act of making data unreadable without the correct key. As such, it is a widely used technique that makes forensic examinations very hard (Vincze 2016). While using various attacks on seized devices is widely accepted as forensic techniques, and asking the owner of a device to give up the keys willingly is common practice, several governments are designing laws to force suspects to give up their encryption keys or face prosecution for the act of keeping the data encrypted and out of the authorities' reach. There are several different ways to implement this kind of law where one is to force a suspect to give up encryption keys and another is to force the suspect to decrypt encrypted data.

While a key disclosure law would, undeniably, be helpful for law enforcement, it is not blindly accepted by the public. Looking at recent debates, in, for instance, Australia, there are at least three big objections. First, and perhaps most relevant from an ethical perspective, critics claim that a key disclosure law is in conflict with the right to not self-incriminate that is used as a fundamental legal principle in many democratic countries. Essentially, the right to not self-incriminate means that a suspect should not be forced to actions that can generate evidence against her, or as everyone heard from American police series such as the CSI or Miami Vice:

> You *[the suspect]* have the right to remain silent. Anything you say or do can and will be held against you in a court of law (FANDOM 2019).

Other objections are the very real possibility of someone forgetting their passwords; what would happen in that case? Or what would happen if a suspect just refuses to hand out his password? A concrete example can be found in Crimes Act 1914 by the Australian Government (2015) that states that a police can get magistrate's order to make someone give out encryption keys. Failing to comply with such an order can result in imprisonment for 2 years. The consequence is worth contemplating on: what would happen if someone that actually committed a murder and the evidence is on his encrypted computer is given such an order? He would most likely accept his 2 years in prison and move on in happiness. The moral of the argument is that a common objection is that having minor consequences will lead to a law that is only efficient against low rank crimes and is therefore unnecessary. And again, what will happen if the key is just forgotten? It would seem harsh to get 2 years in prison for forgetting a password.

Before leaving the topic of key disclosure laws, it should be mentioned that Australia quite recently took a step further. With a new law, the Australian government can now order companies to create technical functions that can give them access to encrypted user information without the user's knowledge. To exemplify, services such as Apple's ICloud allow a user to store data on Apple's servers and that data can (AND SHOULD!) be encrypted. Using the new act from 2019, Australia can force Apple to create a backdoor into the user's data without the user knowing about it (BBC 2018). While the implications on integrity for the targeted user are obvious, this act brings yet another concern as introducing backdoors into a service is a security issue that concerns any user of that service. Well, taking a stance and judging what is right is left to you as a reader, and thus ends this example.

2.3 Police Hacking

The final example concerns governmental spyware or other forms of what some refer to as police hacking. While that headline may sound a bit intimidating, it concerns various ways for the government to spy on what a suspect does on his or her computer using technical aids. As described by Škorvánek et al. (2019) as well as Ohm (2017), laws that allow the police to hack into suspects' computers or plant malware in them have been introduced and discussed in several countries in recent times. It goes without saying that this is an action that is highly intrusive and carried out without the knowledge of the suspect. While those in favor of police hacking highlight that it is a tool that can be a very effective way to gather evidence, the con side talks about the obvious privacy concerns.

Looking at the technical aspect of police hacking, it is essentially about hacking. Even if the hacking operations carried out by the police would be attacks that are performed with the government's good mind, it is still hacking using the same tools and conditions as an evil hacker that wants to destroy the world. The reason for why that insight is important is that any police hacker would face the same challenges that an evil hacker would—security measures. There are two sides to this coin, which is sometimes proclaimed by those that are against police hacking. First, one can argue whether or not it is reasonable for governmental agencies to hunt for vulnerabilities and exploits. Since they would be used to solve crimes, it would be unlikely that the vulnerabilities discovered would be disclosed so that they can be fixed. The other side would be that if police hackers need to deface security measures, they will have a hard time and may have a slim chance of succeeding. The question becomes: Is it reasonable to use highly intrusive techniques with only slim chances of succeeding? Well, the author's opinion will remain hidden and the reader can form his own.

As a final note, before discussing ethical guidelines, there is a pattern in different measures that needs to be highlighted. There are measures that the suspect will be aware of and measures that the suspect will not be aware of. In terms of integrity, this difference is important. If you are aware of an action that will be taken against you, you have a chance to appeal. Something that all actions that are happening without the suspect being aware of have in common is that they are effectively impossible to appeal since, well, the suspect does not know that they are happening. It could also be mentioned that, as of today, democratic legislation does not typically let the forensic expert of police officer to rampart with the powers just described. Rather, most action will, in most legislations, require approval from an attorney, judge, or court.

2.4 Ethical Guidelines

The author of this book is not a moral philosopher or someone who can claim the title of an expert in ethics, privacy, or integrity. But it still seems important to conclude this chapter with some ethical compass that could, and perhaps should, be used when conducting forensic work. So based on experience as a forensic expert and information security research, here comes a discussion on ethical guidelines for forensic examinations.

Ethics in digital forensics is indeed an interesting topic. Whether you are doing forensics in a corporate environment or criminal investigation, you are doing something that is breaching privacy of someone, at least very likely. There will of course be regulations to follow, and those will serve as the first rule. Regulation in this sense can be local laws (in criminal investigations) or agreements such as nondisclosure agreements (common in the corporate world). However, regulations may say what you can do, but do they also say what you should do? That may not always be the case; for instance, a bachelor thesis from the University of Skövde concluded that the integrity of those subject to forensic examinations in criminal investigations, in Sweden, is to a large extent up to the people involved in investigation of the case (Olsson 2019). The same thesis concluded that solving crimes is prioritized over the integrity of someone whose devices are seized.

Looking at the research community, Schrittwieser et al. (2013) discuss the following four guidelines for information security research:

- Do not harm humans actively.

  While the intent of this guideline was to make researchers avoid studies where someone got harmed during the study, it works for forensics as well. For a forensic examiner, this guideline could be interpreted as "Do not do more harm than you must" and could, for instance, include making sure not to include personal data of someone that is not of interest in an examination when writing a report.
- Do not watch bad things happen.

  This guideline essentially says that if you see something bad and have the power to fix it—fix it. One could argue that the forensic interpretation would be to stop crimes or illicit activity as soon as you can rather than to wait for something to play out to get more evidence. It could also mean that if you find something that is illicit but not in the scope of what you are asked to do, you should report it to a supervisor.
- Do not perform illegal activities to harm illegal activities.

  Well, one should avoid doing anything illegal and follow local laws and regulations.
- Do not perform undercover research.

  This guideline says that you should not do anything to unknowing subjects. As we previously explored in this chapter, such actions are in conflict with integrity. However, they are perhaps necessary at times but should be used with caution.

Bassett et al. (2006) discuss ethics specifically in regard to digital forensics and can be summarized in the following bullets:

- Avoid irrelevant information.
  This bullet basically states that you should avoid information that is not relevant to your task. This could involve information about inappropriate behaviors, medical history, or basically anything.
- Be honest about your errors.
  This bullet depicts that if a forensic expert makes errors, he should own up to them. As you will notice, a forensic examination is a process where it is possible to well, screw up, and in some legislations that will lead to results being questioned. However, it is very important that a forensic examiner reports on what happened during an examination, even if that means that errors are reported.
- Be objective.
  This bullet says that a forensic examiner cannot be biased. A forensic examination should be carried out with an open objective mind and aim at uncovering the truth.

Finally, the International Society of Forensic Computer Examiners, a private organization concerned with forensic training and certification, provides a code of ethics that can be summarized as follows (The International Society of Forensic Computer Examiners 2019):

- Be objective and accurate in all investigations.
- Always be truthful about your findings.
- Be truthful about your competence and training.
- Base examinations on established and validated principles.
- Examine all evidence in the scope of the task.
- Never do anything that could appear to be a conflict of interest.
- Never withhold any evidence or express opinion on guilt.

While compiling a granular list of bullets for everyone to follow is a job that is hard and should perhaps be performed by some organizations with influence over the entire world, the aim of this chapter is to highlight some aspects of ethics and privacy in forensic examinations with the purpose of making the reader, you, aware of them. Such a list would also be impossible since there are different rules in different regulations. For instance, you may or may not gather data from cloud services, depending on where you work. However, there are some abstract boundaries that should never be overstepped. They will conclude this chapter:

- Follow local regulations and law.
  First and foremost, the law is the law and should be followed. After the law come directives and agreements that should also be followed. However, while the law must always be obeyed, one could think of a situation where an agreement

would break the rest of the ethical guidelines. Will your ethical compass allow you to sign it?

- Be objective and thorough.

  The task of a forensic expert is to find out what happened in a digital environment, not to build a strong case. As such, all examinations should be thoroughly executed with an objective mind.
- Be honest about your competence, training, and mistakes.

  A forensic expert should not lie about his or her competence or mistakes. A report should include what happened during an examination. And on the topic of competence, the task of the forensic expert is to be truthful about competence and findings and let other judge their value.
- Present all facts, but no verdicts.

  A forensic expert should present all findings from a forensic examination. Even if tasked with finding evidence of a crime, all evidence in favor and against that crime should be presented. The judging is the task for the court.
- Ignore irrelevant data and treat it as confidential.

  If data that is irrelevant for the case is encountered, that data should be ignored and treated as confidential. That means that the forensic examiner should not discuss that data with anyone. A reasonable time to step away from this rule would be if the irrelevant data is actually evidence of another crime; in such a case, it would be reasonable to discuss what to do with it with a supervisor.
- Never put yourself in a conflict of interest situation.

  A forensic examiner is dependent on his or her reputation. Never put yourself in a situation that could be seen as a conflict of interest. That will impact your credibility and make you seem unprofessional.

2.5 Questions and Tasks

Ethics and legal matters are often points of discussion. Thus, the end of chapter tasks are oriented as such. Consider the following questions in class:

1. In your jurisdiction, is it ok for the police to hack into your computer or cell phone to acquire the data that is on it?
2. In your jurisdiction, is it ok for the police to require that an Internet service provider discloses who the user of a certain IP address is?
3. Should the police be allowed to place malware in suspects' digital devices to track what they are doing?

References

Australian Government (2015) Crimes Act 1914. In: LEGISLATION FRO (ed). https://www.legislation.gov.au/Details/C2015C00111/Html/Volume_1#_Toc415554770. Federal Register of Legislation

Bassett R, Bass L, O'Brien P (2006) Computer forensics: an essential ingredient for cyber security. J Inf Sci Technol 3:26–30

BBC (2018) Australia data encryption laws explained [Online]. Available: https://www.bbc.com/news/world-australia-46463029. Accessed 2019

FANDOM (2019) Miranda [Online]. Available: https://miamivice.fandom.com/wiki/Miranda. Accessed 2019

Ohm P (2017) The investigative dynamics of the use of malware by law enforcement. William & Mary Bill of Rights J 26:303

Olsson A (2019) Hanteringen av integritetsperspektiv inom IT-forensik: En kvalitativ intervjustudie med rättsväsendets aktörer

Schrittwieser S, Mulazzani M, Weippl E (2013) Ethics in security research which lines should not be crossed? Security and Privacy Workshops (SPW), 2013 IEEE. IEEE 1–4

Škorvánek I, Koops B-J, Newell BC, Roberts AJ (2019) 'My computer is my castle': new privacy frameworks to regulate police hacking. Brigham Young University Law Review, Forthcoming

The European Court (2016) Judgment of the Court (Grand Chamber) of 21 December 2016, Joined Cases C-203/15 and C-698/15. In: COURT TE (ed). https://eur-lex.europa.eu/legal-content/EN/SUM/?uri=CELEX:62015CJ0203

The International Society of Forensic Computer Examiners (2019) Code of ethics and professional responsibility [Online]. Available: https://www.isfce.com/ethics2.htm. Accessed 2019

Vincze EA (2016) Challenges in digital forensics. Police Pract Res 17:183–194

3 Computer Theory

Up until this point, we introduced what computer forensics is and pretty much concluded that it is about examining and deducing what happened on a computer or in a computer system. That is all well and good, but to move on further, you do need a bit of background knowledge. The intent of this book is not to provide you with a summary of computer science. Rather, the book expect you to have a fair "know-how" on computer stuff. But there are a few areas that the author found that IT people commonly do not know that much about, but that are important to a computer forensic expert. Those areas are covered, in brief, here. Note that each subsection is an overview. For a complete understanding, follow the references!

3.1 Secondary Storage Media

Secondary storage media refers to media where data is stored for long-term preservation. This is in contrast to primary memory, which includes random-access memory and cache memories, which is used for short-term storage. Secondary storage includes hard drives, CD/DVD, USB flash drives, and memory cards. This discussion refers mainly to hard drives but is also (commonly) applicable for USB flash drives and memory cards.

The first thing that is important to know is the physical size of the storage media. This is because it is important to know that you can account for all the storage area on a computer. Say that you find a computer that appears to have a "C:\" partition of 200 GB but a physical examination of the hard drive reveals that it is supposed to be able to house 250 GB of data. This could mean that there is another hidden partition present on the hard drive or that the hard drive was reformatted. Either way, the remaining 50 GB may contain valuable evidence.

This is also a good place to comment on how hard drive formatting is commonly handled by the operating system. It is easy to assume that if you repartition your hard drive, the existing data is overwritten. That is, most times, not the case. Rather, the hard drive is made up from sectors and clusters that can be allocated to a file or a

J. Kävrestad, *Fundamentals of Digital Forensics*,
https://doi.org/10.1007/978-3-030-38954-3_3

partition. When you partition a hard drive, you create a master boot record or GUID partition table (other versions exist as well, but seem rare) that contains a partition table. The partition table houses information about partitions on the hard drive including starting and ending sector for each partition. If you resize your partitions, the only thing that will happen is that the partition table gets updated. The actual data on the hard drive is often unaffected. While this makes the data that was on the hard drive inaccessible by the operating system, it is still possible to recover it using forensic tools.

It should also be mentioned that it is quite common that a hard drive that may appear empty is just reformatted. When a hard drive is reformatted, it happens every so often that only the partitioning table is removed. The partitions, that we will discuss next, still remain on the disk. The reformatting only made it possible for the computer to put new data in the sectors that made up the partitions. But until that happens, the old data is still fully readable and the partitions can be recovered using forensic tools. Further information on hard drives and partition tables is beyond this book, but a good source of information is available at www.ntfs.com/ntfs (NTFS 2017).

3.2 The NTFS File Systems

As we just discussed hard drives and partitions, the next logical step becomes discussing file systems. A file system is essentially a structure used to control how data is stored and retrieved on a storage device and is the common content of a partition. So to make things clear, a hard drive contains partitions, a partition commonly contains a file system, and a file system is used to structure data. I am saying that a partition *commonly* contains a file system because that is not always the case. For instance, a partition may contain some semiorganized data such as swap space, that is, the case for swap partitions in the world of Linux—but that is another story.

As for the file system, there are several different file systems out there such as ext4 (common on Linux), NFS (common for network storage), and FAT32 (common on surveillance video and thumb drives). However, we will dig into the NTFS file system that is used on modern Windows-based computers for the sole reason that NTFS is the most common encounter for a forensic examiner and this book is aimed at examinations of Windows-based computers.

As previously discussed, the partitions are stated in the partition table found in the master boot record. Next, a partition formatted with the NTFS file system begins with a metadata file called the partition boot sector. What we need to know about this file is that it contains the Master File Table (MFT) that is basically a dictionary of all files and folders on the NTFS partition. The most important content, for a forensic examiner, in the MFT is the file records. All files and folders on the partition have one! For each file or folder on the partition, the MFT record contains information about the name and the actual file data. However, a MFT record cannot be bigger than 1024 bytes, so files that are bigger than about 600 bytes (about 400 bytes are reserved for file name and such) cannot reside in the record. In these cases, the MFT record describes what clusters on the hard drive that house the file (Guidance Software 2016). Files contained in the MFT are called resident, and files not contained in the MFT are called nonresident. Before we move on, you should also know that there is a backup MFT, commonly located at the end of the partition (TechNet 2017).

So how are files created and deleted? Well, when you create a file or folder it will get a MFT record. If the file is small enough, it will be stored in the MFT, and if it is too big, the computer will allocate clusters and store the file in the clusters. When you delete the file, it is actually the MFT record that gets deleted, and the data in the allocated clusters remains there until they are overwritten. This allows a forensic examiner to recover deleted files using forensic tools.

While the paragraph above describes how an NTFS file system will typically operate, the ability to recover deleted files is also affected by the type of hard drive that is used. When using a mechanical hard drive, it makes sense to not delete data on disk because the action of marking it as deleted enables the hard drive to overwrite the affected area with new data, thus deleting the data would be an unnecessary action, However, Solid-State Drives (SSD) cannot write new data into areas that are already occupied. Thus, writing data into an area of an SSD that is marked as deleted but still contains data would include two operations. First, the old data is deleted and then the new data can be written in its place. To improve the speed of SSDs, they commonly use techniques to periodically delete data that has been marked for deletion. Thus, one can expect to find less deleted files on an SSD compared to a mechanical disk.

3.3 File Structure

To be able to recover and understand files, you need to know a little bit about how files are commonly structured. You should know that a file does not need to follow a certain structure so what you read here is not always the case. Well then, the common structure of a file is that it begins with a header containing metadata and then comes the actual data and finally a trailer. The metadata commonly contains what is called a file signature that tells the computer what kind of file the file is, such as a JPEG or PDF. By knowing this, you can search a hard drive for headers and trailers to find files even if they are deleted from the MFT. You can do this by searching for the hexadecimal or alphanumerical file signature depending on your software.

An example of a file signature is given in Fig. 3.1, which shows the file signature for a JPEG file. The left-hand side shows the file offset in hexadecimal (not relevant

```
0000 | FF D8 FF E0 00 10 4A 46-49 46 00 01 01 01 00 78 | ÿØÿà··JFIF·····x
0010 | 00 78 00 00 FF DB 00 43-00 02 01 01 02 01 01 02 | ·x··ÿÛ·C········
0020 | 02 02 02 02 02 02 02 03-05 03 03 03 03 03 06 04 | ················
```

Fig. 3.1 Header of a JPEG file

```
000000 25 50 44 46 2D 31 2E 34-0D 25 E2 E3 CF D3 0D 0A %PDF-1.4·%âãÏÓ··
000016 34 20 30 20 6F 62 6A 0D-3C 3C 2F 4C 69 6E 65 61 4 0 obj·<</Linea
000032 72 69 7A 65 64 20 31 2F-4C 20 35 30 31 35 32 37 rized 1/L 501527
000048 2F 4F 20 36 2F 45 20 34-39 38 31 31 31 2F 4E 20 /O 6/E 498111/N
000064 31 2F 54 20 35 30 31 33-32 38 2F 48 20 5B 20 34 1/T 501328/H [ 4
```

Fig. 3.2 Header of a PDF file

at the moment), the middle column shows the file data in hexadecimal, and the right-hand side shows the file data in alphanumerical format. As you can see, the file begins with FF D8 FF E0, and this is what you would search for if you wanted to look for deleted JPEG files. You could also search for JFIF which is part of the alphanumerical file signature. Another example is given in Fig. 3.2, which shows a part of the header for a PDF file. In this case, you would search for 25 50 44 46 2D or %PDF-1.4 since that is the file signature for a PDF file in hexadecimal and alphanumerical.

It is also worthwhile to mention that there are different approaches on how to store files. Most file formats, including plain text files and many picture formats, store files as plain files. However, some files including Microsoft Office files and compressed file formats such as ZIP are stored as compound files. Compound files are files that maintain some structured storage approach of their own (Microsoft 2017a). That means that there is a local file structure within the compound file. This is the common case for compressed files. What is special about compound files is that they cannot be fully examined when they are in their "packed" state. Instead, they must be unpacked to be fully analyzed. The reason is that the data in the compressed state is represented in a different way than in the original, unpacked state.

3.4 Data Representation

This section contains a very brief discussion on how data is stored and represented in a computer system. This is simply to make you understand that the data may have different meaning depending on how you interpret it.

To begin, the data stored on any storage media is stored in binary, with zeroes and ones. You may group the bits into groups of eight called bytes, and a byte may also be represented with two hexadecimal signs. To make life complicated, different applications may store data in different order. To begin, when we are looking at a single byte, containing 8 bits, the order is always the same. You interpret the bits with the leftmost bit having the highest significance and the rightmost having the lowest, as depicted in Fig. 3.3.

That is all well, but when you have a data set consisting of more than one byte we get in trouble. There are two ways to store consequent bytes. The first is called big-endian, storing bytes with the biggest end first making the first byte the most significant. In contrast, we have little-endian storing data with the smallest end first,

Bits:	1	1	1	1	1	1	1	1	1
Value:	256	128	64	32	16	8	4	2	1

Fig. 3.3 Bits and values

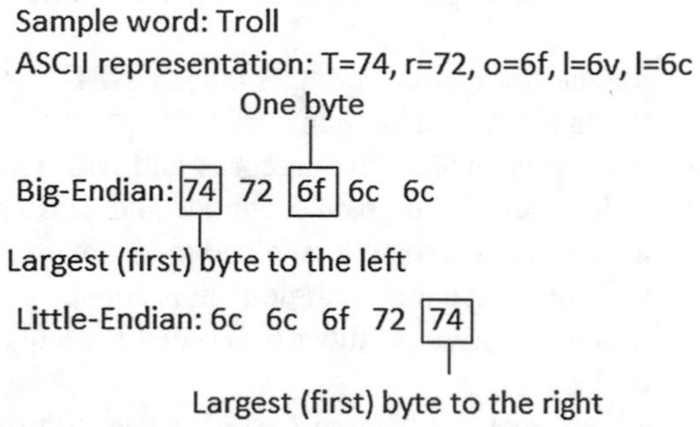

Fig. 3.4 Example of little- and big-endian

Sample word: Troll
ASCII representation: T=74, r=72, o=6f, l=6v, l=6c
One byte
Big-Endian: 74 72 6f 6c 6c
Largest (first) byte to the left
Little-Endian: 6c 6c 6f 72 74
Largest (first) byte to the right

reading from left to right (Cohen 1980). To give an example—consider the word "troll" in little- and big-endian in Fig. 3.4.

That is that on binary and hexadecimal representation. You should just know that depending on what kind of data you are looking at you may want to look at it in binary or hexadecimal.

The final part on data representation is that you should know that computers have different ways of representing characters, called different ways of encoding data. While I have no intention of discussing different ways of encoding text or data, you should know that different ways of encoding data exist, such as ASCII, UTF-8, and UTF-16. What the encoding decides is basically how a sign is represented in binary or hexadecimal code. For instance, the letter "A" is represented as "feff0041" in UTF-16 and as "41" in ASCII, using hexadecimal code. The reason for why this is important is that if you open a data set that is encoded in ASCII with a program that expects something else, the result will be screwed up.

3.5 User Accounts in Windows 10

Undeniably, a big part of digital forensics has to do with examining the behaviors of different user. It is therefore important to understand a bit about how users are stored and referred to in the Windows OS. In essence, users in any Windows system are identified using a username and a security identifier (SID). Actually, the username string is just informational and can be modified at will while the SID is completely unique and can never be changed. Whenever a user is created, he is assigned a SID. That SID can never be assigned to another user. Further, SIDs follow a very hard structure and are assigned starting from a certain number that is incremented by one for every new user. Below is an example of a SID:

S-1-5-21-1453882016-3398588568-228745471-154059

The SID follow a standardized structure as follows (Microsoft 2019):

S-R-A-D1-D2-Dn-R

The different parts of the SID have the following meaning:

- S identifies that the string is indeed a SID.
- R denotes a revision number.
- A denotes an identifier authority and will typically be set to 5.
- D field are the domain identifier and will show were the user is created. For instance, if a computer is joined to a domain, this field can be used to distinguish local user accounts from domain accounts.
- R is the relative identifier (RID) that is unique within a domain (D).

Given what has been discussed so far, all users created on a local machine will have identical SID values, except for the RID-part. The RID will work as a unique identifier on the local machine. The same is true for a domain environment, but in that case the RID will be unique in the domain. Further, the RID values are assigned in a predeterminable way where RID values from 500 to 999 are reserved for system users. Most notable is 500 that is reserved for the administrator account and 501 that is reserved for guest. Accounts created by the user will start at 1000, meaning that the first user created will get RID 1000, the second will get RID 1001, and so on. Note that RID values are never reused, so if a computer only contains one user with a RID of 1002, that shows that the system previously contained two other users. Likewise, if a system only contains a user with a RID of 1000, that is a very strong indication that the system only ever contained one user, except for the built-in accounts. It is worthwhile to stress that the SID for a user account is never modified while the account name can be changed at will, including the name of the administrator account.

3.6 Windows Registry

The Windows registry is a hierarchical database that stores information about users, installed application, and the Windows system itself (Microsoft 2017b). That makes it a very important place for forensic examiners to look and something for this book to provide an overview of.

To begin, the Windows registry is a tree structure where each node in the tree is called a key and every key may have a value or sub-keys. A registry tree can be as deep as 512 keys (Microsoft 2017b). The values that a key can contain are just arbitrary data, and it is up to the application that stored the value to decide the format and how it is to be interpreted. The registry is made up of several files, so-called hives (Guidance Software 2016). Each hive contains a set of data; the hives that are most commonly of interest to a forensic examiner are called SAM, SECURITY, SYSTEM, and SOFTWARE. There is also another file associated with each user

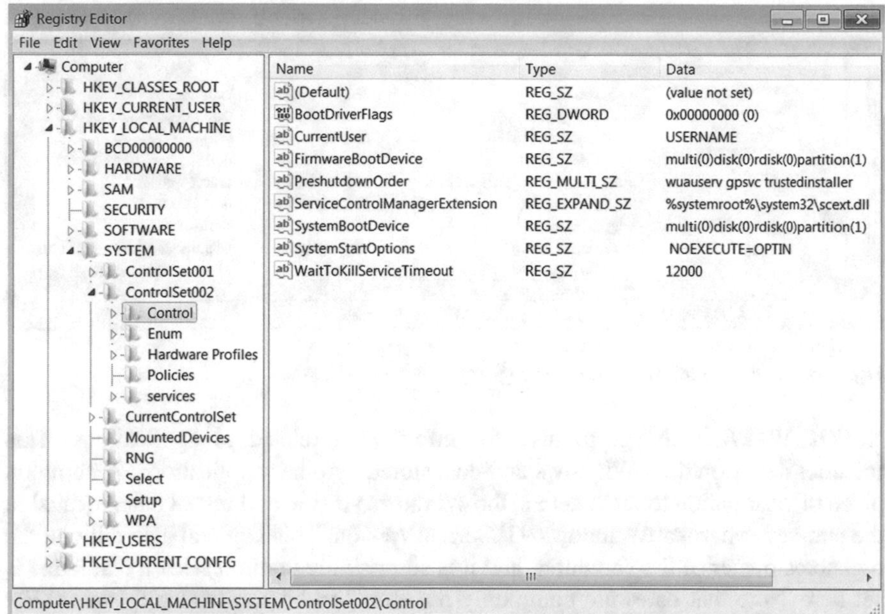

Fig. 3.5 Regedit overview

called NTUSER.dat. There is one NTUSER.dat for each user on the system, and this file is located in the user directory (. . .\Users\ < username>). The other registry hives are located in the . . .\System32\config\folder. You may extract the hives and analyze them with a forensic tool, such as AccessData Registry Viewer or Registry Explorer as done in later sections of this book. You may also examine the registry of a running Windows system through the built-in utility regedit. In Fig. 3.5, presenting an example of regedit, you can see that it presents the registry hives in a format that is a bit different than you may think. This is because regedit shows the registry as seen by the running computer. HKEY_CURRENT_USER contains the data stored in NTUSER.dat for the current user, and data from the other hives is present in HKEY_LOCAL_MACHINE. In the picture, you can see that there are several keys in the tree at the left and some values in the pane at the right. In this case, the values are located under the key "Control" that in turn is a sub-key to the key ControlSet002 that is in the SYSTEM hive.

As you may understand, the registry can be a huge database and many programs store data in the Windows registry. It is strongly suggested to work with the registry to learn what kind of information that can be found in it. The rest of this section will cover each registry hive and the information found, in brief.

NTUSER.dat is a hive that stores information about a specific user account. This hive can, for instance, contain information such as the user's browser settings and history and data related to user applications.

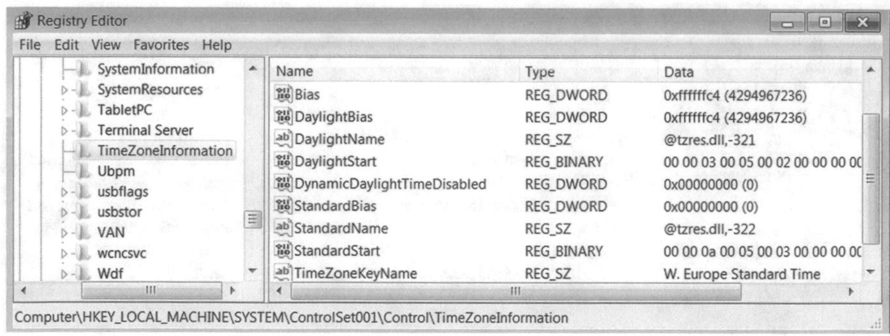

Fig. 3.6 Time zone information in the registry

SOFTWARE is the go-to hive for information related to applications. This includes data stored by Windows and data stored by other applications. A common piece of information to fetch here is the Windows version and install date, located in the sub-key \Microsoft\WindowsNT\CurrentVersion. This key will also tell you the registered owner of the computer, and it is surprisingly common that a real name is set here. Note that dates are commonly not stored in human-readable format. For instance, the install date is stored as a UNIX time stamp—seconds that have passed since midnight on the first of January in 1970—this needs to be converted.

SYSTEM will contain information about the system including USB devices that have been connected to the system, time zone settings, and information about networks that the computer has been connected to. An example is given in Fig. 3.6 that shows you time zone information stored in the key \SYSTEM \ControlSet001\Control\TimeZoneInformation\TimeZoneKeyName.

The *SAM* and *SECURITY* hives are protected by the Windows system and cannot be browsed using regedit on a running computer. However, extracting them from a forensic image and browsing them using a forensic tool is no problem. The *SAM* hive basically stores information about users. Examining this hive you can, for instance, find the users on the local machine, information about when they last logged on, when each account was created, and password hashes. This hive contains the information you need to map a RID to a username, located in the key *SAM \Domains\Account\Users\Names*. As seen in Fig. 3.7 (Registry Explorer), the field "Value Type" holds the RID (in this case 1003) for the user TheDDDUDE.

Finally, we have the *SECURITY* hive that stores some information about the system, perhaps mainly the system audit policy, and the Syskey that you will need in addition to the *SAM* hive if you need to crack user passwords.

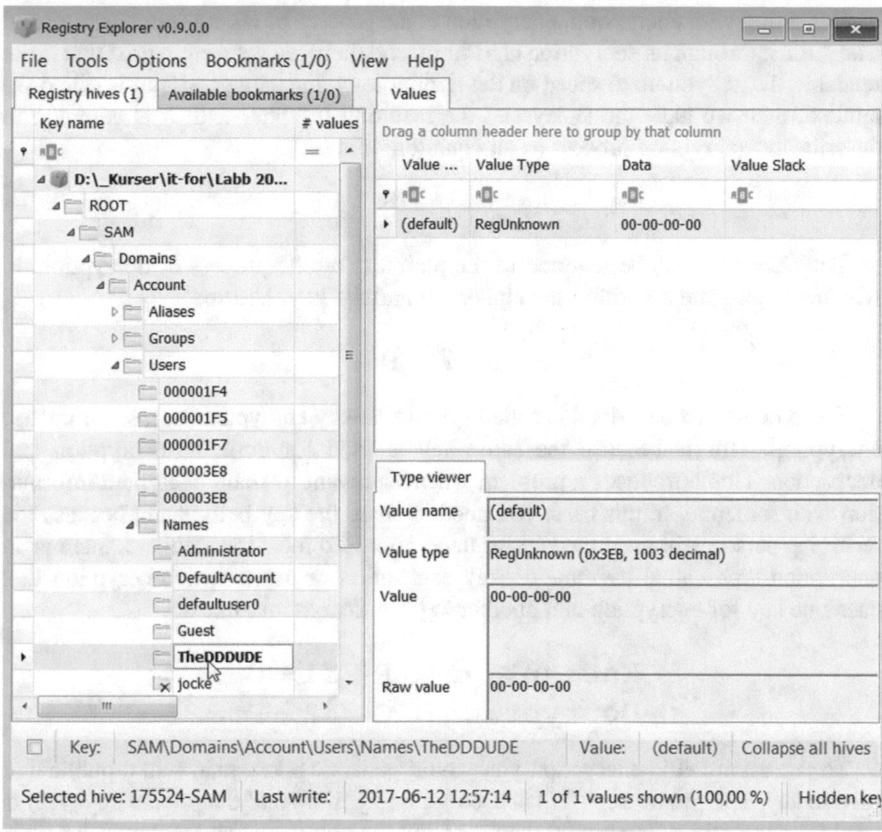

Fig. 3.7 Username in the SAM hive

3.7 Encryption and Hashing

There are tons of good books for you to read if you want to get down and dirty with encryption and hashing, but for the purpose of this book I will just discuss the terms very briefly at an abstract level. Encryption and hashing are cryptographic techniques used to hide data. Understanding how this works is crucial for a forensic expert because, well, criminals usually do not want their data to be found and analyzed. Also, in modern computers, encryption and hashing are usually built-in, fundamental parts of the normal computer behavior making encrypted data a normal part of the forensic examiners daily work.

Beginning with encryption, encryption is the process of taking some data set and a key, run it through an encryption algorithm, and then you get a ciphertext that is not readable. To get you up to speed on the terminology, the data you input is called (P) laintext, then we have the (K)ey and the resulting (C)ipher text. It is common to describe the encryption process as an equation, like so:

$$\mathtt{P} + \mathtt{K} = \mathtt{C}$$

The ciphertext can be reverted to the plaintext by the process of decryption, in which you pass the algorithm the ciphertext and the key, like so:

$$\mathtt{C} + \mathtt{K} = \mathtt{P}$$

The process just described is called symmetric key encryption or just symmetric encryption. This is because the same key is used for both the encryption and decryption. This introduces a problem when you want to share encrypted information with someone. In this case, you need to share the key beforehand because the receiving person will need the key for decryption. To meet this demand, there is an encryption type called asymmetric key encryption or asymmetric encryption that uses one key for encryption and another key for decryption, like so:

$$\begin{aligned} &\mathtt{Encryption:} \quad \mathtt{P} + \mathtt{K1} = \mathtt{C} \\ &\mathtt{Decryption:} \quad \mathtt{C} + \mathtt{K2} = \mathtt{P} \end{aligned}$$

To use asymmetric encryption you would generate a key pair with a public and private key. The public key (K1) is used for encryption, and the private key (K2) is used for decryption. You would then send out the public key and anyone who want to send you encrypted information, and they would encrypt it using your public key. The only key that can be used to decrypt something encrypted with your public key is your private key, you keep that to yourself. Asymmetric encryption has several other usages, well beyond the scope of this book.

Hashing is a cryptographic technique that is used more for storage of sensitive data and validating data integrity than sharing encrypted information. A hash algorithm is basically a one-way function that takes a (P)lain text as input and produces a (H)ash value or digest. What is important about a hash function is the property of it being one-way, meaning that it is impossible to derive the P from the H. The hash function can be described like so:

$$\mathtt{P} \rightarrow \mathtt{H}$$

For a hash algorithm to be considered secure, it must have the following properties:

- Collision resistant meaning that there is only one H for each P.
- Irreversible meaning that it is impossible to derive P from H.

The two main usages for hashes are storing some kinds of sensitive data, like passwords, and to fingerprint data in order to ensure data integrity. In terms of ensuring data integrity hashing is used as a fingerprint. If you want to send someone a message, you can create a hash value for the message and send the message and the hash to the recipient. The recipient can then hash the message and compare his hash value to the one you sent to him. Since the hash algorithm is collision resistant, matching hashes will ensure that the message was not altered. In terms of storing passwords, they are commonly stored in a hashed format, and this is the case in the Windows operating systems. When a user wants to log in, she will submit her password to the system and the system will run what she enters through the hashing algorithm and compare that hash value to the one stored in the user database. If the hashes match, the password must be correct and the user is allowed to enter the computer.

3.8 SQLite Databases

SQLite database are database files that are very commonly used by various applications. They are databases and used to store data in a structured way. In essence, SQLite is an C library that implements n SQL database engine that can be bundled with an application and does not require a separate database process. It is very widely used in computer and mobile applications and thus, of interest for forensic examiners. In essence, a SQLite database is a relation database with tables containing data. Since the application developer may choose to build the database as she pleases, analyzing them can be a bit of an experiment but it is usually worthwhile. Also, SQLite databases for more widely used applications such as Web browsers, common chat clients, and SMS applications can often be analyzed automatically by forensic software. A sample manual examination of a SQLite database is described in REFTEXT.

When we are concerned with databases, it is important to know how data is written on and deleted from the database. In terms of writing to a database, SQLite uses a "write-ahead log" or "rollback-journal"; both approaches are similar, at least for the purposes of this book. When data in the database needs to be modified, the changes are written to the "write-ahead log" or "rollback-journal" or the actual database. This approach lets several programs read the database simultaneously and provides a layer of protection against data corruption. Whenever the application is ready to commit changes in the "write-ahead log" or "rollback-journal," or when they get full, changes are written to the database. The forensic implication of this approach is that a SQLite database that is subject for analysis may not contain all the most recent data, since there may be uncommitted changes in the "write-ahead log" or "rollback-journal." Thus, those files should be included in the forensic analysis. Luckily, they are usually stored in the same folders as the database, with the same name followed by –WAL (write-ahead log) or –journal (rollback-journal).

3.9 Memory and Paging

Finishing up the part on computer theory, I just want to mention some things about the memory and paging. The memory is an extremely valuable piece of information for the one reason that this is where the computer stores information relating to what it does at the moment. Also, the memory is emptied every time the computer restarts, so the content in memory relates only to what the computer was up to since the last reboot. This makes information in the memory extremely good because it is hard for a suspect that was arrested sitting in front of his computer to claim that someone else was responsible for the information found in the computer memory.

Further, when you are viewing encrypted data in a decrypted format, the decrypted version of the data is temporarily stored in memory—this makes the memory a good place to find encrypted information in a decrypted state. During my personal forensic work, I found passwords, encrypted e-mails, and several pieces of incriminating evidence in memory.

Before leaving this topic, I want to mention that whenever the computer needs to hold more data in memory than the memory can hold, part of the memory is stored on the hard drive. This is a process called paging. On Windows systems, the "paged-out" parts of the memory are stored in the file called "pagefile.sys," and it can contain the same type of information as the memory. There are several methods on how to examine computer memory and that topic is explored in REFTEXT of this book. However, it should be noted that, to some extent, the data in memory can be treated like a big blob of unstructured data, similar to slack space or unallocated space. In that regard, whatever techniques presented for searching in and reconstructing files from such spaces can be applied to memory data as well.

3.10 Questions and Tasks

Here are the questions for this chapter.

1. Brainstorm on what secondary storage media devices there are that can be of interest during a forensic investigation.
2. What happens when you delete a file from a NTFS file system and how can you recover deleted files?
3. What is meant with resident and nonresident files?
4. Why do you need to know the difference between little- and big-endian?
5. Use regedit to find out what time zone your computer is set to use.
6. What is hashing and what signifies a secure hash algorithm?

References

Cohen D (1980) ON holy wars and a plea for peace. IETF. Available online: https://www.ietf.org/rfc/ien/ien137.txt. Fetched July 6, 2017

Guidance Software (2016) EnCase computer forensics II. Guidance Software

Microsoft (2017a) Compound files. Available online: https://msdn.microsoft.com/en-us/library/windows/desktop/aa378938(v=vs.85).aspx. Fetched July 6, 2017

Microsoft (2017b) Structure of the registry. Available online: https://msdn.microsoft.com/en-us/library/windows/desktop/ms724946(v=vs.85).aspx. Fetched July 6, 2017

Microsoft 2019 Security identifier [Online]. Available: https://docs.microsoft.com/en-us/windows/security/identity-protection/access-control/security-identifiers#security-identifier-architecture. Accessed 2019

NTFS (2017) NTFS—New technology file system designed for Windows 10, 8, 7, Vista, XP, 2008, 2003, 2000, NT. Available online: http://www.ntfs.com/ntfs.htm. Fetched July 6, 2017

TechNet (2017) File systems. Available online: https://technet.microsoft.com/en-us/library/cc938949.aspx. Fetched July 6, 2017

Notable Artifacts

4

Following the discussion on computer theory, it is important to have a discussion on some of the more notable forensic artifacts that can be of great importance during a forensic examination. A forensic artifact is basically a piece of information that holds forensic value, meaning that it can be used to answer the question or aim of the examination. Quite often the forensic artifacts are pictures, word documents, text messages, or some other information where the importance is quite evident. A picture showing drugs will always be a picture showing drugs. However, in a Windows operating system, there are several artifacts that track the usage of the computer in a way that can be of great interest for a forensic examiner that needs to explain how a computer has been used. What is interesting, and often problematic, about those artifacts is the fact that Microsoft provides little or no documentation about how those pieces of information actually work. Thus, the function of the artifacts described in the remaining of this chapter has been examined, tested, and understood with experience. The chapter is written based on Windows 10 version 1709, and there may be some differences in how the artifacts work in earlier and later versions of Windows. It is important that you, as a forensic expert, ensure that you understand the artifacts that you use to draw conclusions on your own, and research is necessary if you are uncertain.

In combination to this chapter, Chap. 14 presents even more artifacts in a more hands-on manner, including guides on how to find them using forensic tools. The rest of this chapter is devoted to descriptions and explanations of common important forensic artifacts.

4.1 Metadata

One of the single-handed, most important sources of forensic information is metadata. Metadata is basically information about information, and most objects such as files and folders on a computer system will have metadata. On a computer running Windows and the NTFS file system, the file system will record metadata for

J. Kävrestad, *Fundamentals of Digital Forensics*,
https://doi.org/10.1007/978-3-030-38954-3_4

every file created on the computer. The metadata will include information such as when the file was created and last modified and who created it. Several file types will store additional metadata. For instance, Microsoft Office files will store information about the author name, title of the document, how many times it has been modified, and more. The author name is the name that was registered as the owner of the office application that was used to first create the document in question. To view file metadata in Windows, you can open the properties menu and select the "details" tab; however, this view will only provide a subset of the metadata that is actually stored. However, most forensic software will parse and present all available metadata. A more practical discussion on what the metadata can tell you is provided in Chap. 14.

4.2 EXIF Data

EXIF data is metadata stored in pictures and deserves a section of its own because of its great importance for computer forensic experts. It is very common for a forensic examination to include looking for certain pictures, and when finding interesting pictures, a given follow-up question is to determine where, when, and with what device the pictures were taken. This is done by examining the pictures EXIF data.

EXIF data was originally developed to help photographers record when they took a certain picture, what camera they used, and what settings they used (Mansurov 2018). However, the data stored as EXIF data is also very valuable to a forensic examiner. But just to be clear, it is up to the camera manufacturer to decide what information to store as EXIF data, and it is often possible for a user to turn off the storage of this information. Also, Web sites commonly exclude EXIF data when pictures are published online. However, when you find interesting pictures on a computer, it is often possible to find important information about it by examining the EXIF data. You may access this data as you would any other metadata but there are also special built parsers and forensic tools available for EXIF data analysis. Among the more important pieces of information that is commonly recorded as metadata is:

- Camera make and model
- Device name
- Time when the picture was taken
- GPS coordinates describing where the picture was taken
- Serial number of the device that took the picture
- Name of the person who took the image

Note that the information stored in the EXIF data is, of course, the information that was available to the device when the picture was taken. If the user configures the device name to be "Jacksons Iphone," then that will appear in the device name field. Figure 4.1 shows sample metadata including EXIF data viewed through Windows.

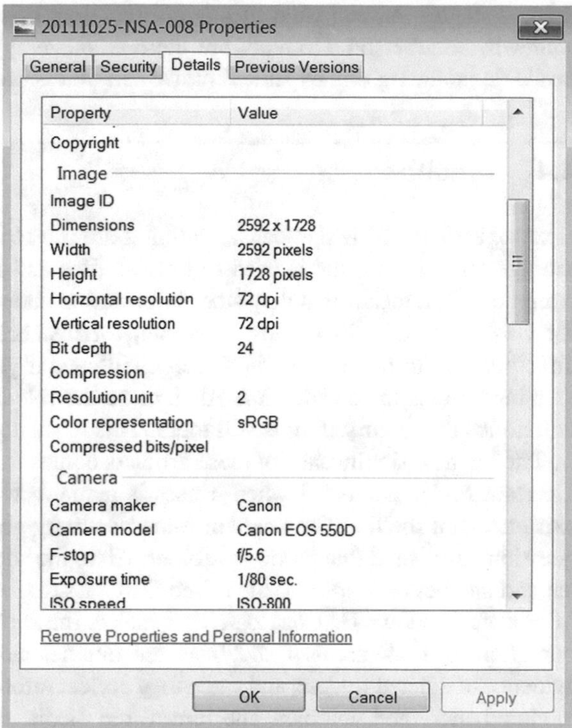

Fig. 4.1 Picture metadata including EXIF data

4.3 Prefetch

Prefetching, in Windows terminology, is the process of bringing data and code pages into memory before it is needed. The idea is to track normal application usage and load the data that an application usually needs during runtime when the application is loaded. This process was implemented to increase performance of applications that are used in a similar manner every time they are used (Nair 2012).

Prefetch data is stored in prefetch files located in the "Prefetch" folder under the system root (commonly c:\Windows). The most significant function of the prefetch files, from a forensic perspective, is that they contain information about how many times an executable was run, and when it was last run. The file name of a prefetch file begins with the name of the executable followed by a hash of the location where the executable is stored. For instance, a prefetch file for FTK imager could be named "FTK IMAGER.EXE-1B23CEFA.pf". If there is a second instance of FTK imager installed somewhere else, there would be a second prefetch file with the same executable name but another hash value. There will be a "modified" time stamp for the prefetch file, and that time stamp reflects the last runtime of the application, as the prefetch file is updated when the application is executed. The data in the prefetch file contains information about how many times the application was used, what hard drive it resides on, and what files and directories it referenced. The data format is somewhat cumbersome to read, but there are several good and free to use parsers available including one by Erik Zimmerman that is presented in Chap. 14.

4.4 Shellbags

Next topic to handle is shellbags. Shellbags are used to store information about GUI settings for explorer that is used to browse files and folders on a Windows-based computer. That means that they store information about what preferences a user sets for viewing certain directories. This can, for instance, be how to list files in the directory. To further explain the use of shellbags, if you browse to a folder and set viewing options to "detailed list," then close the folder, and browse back to it, you will notice that your setting is still there. This is shellbags working for you.

The forensic significance of these artifacts comes from the fact that a shellbag for a certain folder is created when a user is actually viewing that folder. Thus, the existence of a shellbag for a certain folder is a very good indication that the user in question has visited that particular folder. Also, the shellbags are stored in NTUser.dat and another user-specific file called UsrClass.dat, located in . . ./AppData/Local/Microsoft/Windows/UsrClass.dat. That makes the shellbag data user specific. On a third notice, it seems as if shellbags are not deleted and can therefore serve as evidence of deleted folders, and since they collect information about network shares, mounted encrypted volumes, and removable media, they can provide information about that as well. Further, experiments done by the author indicate that for Windows 10 version 1709, UsrClass.dat is the best source of shellbag data. However, both locations should be examined.

As said, shellbags are stored in registry in the following keys:

- USRCLASS.DAT\Local Settings\Software\Microsoft\Windows\Shell\BagMRU
- USRCLASS.DAT\Local Settings\Software\Microsoft\Windows\Shell\Bags
- NTUSER.DAT\Software\Microsoft\Windows\Shell\BagMRU
- NTUSER.DAT\Software\Microsoft\Windows\Shell\Bags

However, the names of the shellbag keys are numbers and the values of the keys are in binary format making manual interpretation hard. It is more feasible to use a tool designed to parse shellbags, and there is one made my Erik Zimmerman that will parse out shellbag information from a registry hive. The tool is called "Shellbags Explorer" and is presented in Chap. REFTEXT. Sample output from this tool is presented in Fig. 4.2.

As shown in Fig. 4.2, there are traces of the computer being used to browse several folders on several drives. Also, in the right pane, there are time stamps that provide additional information. "Created on" would reveal the first time that a folder was visited, and "Modified on" should be updated if the user makes changes to the appearance of a certain folder. Except for being useful for criminal forensics, shellbags can also be useful in intrusion detection to, for instance, reveal if a user

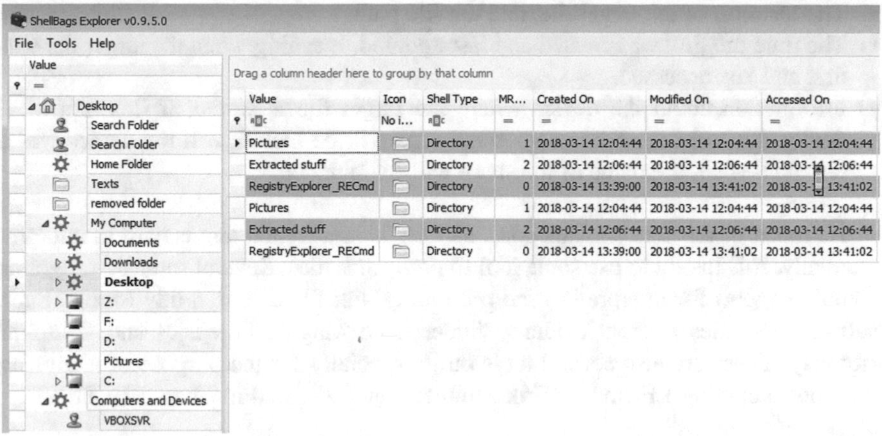

Fig. 4.2 Shellbags explorer sample output

account was compromised and used in an enumeration attempt. In such a case, the shellbags would reveal an unusual pattern in folder visits. For instance, shellbags indicating visits to system folders that a user would not normally visit in a limited time period could indicate an enumeration attack.

4.5 .LNK Files

Continuing on the topic of exploring what files and folders that were accessed using the computer subject to examination, there are some neat artifacts called .lnk files. In essence, .lnk files are shortcuts within Windows. From a regular users' point of view, they are most commonly used to access applications and placed on the user desktop. The common case is that when you install an application, the actual executable is placed somewhere down under the "c:\program files" directory, and an .lnk file is located on the user's desktop. However, there are several other reasons why the operating system would create .lnk files that makes them useful during forensic examinations. For instance, .lnk files are created whenever a user opens a file, local or remote (Magnet Forensics 2014).

The .lnk files are created in different locations, and .lnk files created when a user opens files are located in the path *[userhomefolder]\AppData\Roaming\Microsoft \Windows\Recent*. As for the information located in the files, they are named *targetfilename*.lnk. For instance, the name of an .lnk file related to a file called "test.txt" would be "test.txt.lnk". What makes .lnk files very interesting for forensic examiners is that they are not deleted when a remote drive containing the target file is removed, or when a file is deleted. That makes them a good source of information about network storage, removable storage, and deleted files. As for the actual content of the .lnk files, they will include information about:

- The location of the target file, i.e., the file path.
- The time the link was created and last updated, meaning when the target file was first and last accessed.
- Information about the device where the target file is stored. If this is a local device, the volume serial number and type will be included. If the device was a remote device, the name of the share will be included.

As much of the data contained in .lnk files is in a format that is hard to interpret manually, it is handy to use some tool to parse .lnk files. Several forensic programs contain support for interpreting and presenting .lnk file data in a tidy format. Such software includes Internet evidence finder from Magnet Forensics and sleuthkit/Autopsy. There are also several tools built especially for the purpose of analyzing .lnk files including LECmd by Erik Zimmerman, presented in Chap. REFTEXT.

4.6 MRU-Stuff

The final artifact described here that relates to accessing files and folders is more of a collection of different keys in the Windows registry that can be called most recently used (MRU) keys. They are exactly what the name suggests, namely, keys describing when something was last accessed. There are MRU keys for a whole lot of things scattered across the Windows registry. In general, the keys containing MRU information can be identified by having MRU included in its name. Most MRU keys contain one entry called “MRUlist” or “MRUListEx” and then several entries named with numbers or letters. Whenever an event that is tracked by a MRU key occurs, an entry will be placed in the MRU key, named with a letter or number. The letter or number will tell you in what order the event first occurred and was recorded in the MRU key. However, “MRUlist” and “MRUlistex” will describe when the event occurred last. As one example, consider the example in Fig. 4.3 where the key “Map Network Drive MRU” is examined.

In this case, there is only one entry called “a” that tells us that a network drive located at \crVBOXSVR\VMDShare was mounted to the system. “MRUlist” will tell us that it was the last mounted network drive. If another network drive was to be mounted, it would be given the MRU entry “b” and added as number one in “MRUlist”, as in Fig. 4.4.

Then, if \crVBOXSVR\VMDShare was to be mounted again, “MRUlist” would be updated to reflect that. This is demonstrated in Fig. 4.5, using Windows built-in regedit.

Value Name	Value Type	Data
a	RegSz	\\VBOXSVR\VMDShare
MRUList	RegSz	a

Fig. 4.3 Map network drive MRU

Value Name	Value Type	Data
a	RegSz	\\VBOXSVR\VMDShare
MRUList	RegSz	ba
b	RegSz	\\VBOXSVR\My_Pictures

Fig. 4.4 Map network drive MRU again

(Default)	REG_SZ	(value not set)
a	REG_SZ	\\VBOXSVR\VMDShare
b	REG_SZ	\\VBOXSVR\My_Pictures
MRUList	REG_SZ	ab

Fig. 4.5 Map network drive MRU yet again

Drag a column header here to group by that column

Value Name	Valu...	Data
0	Reg...	54-00-6F-00-20-00-62-00-65-00-20-00-64-00-65-00-6C-00-65-00-74-00-65-00-64-00-2E-00-74-00-78-00-74-00-00-00-80-00-32-00...
MRUListEx	Reg...	03-00-00-00-05-00-00-00-04-00-00-00-02-00-00-00-01-00-00-00-00-00-00-00-FF-FF-FF-FF
1	Reg...	72-00-65-00-6D-00-6F-00-74-00-65-00-74-00-65-00-73-00-74-00-2E-00-74-00-78-00-74-00-00-00-78-00-32-00-00-00-00-00-00-00...
2	Reg...	6C-00-61-00-73-00-74-00-2E-00-74-00-78-00-74-00-00-00-66-00-32-00-00-00-00-00-00-00-00-00-00-00-00-00-6C-61-73-74-2E-74-78-74...
4	Reg...	66-00-69-00-72-00-73-00-74-00-20-00-63-00-72-00-65-00-61-00-74-00-65-00-64-00-20-00-6C-00-61-00-73-00-74-00-20-00-6F-00...
5	Reg...	69-00-6E-00-20-00-74-00-68-00-65-00-20-00-6D-00-69-00-64-00-64-00-6C-00-65-00-2E-00-74-00-78-00-74-00-00-00-80-00-32-00...
3	Reg...	6C-00-61-00-73-00-74-00-20-00-73-00-61-00-76-00-65-00-64-00-2E-00-74-00-78-00-74-00-00-00-78-00-32-00-00-00-00-00-00-00...

Type viewer | Slack viewer

```
         00 01 02 03 04 05 06 07 08 09 0A 0B 0C 0D 0E 0F 10 11 12 13 14
00000000 6C 00 61 00 73 00 74 00 20 00 73 00 61 00 76 00 65 00 64 00 2E  l.a.s.t. .s.a.v.e.d..
00000015 00 74 00 78 00 74 00 00 00 78 00 32 00 00 00 00 00 00 00 00 00  .t.x.t...x.2.........
0000002A 00 00 0C 01 73 74 20 73 61 76 65 61 2E 71 70 71 2E 6C 6E 6B 00    last saved txt lnk
0000003F 00 56 00 09 00 04 00 EF BE 00 00 00 00 00 00 00 00 2E 00 00 00  .V.....ï¾...........
00000054 00 00 00 00 00 00 00 00 00 00 00 00 00 00 00 00 00 00 00 00 00  .....................
00000069 00 00 00 00 00 6C 00 61 00 73 00 74 00 20 00 73 00 61 00 76 00  .....l.a.s.t. .s.a.v.
0000007E 65 00 64 00 2E 00 74 00 78 00 74 00 2E 00 6C 00 6E 00 6B 00 00  e.d...t.x.t...l.n.k..
00000093 00 22 00 00 00                                                  ."...
```

Fig. 4.6 RecentDocs\.txt in Registry Explorer

To complicate matters a bit more, the MRU keys containing the entry "MRUListEx" work in a similar manner but look quite different. Instead of naming the values with letters, numbers are used, and the data format is in hexadecimal. For this reason, using a Registry Explorer that is capable of interpreting this data is very handy. Examples of such tools will be given in Sect. 4.2. However, even if the format of these MRU keys is different, they work in the same way. Whenever an event occurs, an entry is created with a number. The order of the events is recorded in numbers stored in DWORD (four bytes) format in "MRUListEx". The order in "MRUListEx" can tell in what order the events recorded in the listing appeared. As an example, consider Fig. 4.6 that shows the MRU key for opened.txt files.

As seen in "MRUListEx", the entry with number 3 reflected the last recorded event, in this case a text file being opened. Further, Fig. 4.6 shows that the values are

Table 4.1 Listing of MRU keys and their function

Key path	Purpose
Software\Microsoft\Windows \CurrentVersion\Explorer\RecentDocs*	In this key, there are sub-keys for a multitude of file extensions. Each sub-key tracks the most recent files that were opened by the user on a by file-type basis
Software\Microsoft\Windows \CurrentVersion\Explorer\Map Network Drive MRU	This key tracks the most recent network drives that were mapped as network drives by the computer
Software\Microsoft\Windows \CurrentVersion\Explorer\ComDlg32 \OpenSavePidlMRU	The values recorded here are recorded when a file is saved using the "Save as" dialogue
Software\Microsoft\Windows \CurrentVersion\Explorer\ComDlg32 \LastVisitedPidlMRU	This key tracks recently used applications and the folder paths used by these applications to open a file. After testing done by the author at Windows 10 version 1709, it appears as if only applications used to open files using the file explorer (i.e., when the user clicked "Files → open" and browsed for a file) are tracked. So, these keys will not tell you what applications that were used, rather what applications that were used to open files using the method just described. Also, if you right click a file and select "open with X", this action will not be tracked by this key
Software\Microsoft\Windows \CurrentVersion\Explorer\RunMRU	This key will track the most recent stuff the user typed into the "Run" dialogue
Software\Microsoft\Office*	This key will hold sub-keys for different version of Microsoft Office and then for the different office applications. Digging down this sub-key, you can find a multitude of MRU information relating to the usage of office applications

recorded in hexadecimal format, but the software used to examine this key can interpret that the name of the file referenced in the entry is "last saved.txt". The name of the software is Registry Explorer and will be described in Sect. 4.2. Now that you know how to read MRU keys, the next step is to find them. Table 4.1 provides a listing of some noticeable MRU keys located in NTUser.dat on Windows 10 version 1709 and a description of what they do. Note that many keys exist on many versions of Windows, but there may be minor differences from different Windows versions.

4.7 Thumbcache

Lets move on to an artifact with a different use than the prior, namely, the thumbcache. The thumbcache is a Windows feature with the purpose of making previewing of pictures quicker. When you list the content of folder in Windows containing pictures, the icons will be miniatures of the pictures. To mitigate the need

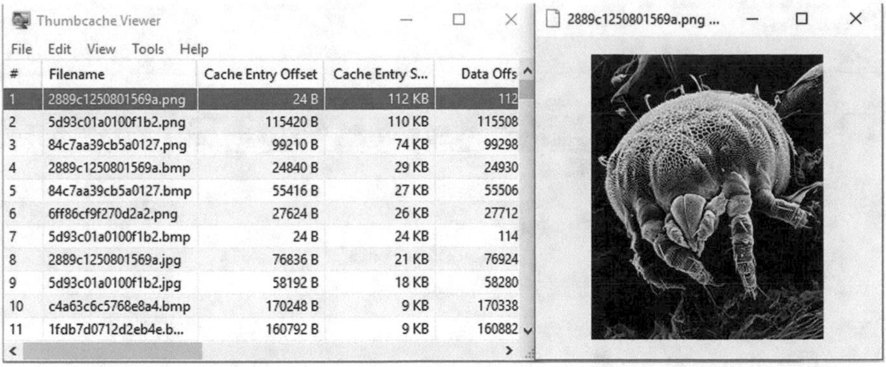

Thumbcache Viewer

File Edit View Tools Help

#	Filename	Cache Entry Offset	Cache Entry S...	Data Offs
1	2889c1250801569a.png	24 B	112 KB	112
2	5d93c01a0100f1b2.png	115420 B	110 KB	115508
3	84c7aa39cb5a0127.png	99210 B	74 KB	99298
4	2889c1250801569a.bmp	24840 B	29 KB	24930
5	84c7aa39cb5a0127.bmp	55416 B	27 KB	55506
6	6ff86cf9f270d2a2.png	27624 B	26 KB	27712
7	5d93c01a0100f1b2.bmp	24 B	24 KB	114
8	2889c1250801569a.jpg	76836 B	21 KB	76924
9	5d93c01a0100f1b2.jpg	58192 B	18 KB	58280
10	c4a63c6c5768e8a4.bmp	170248 B	9 KB	170338
11	1fdb7d0712d2eb4e.b...	160792 B	9 KB	160882

2889c1250801569a.png ...

Fig. 4.7 Thumbcache example

of reading all picture and turning them to miniatures every time such folder is viewed, Windows stored the miniatures as thumbnails when they are first created. The thumbnails are stored in database files called thumbcaches located in the folder *[userhomefolder]\AppData\Local\Microsoft\Windows\Explorer*. The thumbcache database files are called thumbcache_x.db where x is the thumbcache for a certain folder listing mode.

There are two things that are particularly neat about the thumbcache from a forensic perspective. First, they contain the actual thumbnails produced when a user is viewing the content of a folder, and that is a fact that makes them quite smooth to analyze. Second, they are not deleted, and therefore thumbnails of pictures that were deleted or stored on a storage device that is removed are still there.

As the thumbcache is stored in a database format, you need a program that is able to interpret the database in order to view them. One such viewer is Thumbcache Viewer that was used to produce the thumbcache example in Fig. 4.7, and that is further presented in Chap. REFTEXT.

As shown in Fig. 4.7, the thumbnails are stored with arbitrary file names, and it appears as if there are no easy ways to deduce the original file path of a thumbnail. One way to map the thumbnails to actual paths is by examining the Windows internal search database called *Windows.edb*, located in the folder [systemroot]\ProgramData\Microsoft\Search\Applications\Windows. The attempt to map can be done in, for instance, Thumbcache Viewer.

4.8 Windows Event Viewer

As we declared in the beginning of this book, digital forensics is about figuring out what a computer was used for. What can actually be seen as the golden ticket to that goal is the built-in Windows Event Viewer, the internal logging tool in Windows. As stated by Microsoft Technet (2018), Event Viewer "maintains logs about program,

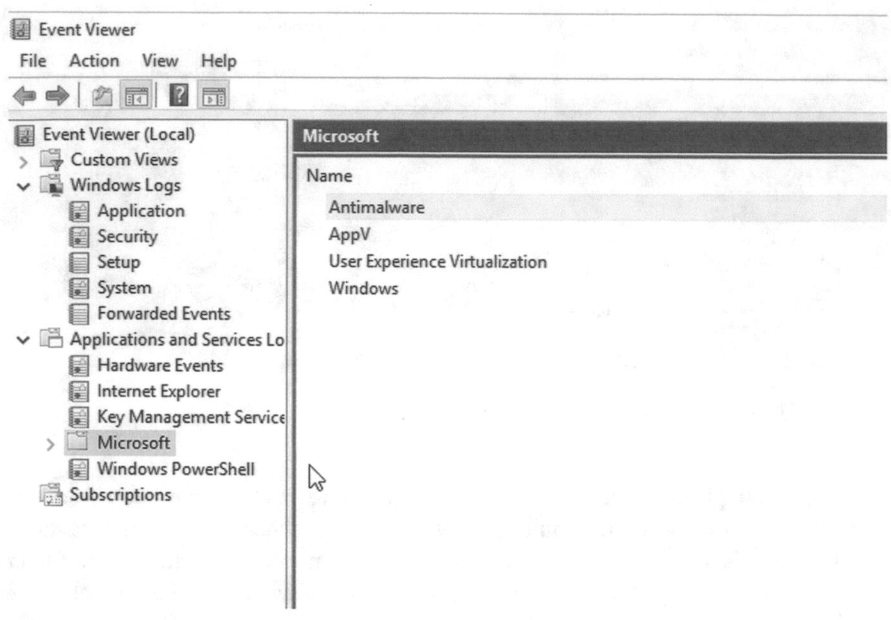

Fig. 4.8 Windows Event Viewer

security, and system events on your computer." As such, it is a great place to figure out what happened on a computer.

Windows event logs are commonly analyzed using Event Viewer, which is built into Windows. The actual logs are stored in files, and there can be loads of different log files. Looking at Event Viewer, shown in Fig. 4.8, you will notice that the logs are classified into "Windows logs" and "Application and Service logs." The log files under "Windows logs" are the most commonly used and work as follows:

- Application: Logs sent from applications are located here. Windows applications logs will usually end up here, and logs from other applications may end up here. It is up to the application developer to decide how logging is managed.
- System: Logs sent by system components will end up here.
- Security: Security events such as user log-ons will end up here.

Further, for the application and service logs, there are log files for virtually everything that is built into Windows, and it is possible to browse those logs on an application-by-application basis.

Next thing to know about the actual entries in the log files is that they can be of different types. The logs filed under Security will be audit logs that can be Audit Success or Audit Fail. The other logs will concern how applications and hardware perform and can be information, warning, or error.

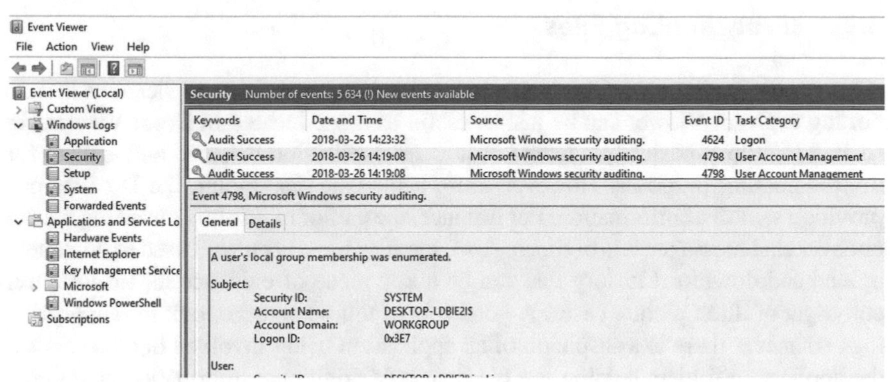

Fig. 4.9 Windows log entry

Table 4.2 Some event IDs of forensic interest

Event ID	Description
4624	Tracks user log-ons; the log entry will contain a log-on type that will tell you if the user logged on locally or remotely and more. Type 2 indicates a local log-on and 10 indicates a remote log-on
4634	Tracks user logoffs
4116	Tracks time changes and will describe the name of the user account that changed the time settings
11,707	This event tracks software installations

What may be of more forensic interest is how to understand what kind of events the logs actually describe. A log entry is shown in Fig. 4.9.

As shown in Fig. 4.9, every log entry comes with a set of attributes. First, the keyword will describe the log type as described above, and it is followed by a time stamp indicating when the entry was written. The next value identifies the source indicating where the log came from. This can be some Windows process as in this case, or some application. Then the log has an event ID, and the event ID will classify the event into some category. Actually, many events that are logged have predetermined event IDs enabling a forensic examiner to search for interesting event IDs in order to identify events of interest for a forensic examination. Some of the more interesting event IDs from a forensic standpoint are listed in Table 4.2.

As for analyzing the log files, using Event Viewer seems like a well-working option; it is possible to extract log files from a computer and import them into Event Viewer on another computer used for analysis. The log files are located in *[SystemRoot]\Windows\System32\winevt\Logs.*

4.9 Program Log Files

While on the topic of log files, it should be noted that logs from applications that do not log to Event Viewer can be just as useful as those located in Event Viewer. As such, a log file is basically a listing of how an application behaved and is there for troubleshooting purposes. However, from a forensic standpoint, the log files can provide a wealth of information. For instance, the author of this book used log files to uncover chat messages lots of times. Also, log files have been well used to document upload and download history that can be a key piece of evidence in, for instance, copyright of illicit picture cases. A good rule of thumb is to go look for application logs whenever there is a suspicion of an application being involved in a case. Also, the application folders holding log files can hold additional information about how the user used the application.

As for where log files are stored, it is impossible to provide a golden rule as the decision is up to the application creators. However, a very common place to find application logs is the user AppData folder ([UserHomeFolder]\AppData). Another common location of log files is in the application folder located under [SystemRoot]\ProgramData. Interpreting the log files can also be cumbersome and does not follow a standard practice as they can be structured in any way that you can imagine. However, experimenting with a program to see what logs they output during a known use case can help. This practice is further described in Sect. REFTEXT.

4.10 USB Device History

In modern-day usage of computers, it is extremely common to use USB devices to store data. As such, being able to detect and examine how USB devices have been connected to a computer can be very important during a forensic examination. Fortunately, Windows will track quite a few events in relation to USB devices being connected and disconnected from a computer. Identifying what USB devices that have been connected to a computer running Windows would involve combined information from three sources: setupapi.dev.log, the registry, and the system logs.

Setupapi.dev.log is a log file located in the folder [SystemRoot]\Windows\INF. It logs events related to installation and uninstallation of devices, and when a USB device is inserted, it is installed before use making this log file one source of information. Figure 4.10 shows the beginning of an entry relating to a USB stick being inserted.

As shown in Fig. 4.10, the first line shows that a device is being installed, and one could use the term "USBSTOR\Disk&Ven" to search for events relating to USB storage devices. Following that line is the device vendor, in this case Kingston, followed by the product name, in this case DataTraveler 3.0. It should, however, be noted that vendor name and product name is up to the manufacturer to specify, and it is quite common that they do not; instead, these fields may hold more generic information. For the purpose of tracking the USB device, the most important piece of information revealed is the device serial number, residing at the end of the first

```
>>>  [Device Install (Hardware initiated) - USBSTOR
\Disk&Ven_Kingston&Prod_DataTraveler_3.0&Rev_PMAP\08606E694934BEA1B7057E9D&0]
>>>  Section start 2018/03/27 11:07:13.879
     ump: Creating Install Process: DrvInst.exe 11:07:13.882
     ndv: Retrieving device info...
     ndv: Setting device parameters...
     ndv: Searching just Driver Store...
     dvi: {Build Driver List} 11:07:13.902
```

Fig. 4.10 USB entry in setupapi.dev.log

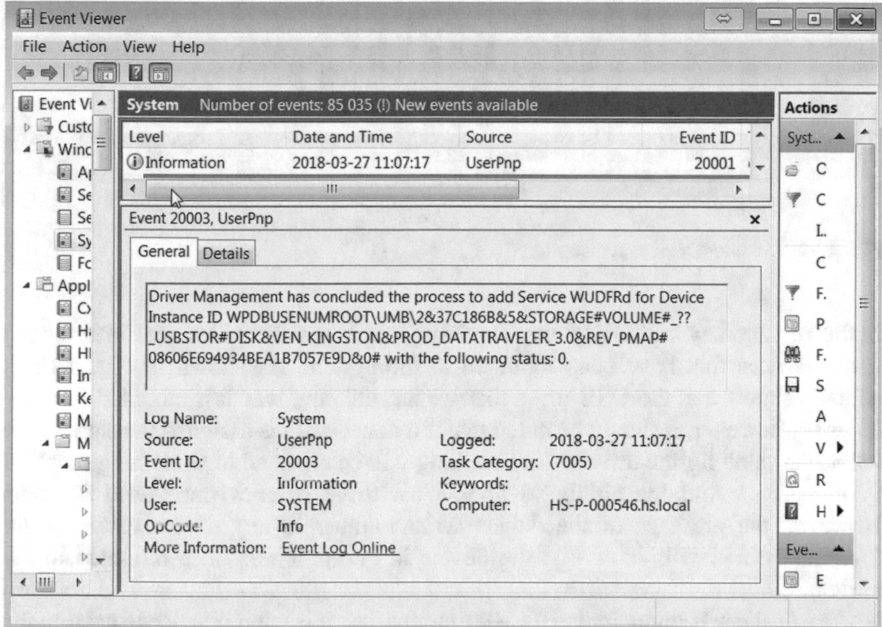

Fig. 4.11 USB installation in Event Viewer

line. In this case, it is 08606E694934BEA1B7057E9D&0. The same information can be found through the Windows system logs, with event ID 20001, as shown in Fig. 4.11.

Having gathered the information from the above-described logs, additional information can be found in the Windows registry. Using USB thumbs will leave several traces in the registry, all in the system hive. The first point of interest is the sub-keys to *ControlSet001\Enum\USBSTOR*. This key will hold sub-keys for different vendor and product name combinations that in turn contains sub-keys for the different USB devices that have been connected. The sub-keys will have the device serial numbers as name. This information can serve as a confirmation or alternative path to reveal the information that we just found using logs. There are several other places in the registry where similar information can be found, but what would be the next step is to figure out the mount point that was used for the USB drive. The first place to look

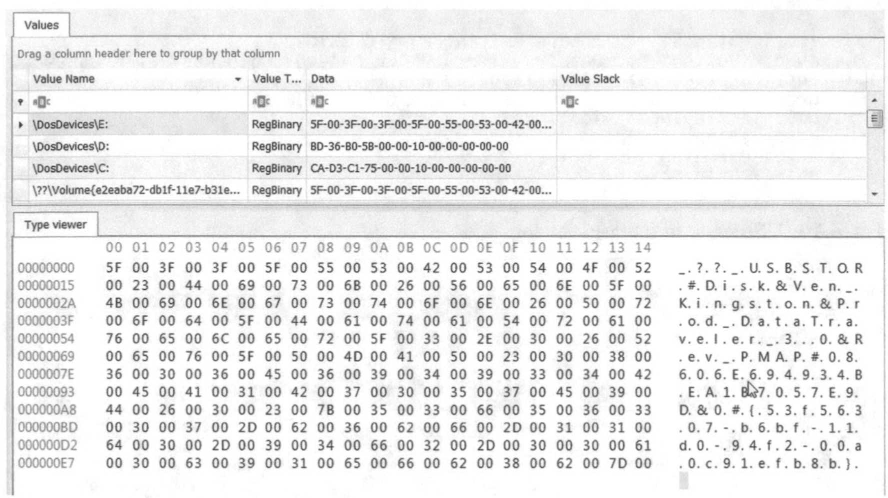

Fig. 4.12 MountedDevices registry key

is the registry key called *MountedDevices*. This key will hold useful information about devices that have been mounted to the system. As shown in Fig. 4.12, it actually shows that the USB drive that we are tracking was last mounted as drive letter E:. However, it should be noted that if a new device is assigned the same drive letter, the value for the drive we are tracking will be changed to something like "\?? \Volume. . . ." And the ability to track what drive letter it once used is gone. However, the presence of the device serial number in any of the values under *MountedDevices* will show that the device in question was once mounted to the system.

As a final mark, upon finding a USB thumb drive, it is good practice to capture the serial number from that device in order to be able to tie that drive to the computer that is subject to examination.

Note that the examples relating to USB device history were created using a computer running Windows 7. However, as discussed by Arshad et al. (2017), the artifacts are the same for Windows 10.

4.11 Questions and Tasks

1. What is file metadata and EXIF information?
2. Prefetch, Shellbags, .lnk file and MRU data will provide insight into how a computer system was used. How and why are these artifacts on interest during a forensic examination?
3. How can thumbcache help detect pictures that have been deleted from a computer?

4. Why would a forensic examiner care about Windows internal and program specific log files?
5. Discuss when it can be important to detect if a certain USB device has been connected to a computer.

References

Arshad A, Iqbal W, Abbas H (2017) USB storage device forensics for Windows 10. J Forensic Sci 63:856–867

Magnet Forensics (2014) Forensic analysis of LNK files. Available online: https://www.magnetforensics.com/computer-forensics/forensic-analysis-of-lnk-files/. Fetched March 22, 2018

Mansurov N (2018) What is EXIF data? Available online: https://photographylife.com/what-is-exif-data. Fetched March 12, 2018

Nair R (2012) What is app launch prefetching and how does it help? Available online: https://social.technet.microsoft.com/wiki/contents/articles/13011.what-is-app-launch-prefetching-and-how-does-it-help.aspxaspx. Fetched March 13, 2018

TechNet (2018) Event viewer. Available online: https://technet.microsoft.com/en-us/library/cc938674.aspx. Fetched March 26, 2018

5 Decryption and Password Enforcing

A common task during any forensic examination is to attempt to decrypt encrypted data in different forms ranging from encrypted files or folders to encrypted communication such as e-mail and chat or even complete hard drives that have been encrypted, full disk encryption (FDE). Data can be encrypted following a user's active choice to encrypt data, but it is also common for modern devices to employ data encryption as default behavior. As such, encryption is one of the major obstacles in forensic examinations, and as a forensic examiner, it is vital to have some know-how on how to crack encrypted files and passwords. The methods for breaking encryption and hashing can roughly be divided into two different methods—decryption attacks and password cracking. The rest of this section will describe them both, after presenting some theory around passwords.

Before dwelling into the interesting parts, there is some terminology that we need to understand, as repetition from the discussion on encryption, the encrypted data is called cipher (denoted C) and the readable version of the data is called plaintext (denoted P). The password, or key, used in the encryption and decryption process is denoted as K. During a forensic examination, we usually find a cipher, and we need to figure out K in order to get the readable plaintext. Hashing is commonly used to store plaintext (P) in an unreadable format called digest (H). From a forensic standpoint, we can usually get hold of the digest and want to figure out the plaintext. The rest of this chapter will provide a theoretical background to approaches used for cracking. It is accompanied by a practical description on the topic, presented in Chap. 13.

5.1 Password Theory

Before getting into how to crack passwords, let's review some background about how passwords are created and why. This knowledge is very important in order to enable efficient passwords cracking. In essence the research and practitioner community is coming to an understanding around the fact that there are two major factors

J. Kävrestad, *Fundamentals of Digital Forensics*,
https://doi.org/10.1007/978-3-030-38954-3_5

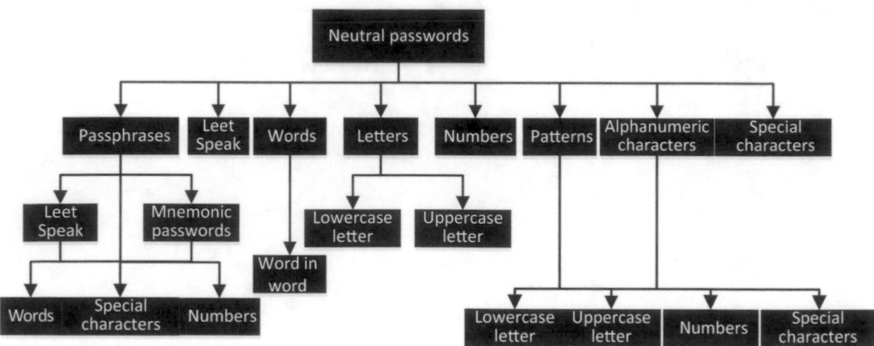

Fig. 5.1 Password classification model. (Kävrestad et al. 2018)

that affect passwords security, computational security (how hard they are to crack) and memorability (how easy they are for users to remember). There are two district approaches to creating passwords with different drawbacks and benefits to security. Those approaches are user-generated passwords that a user is creating himself and system-generated passwords where the user is using some software to create a password that is often random. When users are creating passwords using a software or are faced with password complexity requirements, they commonly employ some strategy to ensure that they remember their passwords. Those can be to write them down or possibly use a password manager. A common practice to cope with complexity requirements is to simply add whatever is required, such as a special character, to the end of a password to make it comply with technical demands.

Looking at passwords created by users, it is very common for users to employ some strategy to make the passwords easy to remember. Understanding what strategies that can be used to create passwords, The Development of a Password Classification Model by Kävrestad et al. (2018) is a good starting point. The main contribution in that paper is a model used for categorization of passwords according to strategies used to create the password. The model is partially presented in Fig. 5.1.

The idea with the model presented in Fig. 5.1 is to outline the different strategies that can be used for password creation as characteristics where a password may hold one or more of them. The model was designed by interviewing forensics experts that worked with password cracking as a part of the work duties. It has also been tested against 5000 real passwords from leaked databases. From left to right, the categories are explained as follows.

Passphrases are simple phrases put together to form a password. It may include words, special characters, and numbers, and one example could be *joakim@trimroad1*. Passphrases may be further modified using leetspeak, where characters are changed into other characters according to a leetspeak alphabet, or be mnemonic, meaning that the first letter or every word in a sentence is used to form a password. A sample of a mnemonic password can be to use the phrase *my little cute red car* to form the password *mlcrc*.

Table 5.1 Leetspeak alphabet (Kävrestad et al. 2018)

Table of leetspeak alphabet		M = /\/\	T = 7 or +
A = /\ or 4	G = 6	N = |\\\|	U = |_|
B = |3 or I3 or 8	H = |-|	O = 0	V = \/
C = (or [	I = |	P = 9	W = |/\\|
D = |) or |>	J = _|	Q = (,)	X = ><
E = 3	K = |<	R = |2	Y = \-/
F = |=	L = |_	S = 5	Z = 2

Moving from passphrases, leetspeak can be a characteristic of any password, not just passphrases. As just mentioned, using leetspeak to create a password involves taking a word and changing some or all signs according to a leetspeak alphabet. A leetspeak alphabet is presented in Table 5.1. Using the leetspeak approach, the password *Joakim* could be transformed into *j04ki/\/*.

The next characteristic, words, is quite self-explanatory. It would be passwords made up of words and includes the sub-category that is called word in word. A word in word password is a password made up of two words where one is inserted into the other. For instance, using *red* and *car* to create a word in word password could result in *credar*.

Next category is letters that can be upper- or lowercase followed by numbers that are, well, numbers. Then, we have the category patterns. Using patterns would mean using patterns on a keyboard as passwords; for instance, *QWERTY* would be a pattern with six letters in a row starting from q on a QWERTY keyboard. A more complex pattern could be *¨´å + p0o9i* created by doing a zigzag pattern from right to left starting with ¨ and ´. As depicted by the sub-categories, the patterns may hold letters, numbers, and special characters. The same goes for the next category called alphanumerical characters. This is a category for passwords that does not fit any other category, namely, those that appear to be random. The model ends with a category for special characters.

As mentioned, the model presented in Fig. 5.1 is only a part of the model presented by Kävrestad et al. (2018). The model presented in their paper included two more main categories. The main category presented in Fig. 5.1 is neutral passwords; the model presented by Kävrestad et al. (2018) also includes biographical and system generated as main categories. Neutral and biographical passwords are created by the users, while system-generated passwords are created by a computer. Further, biographical passwords will contain some information relating to the person who owns the password, while neutral passwords will not. Including information that relates to the password, owner seems to be a common approach when creating passwords. While the described strategies can help users remember their passwords, the obvious drawback is that they are not at all random. That is knowledge that can be leveraged in forensic examinations.

The final topic to discuss under the headline of password theory is password reuse. An average user will have many different accounts and passwords for different uses, and remembering them all is extremely hard. In addition to using coping techniques, users tend to reuse passwords, or parts of passwords, over many different places. In practice, this means that a password for a given purpose, such as file encryption, can be compromised if it is used somewhere else. A very common way for passwords to be compromised is via password leaks. Passwords leak from various sites all the time and can be easily downloaded by anyone.

5.2 Decryption Attacks

A decryption attack is where you attack the encryption or hashing algorithm or implementation of it in order to deduce the plaintext from the cipher or digest. Using this kind of attack will save you the trouble of trying to guess the password, a time-consuming approach. However, the most commonly used algorithms do not suffer any weaknesses that make an attack against the algorithm feasible. There are algorithms that are considered to be cracked, but in a forensic context, you are usually limited in time, meaning that for an attack to be considered successful, it must be successful within the provided time scope. For that reason, being able to crack an algorithm in matter of years or months is commonly not good enough. You should, however, know about the existence of this approach because every so often you stumble upon some old and weak algorithm. Whenever you are about to attack some application or algorithm you are not familiar with, be encouraged to research it to determine the best point of attack.

Even if you are not able to attack the actual encryption algorithm, there may be weaknesses in how it was implemented. You may uncover such a weakness by experimenting on how a software works and then be able to find something to exploit. This was actually the case for me and a colleague of mine a couple of years back. We worked a case where the suspects used a Web site called Privnote to send encrypted messages that destroyed themselves upon being read. We could find traces of the messages on the suspect's computer, but they were encrypted. After examining Privnote, we realized that when you sent someone a link to a Privnote message, you had to give them a URL, and the URL contained the key used for encryption. We could also deduce that the AES algorithm, which is a symmetric encryption algorithm, was used for encryption. The experiment told us that we should be able to harvest possible keys from the computer's browsing history and then use whatever we found to decrypt the messages we uncovered, and we could.

From a practical standpoint, there are forensic password cracking software that can help you analyze files and tell if a decryption attack is possible. As always, another practical tip is to analyze the software and algorithm you are about to crack. A Google search will commonly reveal if there are any known weaknesses.

Before looking at password guessing attacks, you should be aware of the existence of attacks that are similar to decryption attacks, called side channel attacks. A side channel attack can be described as an attack where you find information by looking at sources that the creator of a system did not expect for you to look at. It can also be about looking somewhere or at something that the creator did not even anticipate that you could look at in order to retrieve information. In computer forensics, a common side channel would be the computer memory. Consider a case when someone is using some encryption software in order to encrypt files. Whenever the files are to be used, they have to be decrypted, meaning that the computer has to store a temporary decrypted version of the file in the memory. If you have access to a memory dump, you may just uncover the decrypted version of the file instead of going through the trouble of decrypting it.

Adding the knowledge that parts of memory are sometimes paged out and stored in a file on the hard drive that is called *pagefile.sys*, it becomes evident that it is also a location where side channel data can be retrieved. A quite common artifact to recover in this manner is, in the experience of the author, fragments of e-mails sent using a Web-based e-mail client such as Hotmail or some encrypted e-mail provider. No matter if those e-mails are sent and/or stored encrypted or decrypted, they will always be in a decrypted state when they are read; otherwise they would be pointless. When an e-mail is read, it must be stored in the computer memory, and there is therefore a fair chance that it is also paged out and stored in *Pagefile.sys* where it can be recovered using forensic tools.

5.3 Password Guessing Attacks

The most common case is that a decryption attack is not possible. In that case, you need to resort to password guessing. Technically, a password guessing attack against an encryption scheme means that you try different keys until you get a result. This works because a basic property of an encryption algorithm is that if you supply an algorithm with the wrong key, it will return nothing or a null value. That way you can know that if you get something, you get the plaintext. You could express this in an equation, like so:

$$\texttt{Unsuccessful attempt}: C + K_{\texttt{wrong}} = \texttt{Nothing}$$
$$\texttt{Successful attempt}: C + K_{\texttt{correct}} = P$$

Password guessing against hash algorithms works a little bit different, because there is commonly no key to submit. Instead, you need to hash different data sets and compare the hash values that you get with the one you want to crack. When you get a hash value matching the value you want to crack, you are done. Consider a case where you want to crack the digest $H_{tocrack}$ by hashing multiple different P, called $P_{test.}$ For a successful attempt, the H for P_{test} would be equal to $H_{tocrack}$, like so:

$$P_{\texttt{test}} \rightarrow H_{\texttt{tocrack}}$$

Given that P_{test} is the wrong plaintext, you would get some other value as H.

Now that you know the basics of password guessing, it is time to get a bit practical. Traditionally, password guessing attacks have been divided into brute force and dictionary attacks. Using a brute force attack, you try every possible combination of signs until you get to the correct one. This attack can be quite feasible on short passwords but totally impossible to succeed with for longer passwords; this is because of the fact that the number of potential passwords will increase exponentially when you add characters to the password length. A dictionary attack involves assembling a list of strings and testing each of them in turn to see if the password is any of the words in the dictionary. The success of the dictionary attack depends on the ability to build a dictionary that contains the password. There are also some other types of attacks that can be used that leverage the fact that users tend to use different strategies when creating passwords or knowledge about what characters that are most commonly used in passwords. Those can be seen as smart brute force attacks or other ways to do dictionary attacks.

In essence, a password guessing attack or the success rate of a password guessing attack is very dependent on the time available to crack a given password. Thus, the attack has to executed as effectively as possible, and that would normally include choosing different attacks based on how fast they are and how likely they are to succeed. To do that there are some values that we need to be aware about in order to crack the given password. The first value is the time needed to execute an attack. The execution time of a single attack would be calculated as the time it takes to exhaust the entropy of the attack. The attack entropy is simply the total number of passwords that will be tested during the attack. The entropy divided with your attack capabilities, the number of passwords you may test per hour, will tell you how long it will take to execute the attack. The attack capability will vary depending on hardware resources and the encryption algorithm to attack; it is, for instance, well-known that it's possible to test substantially more passwords per second against a VeraCrypt container than against a password protected rar file. For the sake of this book, we will consider the attack capability to be 10 billion passwords per hour. In summary, the attack time can be expressed as follows:

$$\texttt{Attack time} = \texttt{entropy/capability}$$

One may argue that the average attack time will only be half of the above, because by chance, we will only need to test half of all possible passwords before finding the one we are looking for. If we test all possible key combinations (brute force), that is true. But if we use some other kind of attack, there is a reasonable chance that the attack will fail altogether, and thus, it is more feasible to calculate the time for a worst-case scenario, which will essentially tell us how much time that we waste if the attack fails.

The first type of attack we will have a deeper look at is brute force attacks. A brute force attack involves testing all possible combinations of characters and will, thus, test all possible passwords. The good thing with a brute force attack is that it will eventually be successful; the caveat is that it is insanely time-consuming and practically impossible for longer passwords—at least until quantum computers are getting used. The entropy for a brute force attack can be calculated as the number of different possible characters to the power of n where n is the password length. Given that a password contains English upper- and lowercase letters and numbers, you get 62 different possible characters. That information can be used to calculate the time to exhaust the entropy or, as in this case, the average time to crack a password. The rules of probability tell us that we will, on average, have to go through half the key

Table 5.2 Sample key space and cracking time for passwords

Password length	Equation	Resulting key space	Sample crack time in hours
4	62^4	14,776,336	0.0014
5	62^5	916,132,832	0.0916
6	62^6	56,800,235,584	5.68
7	62^7	3,521,614,606,208	352 (14 days)
8	62^8	218,340,105,584,896	21,834 (909 days)

space to find the correct password. Thus, the time it takes to crack a password can be expressed like so:

$$(\texttt{Keyspace/attemptsperday})/2 = \texttt{averagecrackingtimeindays}.$$

As an example, key space and cracking time for passwords of different length in our scenario are presented in Table 5.2.

As you can tell from the numbers in Table 5.2, cracking an eight-character-long password using a brute force attack is very time-consuming. Even if we give ourselves computer power enough to test 100 billion passwords per hour, it would still take us about 90 days to crack it. That is way too long, not to mention that passwords containing special characters or even longer will take exponentially longer time to crack. Thus, brute force attacks are often only feasible as a way to test very short passwords.

Fortunately, there are more efficient ways to perform password guessing attacks. Perhaps the most common and widely used is the dictionary attack that is based on you creating a list of words and then testing to see if any of the words is the password. The basics of a dictionary attack are simple—if the password is one of the words in your list, you will crack the password. If the password is not in the list, it won't get cracked. Following that analogy, the successfulness of a dictionary attack is based on the attacker's, your, ability to make a good dictionary. Luckily, there is a method to work with!

The method used for creation of dictionaries, as presented in this book, is based on two well-known facts about computer's password behavior. At a glance, computer users tend to follow common rules when creating their passwords.

1. They use some strategy to help them remember the password.
2. They reuse passwords, or parts of passwords.

The password creation strategies we explored previously taught us that users tend to use different strategies when creating passwords, such as including plain words and biographical information. Moving on to password reuse, it is a well-known secret that computer users tend to use the same passwords or at least similar passwords across multiple accounts (Das et al. 2014). Leveraging this knowledge,

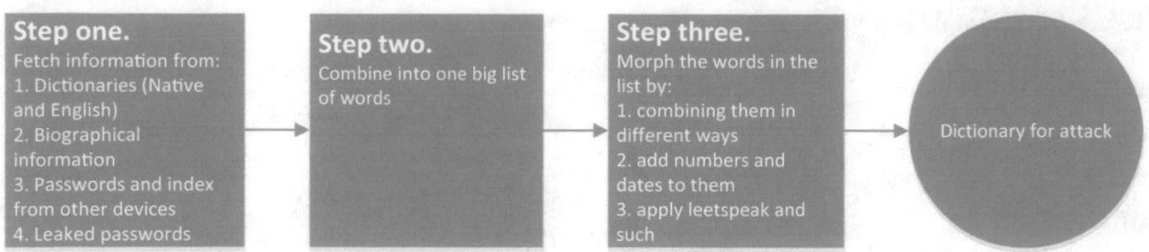

Fig. 5.2 Creating a dictionary for a dictionary attack

it becomes evident that if you know previous passwords owned by the person owning what you are attempting to crack, your success chance will increase.

Using the ideas that people reuse passwords and use certain strategies when they create their passwords, the dictionary creation model presented in Fig. 5.2 was developed. The model begins with a first step where you are looking to your sources to get hold of words that could have been used to create the password you are about to crack. This would involve general sources of words, addresses, and more as well as specific sources relating to your target and sources of leaked passwords. As a general rule, the information fetched in this step would at least include:

- Word lists to get a base of English words and/or words in the language that is of relevance for the attack.
- Biographical information that would include all possible information about the person owning the password you want to crack. This would include name, address, family members, birth dates, words relating to interests, and more. As an example, if you are attacking a computer owned by someone in love with Lord of the Rings, it is a good idea to perhaps include the complete Lord of the Rings book in your dictionary.
- Passwords and indexes from other devices that you have access to or readable data on the device you are working on.
- Leaked passwords are just passwords that have been leaked and published online. There are dozens of databases if you look close enough, and there is a chance that your guy has had a compromised account on one of the leaked sites.

As a practical tip, the leaked databases and language dictionaries are often used in several attacks. It is therefore a smart practice to have one dictionary that contains this general information and create a second dictionary with the information that is specific to the case, namely, the biographical data and the data from other devices. It is also clever to keep wordlists that you create, if your local regulations permit. It does happen that a suspect in a current case becomes a suspect in a future case; if she encrypted files the second time around, it is a fair chance that the new password will be present in one of the old lists. It happened to the author of this book at several occasions.

Moving on, step two is just about merging the lists you gathered in order to get ready for an attack, and step three is about morphing the words in the dictionary according to the password characteristics we just discussed. This would, for instance, involve applying leetspeak, generating phrases, and making phrases mnemonic. You may also include different keyboard patterns, for instance, passwords based on lines on the keyboards (for instance, qwerty of 1q2w3e4r) or zigzag patterns (qazwsxedc) in the word list. As a final note, it should be mentioned that depending on your software, some of the steps in the dictionary process can be about modifying the actual dictionaries or just applying rules that will morph the dictionaries on the fly. This will be discussed further in Chap. 13.

Now I guess that you are saying that you will end up with a very large list of word and mutations, and that is true. In my experience, the size of the list will be up to about two billion words. However, remember that with a reasonable amount of computer power, you can test about ten billion passwords in 1 h making two billion attempts very reasonable.

A final attack approach that can be used is smart brute force attacks. A smart brute force attack would be a brute force attack that uses statistical data about passwords to test more probable password before others. For instance, it is well-known that lowercase letters and numbers are much more frequently used in passwords than uppercase letters and special characters (Kävrestad et al. 2019). The last version of password guidelines from NIST omits complexity requirements from their guidelines, making the current situation likely to remain (Grassi et al. 2017). It is also well-known that uppercase letters, when used, are most commonly used as the first character in the password and that special characters are commonly placed at the end of passwords. Leveraging statistical knowledge of passwords can allow execution of smart brute force attack that is likely to find passwords much faster than a traditional brute force attack.

5.4 Questions and Tasks

1. Describe a decryption attack.
2. What is the difference between a brute force and a dictionary attack?
3. What sources of information can be used to create a dictionary for a dictionary attack?

References

Das A, Bonneau J, Caesar M, Borisov N, Wang X (2014) The tangled web of password reuse. In: NDSS, vol 14, pp 23–26

Grassi P, Fenton J, Newton E, Perlner R, Regenscheid A, Burr W, Richer J, Lefkovitz N, Danker J, Choong Y-Y (2017) NIST special publication 800-63b: digital identity guidelines. National Institute of Standards and Technology (NIST)

Kävrestad J, Eriksson F, Nohlberg M (2018) The development of a password classification model. In Security Conference 2018, Las Vegas

Kävrestad J, Zaxmy J, Nohlberg M (2019) Analysing the usage of character groups and keyboard patterns in password usage. Human Aspects of Information Security & Assurance (HAISA 2019) International Symposium on Human Aspects of Information Security & Assurance (HAISA 2019), Nicosia, Cyprus, July 15–17, 2019

Part II

The Forensic Process

Up until this point, digital forensics has been discussed from a very theoretical and abstract perspective. The second part of the book will be more concrete and discuss the parts of the forensic process that was established in Part I in more detail. This part will begin with a discussion on two major areas where forensic examinations are common, as part of criminal investigations and as part of incident response work. Following the presentation in criminal investigations and incident response, this part will cover different methods of data collection and present a discussion on analyzing evidence and writing forensic reports, and a discussion on forensic triage is also included.

Cybercrime, Cyber Aided Crime, and Digital Evidence

6

Before dwelling deeper into forensics, it seems reasonable to have a discussion on what signifies cybercrime or, maybe more importantly, how and when digital evidence comes into play during criminal investigations. I choose to include this discussion due to the fact that during my work as a forensic examiner, I was often faced with the misconception that my daily work was with cybercrime in the sense of computer hacking and that sort of things. In reality, digital evidence is present in crimes of almost every kind. Even so, it can be of importance to understand the different roles of digital evidence in different types of crimes. On the topic of cybercrime and cyber-related crimes, one could divide the types of crimes in the following way:

- Cybercrime
- Cyber aided crime
- Crimes with digital evidence

To further understand the difference of these different categories, a short discussion on what a crime actually is would be useful. To begin that discussion, it is interesting to look at what Rogers wrote back in 2000 (Rogers 2000). He uses the traditional approach of means, motive, and opportunity to discuss cybercriminals. In this discussion, motive is the reason why someone is committing a crime. Take defrauding as an example, in which the common motive is to earn money. Means would be the tools used to commit the crime, and opportunity could be described as the possibility to commit the crime. One could argue that a crime begins in motive and that the means and opportunity are mere results of the easiest way to achieve what is wanted as motive.

So, for a crime to happen, there has to be means, motive, and opportunity. Further, there has to be someone who is committing the crime, a criminal, and someone who is targeted by the crime, a victim. Finally, there is some kind of relationship between the criminal and the victim; something is happening between them. It should be noted that this is a simplified view that is not always 100%

J. Kävrestad, *Fundamentals of Digital Forensics*,
https://doi.org/10.1007/978-3-030-38954-3_6

accurate, but it is good to have this basic notion of what a crime is in order to dwell deeper into what a cybercrime or cyber aided crime would be.

6.1 Cybercrime

Looking at what a true cybercrime could be, Interpol (2018) provides the following definition:

> Advanced cybercrime (or high-tech crime)—sophisticated attacks against computer hardware and software

Going from that definition, one could say that cybercrimes are crimes where computers are used to do crimes at other computers. This would include, for instance, computer intrusions or denial of service attacks. This gives that cybercrimes are crimes that can only be committed by someone who has a fair knowledge on how computers work. Looking at the discussion on means, motive, and opportunity for a crime and applying those to cybercrime, it is reasonable to say that for a crime to be a true cybercrime, the means and opportunity would involve computerized tools and knowledge for a crime to be cyber. This discussion becomes important when an investigation is trying to find suspects, as the knowledge needed to commit a crime would be part of the suspect's profile. That, however, is not a topic to be discussed in a book about computer forensics.

6.2 Cyber Aided Crime

A much broader category of crimes would be cyber aided crimes. As discussed by Interpol (2018), those are traditional crimes that make use of the Internet in some way. This is exemplified by Kävrestad (2014) who studied the difference between online and offline fraud. In that study, the process of a fraud was modeled as shown in Fig. 6.1.

In brief, Fig. 6.1 depicts that a fraud happens when a fraudster deceives a victim into giving up something of monetary value. For this to be possible, there has to be a delivery method for the actual fraud. The delivery method can be through e-mail, telephone, or real-life contact. What decides if a fraud is online or offline was found to be how the delivery is carried out, an online fraud will be carried out using digital means of communication, and an offline fraud would use offline means of communication. This distinction is important because it helps the forensic expert or the investigator to understand how a crime was committed and thus how to best investigate it, that is, where to look for evidence.

Looking at how crimes are committed today, most crimes have been around for a long time and are committed by criminals who do not necessarily hold any high grade of computer skills. However, the use of computers created a new arena where it appears convenient to embark on criminal activities such as frauds, drug trades,

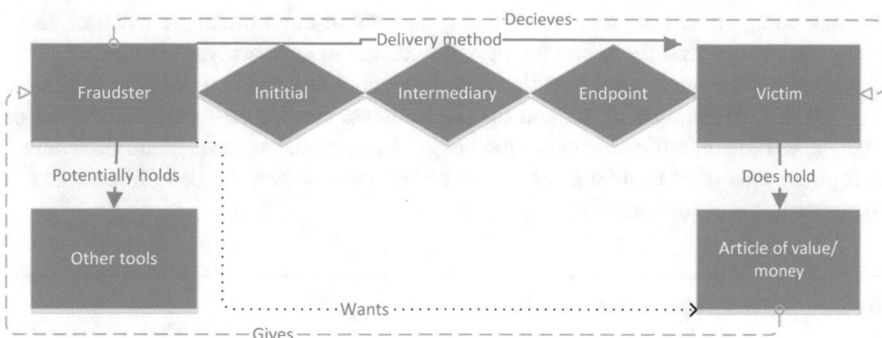

Fig. 6.1 Model of a fraud (Kävrestad 2014)

child abuse, or whatever. As such, the criminals are not typically computer experts; rather, the online and offline fraudsters and drug dealers are the same type of criminals. An interesting result of this development is that cyber aided crimes will leave traces in the digital world, which the suspects are often not aware about.

This view is further discussed by Rogers (2001), who described different types of computer criminals. On the topic of online fraudsters, he argued that online fraudsters are simply fraudsters that commit their crimes online. The same can be said about criminals who sell drugs online and are involved in child exploitation crimes and a wide range of other criminals. They are committing traditional crimes and have traditional motives, but they see the opportunity to commit the crimes from the comfort of their own house, using the Internet. Also, as of today, the means to commit the crimes become owning a computer, and most people have a computer already.

6.3 Crimes with Digital Evidence

It goes without saying that a forensic expert can look for, and expect to find, digital evidence in cybercrimes and cyber aided crimes. Actually, it is interesting to notice how a lot of information that was extremely hard or even impossible to come by in offline crime is quite often captured when the crimes are committed in an online environment. Consider, for example, a drug trade. A traditional drug trade would involve two people meeting in the streets to exchange drugs and money. Oftentimes, there would not be a single trace of that transaction ever taking place unless it was monitored. However, doing the very same trade online would involve e-mail or chat between the buyer and seller as well as a digital transaction of money. This digital communication and money transaction will leave digital traces that can be uncovered and used as evidence.

As an end to this brief cybercrime discussion, we should not forget how digital evidence can play a big role even in crimes that are totally offline. Thing is, in the modern society, it is very hard to do anything without leaving digital traces. Even if you are doing something totally offline, in the heat of the moment or whatnot, there is a great chance that there can be digital evidence to support what happened. This can involve communication logs that can show what the criminal did after the crime was committed. Maybe he looked up punishments for the crime he committed or even talked to some friend about what he did. I have even seen an example where a cell phone was used to tie a suspect to a crime scene, when the cell phone was not even used, it was just present!

6.4 Questions and Tasks

The task of this chapter is to get hold of two verdicts and then read them and consider how digital evidence is used in the cases. Try to get one verdict about a traditional cybercrime such as hacking or copyright infringement and one about something unrelated to the digital world, such as theft. In Sweden, you can call a local court and have them send you verdicts over e-mail, and you can also often find verdicts online, but just make sure you do not break any local laws!

References

Interpol. (2018) Cybercrime. Available online: https://www.interpol.int/Crime-areas/Cybercrime/Cybercrime. Fetched April 9, 2018

Kävrestad J (2014) Defining, categorizing and defending against online fraud

Rogers L (2000) Cybersleuthing: Means, motive, and opportunity. Available online: http://www.sei.cmu.edu/library/abstracts/news-at-sei/securitysum00.cfm. Fetched May 1, 2017

Rogers MK (2001) A social learning theory and moral disengagement analysis of criminal computer behavior: An exploratory study. Doctoral dissertation, University of Manitoba

Incident Response

7

Incident response, as discussed in this book, is basically about managing incidents in IT environments. As such, it is an important part of information security work and is gaining more and more attention; new laws and regulation such as GDPR and the NIS directive are even requiring some degree of incident response capabilities for affected organizations. While incident response is not necessarily a part of digital forensics, it is common to include forensic ideas and processes into parts of the incident response work. As such this chapter will introduce incident response and describe how digital forensics can be used as a part of incident response. The chapter will begin with a discussion on why and when incident response is important and discuss the major parts of preparing by establishing incident response capabilities and actually handling an incident.

7.1 Why and When?

As everyone has heard a thousand times by now, the modern world that we all live in is very dependent on IT and so is almost any organization. However, just as there are physical threats to organizations, such as thieves and natural disasters, there are a number of threats in the digital world. Those threats can actually cause our modern lifestyles to stop working entirely. It is also notable that the threat landscape has changed quite a bit since the early days of the Internet. As exemplified by Srinivasan (2017), hackers in the old days (a whopping 25 or so years ago) can perhaps be best described as pranksters that performed attack for challenge and recognition, while modern attacks often come with more serious motives. In the modern threat landscape, we are facing opponents that are organized criminals with financial objectives or even states engaging in, as exemplified by Connell and Vogler (2017), cyber warfare. Given the strong and organized nature of possible attackers, it is important to develop a capability of strong and organized responses to a potential incident, and that is where incident response plays a key role. To further describe the modern

J. Kävrestad, *Fundamentals of Digital Forensics*,
https://doi.org/10.1007/978-3-030-38954-3_7

threat landscape, this subchapter will end with two examples of attacks before the chapter moves on with incident response work.

The first example is the, by now, very well-known malware Stuxnet which according to Langner (2011) was the first example of a cyber warfare weapon. As described by Langner (2011), Stuxnet was a malware that primarily targeted specific controllers manufactured by Siemens and that was used in an Iranian uranium-enrichment plant. It was primarily spread via USB sticks and local networks and contained a payload that infected specific controllers. The infected code was dormant for a period of time and then triggered by a complex set of times and conditions. What is notable about this attack is that it was clearly targeted at the Iranian uranium-enrichment plant; it infected many Windows computers but would only drop its payload on a very specific set of controllers. It could also do its dirty work without access to command and control servers. All in all, it must be considered an attack at the Iranian nuclear program and not likely the work of a prankster.

Another example of a large-scale attack with high impact was an attack on several Ukrainian electricity providers in 2015. In essence, this attack made up to 225 000 customer lose power for several hours and forces energy companies to switch from manual operations as a result of the attacks (Lee et al., 2016). This attack comprised several components such as malware spread through spear phishing and denial of service attacks. Ultimately, an attack where a SCADA network was hijacked is used to bring down substations (Liang et al., 2016). Anyhow, this attack has been attributed to Russia, and lets for a second regard that as correct (Lee et al. 2016). It is close to other Russian activities in Ukraine, in time, and can then be seen as a part of warfare.

The final example is the WannaCry ransomware which went rampant in 2017 and infected more than 200 000 computers (Mohurle and Patil, 2017). What a ransomware does is that it encrypts data on a targeted machine and demands that the user pays a ransom in order to get the data back. WannaCry infected computer from a number of organizations including companies such as FedEx and hospitals. While it is hard to see a specific target with the WannaCry attack, it has been attributed to North Korea and will serve as yet another example of thc fact that modern adversaries are indeed powerful and motivated entities (Bossert, 2017). Also, it will soon be evident that a ransomware can have a large impact on an infected organization.

7.2 Establishing Capabilities

Whenever an incident occurs, that will be a stressful situation. Consider, for instance, the business impact and stress level at the IT department at MAERSK when they fell prey to the NotPetya ransomware in 2017. They were forced to reinstall close to 9000 computers and reported that they lose up to 300 million dollars due to business interruption (Osborne, 2018). Handling situations where the pressure is that high does indeed require careful preparation. Incidents are considered to be something that does happen, and when they do, it is important to respond fast and effective to minimize losses (Cichonski et al., 2012). Cichonski et al. (2012) and Kral (2011) propose that establishing capabilities is essentially about creating a computer incident response team (CIRT) and developing policies and procedures that allow them to work swiftly. The goal is to have a CIRT that known exactly what to do when it is activated.

When creating a CIRT, it is important to include all roles and competences that can be needed during an incident. This holds not only technical staff but could also include legal expertise, public affairs and media relations, and human resources and management. It is common for an incident to affect an organization in several ways, and it is therefore important for key roles in the organization to be involved in the incident handling. Depending on the incident, there may also be media interest, and it is therefore good to have someone that specializes in media contacts to handle media. Cichonski et al. (2012) also stress the need to have someone that is designated leader for the incident. This person will act as the main contact and coordinator for the incident. This is a role that can be divided between several persons for larger incidents.

Developing policies and procedures would most likely include several steps, which are all meant to give the CIRT the best possible ability to manage an incident that occurred. A policy, or incident response plan, will be an overall document that outlines how to react to an incident, or rather, a possible incident. The common case is that CIRT is activated when an incident is suspected, and a first step is to decide whether or not an incident has occurred. Anyhow, the policy would stipulate the rules of the incident response work within an organization and could include the following:

- Definition of what an incident is. This would include guidelines on when the CIRT should be activated and cover what is an incident that requires the CIRT rather than an incident that can be handled by day-to-day operations. Consider, for instance, the difference between a full-scale denial of service attack that renders the IT services of the organization useless compared to an incident where one employee downloads a file containing some malicious software. The former would require substantial effort and coordination and would indeed be handled by the CIRT. The latter could in many cases be resolved by someone from help desk, by reinstalling the system. In that case, the CIRT would not have to be involved.
- List of CIRT members with contact information and declaration of roles. This is important in order to know who is responsible for what and how to contact everyone. The list should also define authorities, meaning that it should specify who is in charge of what.
- Continuity plan that includes a prioritization of incidents and functions. The idea is to have a predetermined set of rules that describes what the most important assets are. If an incident arises, you do not want to spend time protecting services that are insignificant as the cost of those that are critical to the operations of the organization. In a blunt way of expressing it, the continuity plan should describe what you can sacrifice and what you need to protect at all costs. The continuity

plan could also include action to take in case of some incidents. For instance, if someone has managed to gain unauthorized access to the organization's network, it could be a good idea to plug the Internet cable from machines that store secret information.

- Communication plan that holds guidelines for whom to contact and when. The communication plan should cover internal communication plans as well as plans for when and how to contact outside parties such as media, law enforcement, and others.
- Listing of tools and physical resources that has to be in place.

As identified with the last bullet above, it is important to be prepared, not only in terms of having the right people accessible but also in terms of having the right gear ready to use. Derived from Cichonski et al. (2012) and Kral (2011), the following list includes what could be included in a response kit for incident response:

- The policy as described above
- Laptop(s) containing forensic software, anti-malware utilities, packet sniffers, network monitoring tools, documentation tools, and other tools that can be used to analyze and mitigate incidents
- Internet access that could take the form of some device that is not bound to the organization's network, such as a 4G modem
- Blank removable media
- USB devices or disks with live operating systems with up-to-date anti-malware utilities and other utilities that can be used to analyze devices
- General gear such as USB drives, cables, power cables, etc.
- Portable printer used to print information from devices not connected to the network or not currently available to the network
- Evidence gathering and documentation gear such as camera, audio recorder, evidence bags and tags, etc.

Before leaving this section on preparation, it is necessary to mention the obvious need for appropriate training. While working in IT often includes a fair bit of searching for information as you go, it should be stressed that training CIRT members so that they have the appropriate competence to act on an incident is important.

7.3 Incident Handling

When something that is regarded a possible incident happens, it must be managed in a structured way. Cichonski et al. (2012) and Kral (2011) describe the process of handling an incident in a similar way that can be summarized in three steps:

- Identify
- Contain, eradicate, and recover

- Post-incident activities

The first step, *identify*, contains actions that are designed to collect information that is used to identify if an actual incident that has to be handled by the CIRT has occurred and what the incident actually is. Typical activities performed in this step are to collect data from log files and analyze compromised computers and error messages. It is also common to include information from users and other that actually experienced the incident to figure out how the incident manifested itself and what the user did when the incident occurred. The aim of this phase is mainly to find out the scope of the incident, the type of incident, and the possible impact of the incident. A secondary aim of this phase is to capture data that can be used for later in-depth analysis of the incident and possibly legal processes. To create the best possible foundation for legal actions, information collected during this phase should be considered possible evidence and follow best practices and legal requirements for data collection (Cichonski et al., 2012). Further, Kent et al. (2006) describe that digital forensics techniques are important in incident management and describe several aspects of how digital forensics can be applied in incident response. How data collection should be carried out in practice should be determined in the preparation phase and written down in the policy.

The second step, *contain, eradicate, and recover*, concerns how an incident should actually be managed with the ultimate goal of making the incident case as little harm as possible and making the organization recover, get back to normal operating, as soon as possible. The first part of this step is to contain the incident as well as possible. The idea is to, once the scope of an incident has been established, try to stop the incident from causing any more harm. Containment can actually be seen from two perspectives: contain infected devices or contain uninfected devices. If it is possible to identify specific devices as infected, it would be a simple and good idea to disconnect those from the network. However, it can be equally important to, during an incident, isolate devices that contain important data to ensure that they are not compromised. Depending on the structure of the organization network and the nature of the incident, containment can be handled in a number of different ways, but the goal is always to minimize the damage of the incident.

Next comes eradication and recovery that are steps concerned with removing the incident and recovering from the damage done by the incident. This can include tasks such as resetting or removing compromised user account, reinstalling devices, or applying backup copies to rollback devices to earlier steps. It is good practice to restore machines that are disconnected and put the devices back in the network in a controlled manner under continuous monitoring. This is to ensure that no infected devices are allowed back in the network without being detected. The actual process of eradication and recovery will depend on the network layout, the nature of the incident, and the platforms used and will not be further discussed here.

Following the actual handling of the incident, it is time for post-incident activities. The major parts of this step would involve ensuring that the incident and the incident response are carefully documented. Documentation should certainly be an ongoing process, but after the incident, a report should be written. It is also good and common to have some post-incident meeting to discuss how the incident response worked and use the output of that meeting to, if necessary, update the policy. Perhaps more relevant for this book, post-incident activities will include decisions on whether or not to take legal actions; if law enforcements are to be contacted, it is good to have prepared digital evidence and good reports to give the law enforcement officer the best possible chances of investigating potential crimes related to the incident. It is also common to perform your own forensic examination of gathered data in order to better understand the nature of the incident and how it happened. Such an analysis could answer questions such as how systems were compromised and how malware that infected devices actually worked. While the containment, eradication, and recovery are primarily concerned with figuring out how to stop and recover from an incident, a forensic examination can provide valuable insight that can be used to improve the organization's security and thus prevent future incidents from happening. Best practices and methods for forensic examinations will be discussed throughout the rest of this book.

7.4 Questions and Tasks

The task for this chapter is to examine the NotPetya outbreak and discuss with peers about the intention of that ransomware and how ransomware outbreaks can harm an organization and be stopped.

References

Bossert TP (2017) It's official: North Korea is behind WannaCry. Wall Street J

Cichonski P, Millar T, Grance T, Scarfone K (2012) Computer security incident handling guide. NIST Spec Publ 800:1–147

Connell M, Vogler S (2017) Russia's approach to cyber warfare (1Rev). Center for Naval Analyses Arlington United States

Kent K, Chevalier S, Grance T, Dang H (2006) Guide to integrating forensic techniques into incident response. NIST Spec Publ 10:800–886

Kral P (2011) The incident handlers handbook. SANS Institute, Bethesda

Langner R (2011) Stuxnet: Dissecting a cyberwarfare weapon. IEEE Secur Priv 9:49–51

Lee RM, Assante MJ, Conway T (2016) Analysis of the cyber attack on the ukrainian power grid: Defense use case. SANS Institute/The Electricity Information Sharing and Analysis Center, Bethesda/Washington, DC

Liang G, Weller SR, Zhao J, Luo F, Dong ZY (2016) The 2015 ukraine blackout: Implications for false data injection attacks. IEEE Trans Power Syst 32:3317–3318

Mohurle S, Patil M (2017) A brief study of wannacry threat: Ransomware attack 2017. Int J Adv Res Comput Sci 8:1938–1940

Osborne C (2018) NonPetya ransomware forced Maersk to reinstall 4000 servers, 45000 PCs. Zero day

Srinivasan C (2017) Hobby hackers to billion-dollar industry: the evolution of ransomware. Comput Fraud Secur 2017:7–9

Collecting Evidence

8

Up until this point, the stage has been set with a theoretical background to digital forensics and a description on digital elements in crimes and incident response – the two major areas were digital forensics are used. The reminder of this book will zoom in on forensic practices and begin with describing the steps in a forensic examination as data collection, data analysis, and report writing. The first step in any forensic examination is to collect evidence. This chapter and the next will discuss data collection practices and forensic triage, the process of prioritizing what to collect and analyze in a digital environment.

To begin, it is necessary to discuss what evidence, or more specifically, what digital evidence is. In general terms, evidence as a word means "The available body of facts or information indicating whether a belief or proposition is true or false" (Oxford Dictionaries 2017). This would of course state that digital evidence in turn would be the actual pieces of data that are used to draw conclusions. However, when you refer to a piece of digital evidence, you commonly refer to a hard drive or cell phone or other carrier of digital information. For the sake of this book, digital evidence will mean "data collected from any type of digital storage that is subject to a computer forensic examination."

The key point in that definition is that everything that carries digital information can be subject to investigation, and any such carrier that is targeted for examination should be treated as evidence. This is due to the fact that in order to provide true results in a sound manner, all data that we examine has to be treated as evidence, and there is, generally, no way of knowing what data in a data carrier that will be used to answer the questions in the examination.

Well then, now that that is out of the way, the process of collecting evidence can in general terms be divided into one of two categories. The forensic examiner is either handed the devices subject for examination or is asked to take part in the actual collection. In law enforcement, this is comparable to the inspectors handing you the devices after they conducted a house search or actually asking you to participate in the house search. There is also a number of "in-betweens" were you may be handed devices that are on or you get to do a follow-up hose search. However, from a

J. Kävrestad, *Fundamentals of Digital Forensics*,
https://doi.org/10.1007/978-3-030-38954-3_8

forensic standpoint—what actually makes a difference in data collection is whether the device is powered on or off when the examination starts.

8.1 When the Device Is Off

When the device is powered off, there is only so much you can do. There is only the data stored on the static memory, such as a hard drive, for you to examine. However, there is still some processing that needs to be done before you can analyze the actual data on the storage unit.

When conducting a forensic examination, especially in law enforcement, actions must be taken to eliminate any chance of modifying the actual evidence. Also, if you capture data as part of incident response, you want to capture the data when it is at recent as possible. You can see that starting a computer and browsing about is a big no-no. This is because every action that you take will, in some way, modify the original data and thereby contaminate the evidence. The consequence is that it will be harder to perform a good analysis as you need to differentiate between your actions and actions taken by the computer user. Further, contaminated evidence may not be viable in court. For this reason, we need a way to make a copy of the evidence and then conduct out examination on the copy.

Under different circumstances it is actually impossible or infeasible to not work on the actual evidence, different legislations will have different approaches on how to manage "live evidence"—the rule of thumb is to always document, in detail, what you do to live evidence.

As described by Lazaridis et al. (2016), it is of high importance that the copy is identical to the original data, in terms of content. To achieve such a copy, a so-called disk imaging software is used. The goal of any such software is to create a bit-by-bit copy of the original data and then conduct the examination on the copy. In forensic terms, the copy is generally called a disk image or a forensic disk image.

To create a disk image, the examiner needs to connect the data source that is subject to examination to a special device or an ordinary computer. She will then use a disk imaging software to create the actual disk image. Whenever you are connecting a storage unit to a computer, it should be considered definite that something will be written to that unit. That does not comply with our forensic needs. To make sure that no alterations are made to the original evidence, write blockers are used when connecting a piece of digital evidence to a computer. As described by, for instance, Tobin et al. (2016), a write blocker is a device that is put between the digital evidence and the computer it is connected to and that prohibits the computer from writing any data to the device.

As a final step of creating a disk image, it is essential that you as a forensic expert can actually make sure that the copy is identical to the original. You may even need to testify to it! To make sure that the copy and the original are the same, hash comparison is used. The exact process varies between file formats, but in essence, a hash of the original data is created, and then a hash of the copy is created. The hashes are then compared, and if they match, the copy is identical to the original.

The concept of using disk imaging software and write blockers to create forensically sound copies of digital evidence is crucial in order to perform a forensically sound examination. The process and tools used vary in some sense depending on what type of device you are examining, but the theoretical approach remains the same. A discussion on the tools used is not a part of this book.

8.2 When the Device Is On

In some cases, the device subject to examination is powered on when it comes into the hands of the forensic expert. This is commonly the case in a corporate environment or when the forensic expert is part of the team conducting a house search. When examining a computer or device that is turned on, a live examination, the examiner gets the opportunity to collect volatile data. Volatile data includes information on what the device is currently up to. It also gives the examiner the opportunity to examine if any of the active hard drives are encrypted and collect unencrypted data from them. Common implementations of full disk encryption (FDE) ensure that all data on the hard drive is encrypted when the computer is off. However, the data will be decrypted when the computer is on. Thus, before turning off a computer subject to examination, the examiner must make a thorough search for encryption tools. If any sign of encryption is present, the examiner should create a logical image of the hard drives to ensure that the data is preserved and available for later analysis. Disk imaging can be done logically of physically. A physical disk image is a bit-by-bit copy of the original storage device; this means that a physical image of an encrypted device will be encrypted. A logical disk image will image a partition or storage device as seen by the operating system, meaning that a logical image of a currently decrypted partition will be decrypted. However, a logical disk image provides limited abilities to restore deleted data and should therefore not be used when a physical image is possible.

The ultimate goal of a live investigation is to preserve as much volatile data as possible and ensure that data resting on hard drives is available for later analysis. Further, as a part of the house search, it is vital to ensure that you capture an overview of how the computer was set up, where it was located, and what peripheral devices that were connected to it. Another important part of the house search is to look for any other devices that may be of interest to the investigation. As a part of this discussion, it must be stressed that good communication between the computer forensics expert, forensic experts from other disciplines, and police officers on the case is of utmost importance. Above all else is that you secure the evidence that you need and that you, of course, comply with laws and regulations.

Based on my own knowledge and experience, I created a process for a live investigation that describes the process in full; this is a good place to give thanks to some of my previous colleagues for their review and criticism! The process is designed for live investigations during house searches but is partially applicable in incident response as well, even if more attention is usually given to volatile data in incident response. Encrypted devices are commonly not a big issue in incident response as the organization owning the computer will usually have access to the encryption keys. A graphical overview of the process is presented in Fig. 8.1.

As the figure describes, you can abstract the process into three main steps: preparation, conducting, and afterthoughts. The idea is to visualize that to perform a sound and good live investigation, you need to prepare and to learn from each investigation. The remainder of this chapter is devoted to careful explanation of each step in the process.

8.3 Live Investigation: Preparation

The preparation step is divided into two parts: one that is general (indicated by the tilted top boxes) and one that should happen for every single house search. The general step is divided into creating a process and a response kit. The idea is that you should consider how you want to carry out live investigations in general. You can say that "create a process" concerns putting words on and deciding how to carry out the rest of the tasks in the process. Your process should cover a list of hardware and software you need, persons that are supposed to carry out live searches, and preferably the competences needed. A personal tip learned from carrying out quite a few live investigations is to also compile a list of numbers to persons that you may want to contact during the house search.

Next thing to do is to assemble a response kit. A response kit is nothing more than a bag filled with the software and hardware you need to carry out live investigations. When you are putting together a response kit, you need to make sure that it can be used on any type of system you may encounter. Reading the rest of this book and/or learning about forensics in general will help you gather the knowledge you need to assemble your response kit! Apart from collecting USB thumbs, software, write blockers, and what not, you should remember that you may need supporting devices to make sure that you can get an Internet connection, power, or whatever you need to keep your tools going.

The bottom tilted boxes in the preparation step are concerned with the preparation related to the specific live investigation in question. It is not uncommon that you are requested to an ongoing house search and find yourself in a position where you have to "wing it." However, if you get the possibility, you should carefully plan and prepare for your live investigation. The first planning step is to be requested: hopefully your organization got routines that make sure that you are involved at an early stage in an investigation. If not try to make them put such routines in place!

When you are requested, you have a chance to learn about what you are supposed to expect. Depending on the case and the settings of the house search, you can expect vastly different things. For instance, if you are working in legislation and supposed to do a live investigation of a system belonging to a computer technician suspected of child exploitation, there is a good chance that his system is encrypted. However, if you are working as a private investigator sent to examine the computer of an

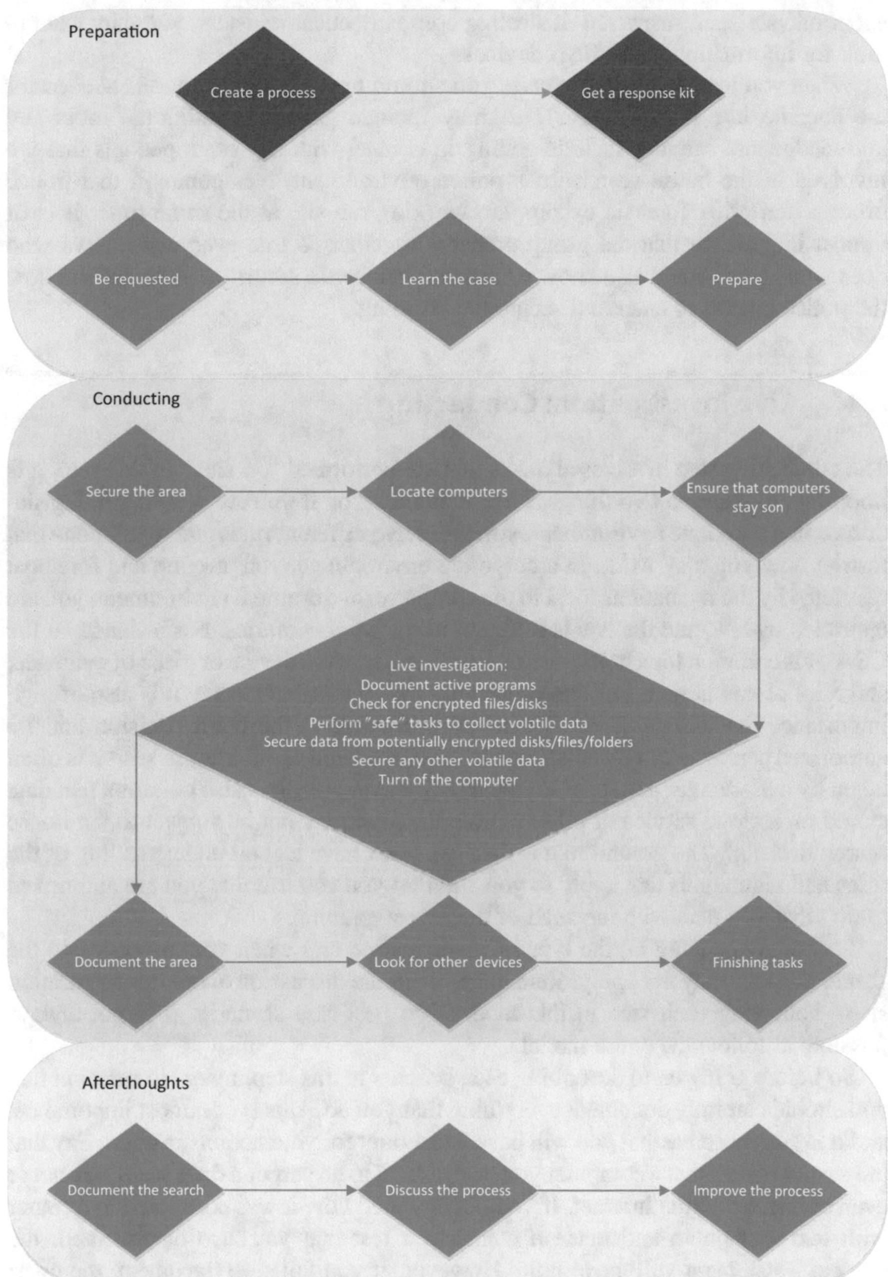

Fig. 8.1 Live investigation process

economic assistant suspected of stealing company client registers, you may want to look for information about USB devices.

When you learned about the case, you should make any preparations needed for the specific live investigation. This may include gathering additional tools and knowledge and can also include getting in contact with any other persons that are involved in the house search. In a police environment, it is common that police officers and other forensic experts are working the site at the same time. It is of utmost importance that the group prepares together so that everyone knows who does what. You should also know what to expect from a security standpoint and how the police intends to enter and secure the building.

8.4 Live Investigation: Conducting

The conducting step involves all tasks that are performed "on-site." In this step, it is important to mention two things. First, depending on if you are working in legislation or in a corporate environment, you will have different rules and regulations that restrict how you may work. In a corporate environment, you are first and foremost restricted by the regulations local to the company. In a criminal environment, you are restricted by law, and the law is different in different countries. For instance, in the USA, it is common for a house search to target a specific device or piece of evidence, and a lot of emphasis is put into preserving the chain of evidence. It is also of high importance that the evidence is handled according to the court decision and by authorized personnel. In Swedish legislation, a decision about a house search is often taken by a prosecutor and regards an entire home or area. It is also common that data stored on a cloud service or other remote location may not be subject to the house search decision. The ground rule is that you must have a good understanding of the rules and regulations that apply to you and that you confirm that you are authorized to do what you plan with the head of the investigation.

Second, depending on the type of investigation and when you are called to the scene, all steps may not apply. Remember from the discussion about the preparation step—following each step in this model is a best-case scenario. It is not always possible to follow the entire model.

So before going on to describing each process in this step, I want to mention that you should carefully document everything that you do. This is of utmost importance, and it is very possible that you will have to account for your actions in court. Say that the suspect states that a computer you determined to be part of a drug scam was never even connected to the Internet. If you documented how it was connected to a router with text and photo and made a connection test that you also documented, the suspect's statement will never hold. However, if you failed to document, the court may find reason to question your findings. We will continue the discussion on documentation in the upcoming chapter.

Well then, before starting any house search, the entire team will travel to the site and enter the building in question. The first tasks at hand are to secure the building, locate any computers that are running, and ensure that they stay on. Depending on the case and background information, this can be done in a variety of ways. In an investigation of a severe crime, where the suspects are likely to possess computer skills, it is not uncommon to break in violently in order to surprise the suspect so that he or she does not turn off any computers as an attempt to hide evidence. In another situation, you may simply knock on the door.

Securing the area is above all else in this step, and it is the duty of the police officers. While the police officers secure the area, it is convenient if they look for computers that are turned on and make sure that they stay on. The computer forensic examiner can then enter the building after it is secured and start working on any computers that are turned on.

At this point, you could discuss if you should conduct the live investigations or document the area first. From my experience, you should never wait with the live investigation, and this is for the sole reason that there are many ways to remotely erase data or there could be some software running that removes data upon certain events. Also, the task of documenting the area could be handed to a police officer.

Looking to the main process in this step, the live investigation, it should have the following ultimate goals:

- Document what is visually present on screen.
- Collect volatile data.
- Check if any data is encrypted and secure data from encrypted storage.
- Provide clues for the continued house search.

Documenting what is actually present on screen is very important as it can prove to be very valuable evidence. This is primarily because of the fact that the stuff up on the screen was, evidently, visible to the person that was last sitting in front of the computer. The high value of this evidence is due to the fact that when you present a suspect with evidence from a hard drive, they commonly claim that they had no idea that they had that particular data on their computer. They may even state that it must have been put there by someone else or that they must have been hacked. However, if you are suspecting a person of selling drugs and you capture him sitting in front of a computer that is in fact being used to sell drugs at the very time that he is sitting there, those claims become harder to make. This corresponds to the first step in the live investigation process, document active programs. This task involves taking photos of all active windows, documenting date and time settings, and extracting other data from active processes, such as log files. This task would also, at least, include mapping of active network connections, documenting currently logged on users, and testing the Internet connection. You may also want to check for connections to remote storage and recently plugged in USB devices. While you are examining what is present on screen, it is a clever idea to record the time and time zone settings on the computer. Usually, these settings are automatically set by synchronization to a time server. However, it does happen that the computer time is wrong, and that is something that you need to be aware of. Also, calculating the time error allows you to correct for the error if you are presenting data where time is important. The same goes for time zone information. If an incorrect time zone is used, time stamps in the computer will appear to be off, and you need to adjust for that in your report.

TIP: To ensure that you collect all data that you want to collect from the operating system, you should create a script for this purpose. In appendix B, you can find scripts to do this collection on Windows, MAC and Linux—feel free to modify to suit your needs!

The next part of the live examination involves checking for evidence of encrypted data. This task would involve checking active processes to see if any process related to encryption is running and visually looking for encryption software. On Windows systems, you can see if a partition is encrypted with BitLocker by visually looking for a padlock on the partition icon in the computer menu. There is also a variety of tools to use to automatically detect encryption software and encrypted partitions. As a final task, you can use imaging software to manually examine raw data for headers associated with encrypted volumes.

If you find that the computer contains encrypted partitions or encrypted data that is currently in a decrypted state, you must secure this data to a logical disk image. However, the process of making a disk image during a live investigation is time-consuming, and you should consider capturing volatile data first. Volatile data is all data that will be lost when the computer is turned off or data that is often changed. Thus, there is a good chance that the volatile data is modified by the disk imaging process. Collecting volatile data involves, at least, taking a snapshot of the computer memory (RAM) and gathering registry files. You should know that there are different ways to gather volatile data, and some ways may risk that the computer crashes. For this reason, it is important to consider your actions. Volatile data, especially the memory, contains information that can help decipher what the computer has been up to since the last reboot. This is valuable information for the same reasons as for the active processes. Also, memory is commonly a good source for finding passwords and data from encrypted communication services in plain text. However, if the computer you are examining contains encrypted volumes and crashes during the memory capture, any potential evidence on the encrypted partition may be lost.

In my own experience, there are tools for memory capture that you can safely use without the computer crashing. One such tool, which is free to use, is FTK imager that will be discussed in greater detail later. My recommendation is to capture any volatile data that you can using these “safe tools” and then create a disk image of possibly encrypted partitions and hard drives. Then you can move on to capturing volatile data in more “unsecure” ways if you need.

When you are done with all the steps, you should make sure that you have documented everything that you have done, and you can turn off the computer and bring it with you for further examination. Also note that in addition to looking for evidence relating to the case, you should also check if any remote storage is connected to the computer and if any USB devices have been connected to it. This information will assist you in your continued house search. Please also note that depending on the type of investigation, you may want to conduct live investigations on networking equipment as well as computers.

When any live investigations of running computers are done, you should make sure that the area is well documented. This would usually involve taking photos. This is important in order to know where stuff was. In the next process, it is time to search the rest of the area for any other interesting finds. In your role as a computer forensic expert, you will commonly look for any other device that can possibly be used to store information. This involves CD/DVD, USB drives, and hard drives. You should also make sure that you look for physical documentation that could be of interest; this could involve passwords, URLs, and other information that have been written down.

As finishing tasks, you should make sure that everything is documented and that all seized evidence is marked according to the regulations and routines that apply to you.

8.5 Live Investigation: Afterthoughts

When the house search is done, there are some finishing touches to attend to. First thing to do is to write a protocol that describes how the live investigation was executed and describe any findings. The responsibility of documenting may vary between different legislations, but at the very least, you should document what you did during the live investigations. A longer discussion on documentation will be held in the upcoming chapter.

After documenting, the team conducting the house search should discuss how the house search was performed. Ideally, this process would be conducted with police officers and any other forensic experts. But at the very least, you should consider the house search from a computer forensic perspective and update your own process as needed.

8.6 Questions and Tasks

Here are the questions for Chap. 8. Again, answering the questions in a group discussion is advised.

1. Why do you want to capture memory during a live investigation?
2. What is a forensic disk image?
3. What is volatile data?
4. Elaborate on the benefits of preparing before a live investigation and give examples on how to prepare.

5. Why would you prefer to analyze a forensic disk image rather than a live computer?

References

Lazaridis I, Arampatzis T, Pouros S (2016) Evaluation of digital forensics tools on data recovery and analysis. In: The third international conference on computer science, computer engineering, and social media (CSCESM2016)

Oxford Dictionaries. (2017) Definition of evidence in English. Available online: https://en.oxforddictionaries.com/definition/evidence. Fetched July 6, 2017

Tobin P, Le-Khac NA, Kechadi MT (2016) A lightweight software write-blocker for virtual machine forensics. In: Sixth international conference on innovative computing technology (INTECH) 2016. IEEE, New Jersey, pp 730–735

Triage 9

A common historical approach to digital forensics has been to examine everything, leave no stone unturned. Unfortunately, that approach is seldom feasible or even possible simply because of the large amount of devices or data that is commonly targeted in a forensic examination. Looking at incident response, all devices in an organization's network can be the scope of an incident. It is virtually impossible to analyze them all in a timely manner. In law enforcement, the number of devices may be lower, but even a standard modern computer will contain large amounts of data, and reviewing all data is very time-consuming. Also, in law enforcement, a forensic expert is usually tasked with several examinations at once and needs to complete examinations fast to avoid a heavy backlog. This is when triage comes into play. The simplest explanation of forensic triage is the process of prioritizing data or devices for forensic examinations (Gielen, 2014). What that actually means is not very clear; if you look to the literature, forensic triage is sometimes discussed as prioritization and sometimes as a separate examination that takes place before the actual examination. It is also sometimes discussed as a part of live investigations and sometimes as a part of the forensic analysis that will be described next. While the aim of this book is not to provide or conduct any research into the area of forensic triage, it is definite that any forensic examination will include prioritization with the aim of ensuring that forensic examinations are performed in a timely manner while maintaining high forensic standards. The remainder of this chapter will discuss a few different practices that could qualify as forensic triage, including some pros and cons with each. In general terms, this book considers triage to be the mindset of prioritization and not a process of its own. However, employing triage in different ways will bring a need to add or remove steps to the forensic process.

J. Kävrestad, *Fundamentals of Digital Forensics*,
https://doi.org/10.1007/978-3-030-38954-3_9

9.1 Specific Examinations

While a historic approach to digital forensics has been to analyze everything, this book and other modern forensic literature are taking a more specific approach. One could call this approach a specific examination, and the idea is essentially to switch mindset from examining the entire devices to answering questions. This approach lets the forensic examiners look for information that is supposed to be used to answer some specific question rather than look at all data in a device to uncover all it has been used for. The idea is that when you are looking for artifacts related to a specific question, you only need to examine a subset of the captured data and that allows for an examination that results in a more specific result. Consider, for instance, a case where someone is suspected of selling drugs online and witness reports claim that the suspect used e-mail as the means of communication. In this case, a forensic expert can focus on e-mail-related artifacts and perform a forensic examination that covers just that. In another example, a computer may be infected with a ransomware on a certain date. It would appear reasonable for an incident response team to focus efforts on events during that day and possibly the few days before. As a final note, using the approach of specific examinations can be a question about only looking at pieces of data; it can also be about being selective in acquiring data. The latter is most commonly employed in situations where complete data acquisition is simply not possible. Consider a case where someone committed a crime from a virtual machine hosted by a cloud service provider. It would not be possible to image the entire could infrastructure; instead, data associated with the virtual machine would be acquired.

The benefits of using specific examinations are that they can be executed much faster than examinations that cover everything. A further benefit is that a resulting report will be focused on what whoever ordered the examination is actually interested in. However, an obvious drawback is that a lot of data will simply not be taken into consideration and that brings the risk of missing important evidence, or evidence of other actions that are interesting for incident response or law enforcement. A way to overcome this is to always include a swift overview examination of the target device, while that does not eliminate the chance of missing important information, the risk is made smaller. Another way to ensure that examinations are actually satisfactory is to employ an iterative approach where new questions are brought to the forensic expert. No matter what, the approach of using specific examinations puts high demands on the forensic reports; they must show what data sets have been examined and why, in relation to the questions asked. In a way, reporting what data has not been subject for examination allows for external parties, such as an attorney, to ask for complementary examinations.

9.2 White and Blacklisting

Another technique that is actually widely used in law enforcement is white and blacklisting, often using lists of hash values. The idea here is to automatically mark files that are known to be interesting or not interesting to the forensic examination. What you do is that you compile and maintain lists of hash values belonging to files that are known to be uninteresting and interesting. You can then create hash value of all files in a machine that is targeted for analysis and compare to your lists of hash values; the lists are commonly called hash sets. In law enforcement, this approach is commonly used in two ways. The first implementation is to create white hash sets containing hash values of files that you are never going to be interested in. This can include executables, operating system files, and more. Upon starting a new examination, you let the forensic software remove all of those files from the case, leaving you with a much smaller data set to analyze. Blacklisting is the opposite, automatic detection of interesting files. This is very commonly used in child exploitation cases where large lists of hash values are calculated for media that is considered child pornography. Applying such a list to a case would allow for automatic detecting of such material and will save the forensic expert from having to do that classification manually. That will not only save time but also the mind and sanity of the forensic examiner. It is also possible to use blacklisting in other scenarios. For instance, it can be a good way of analyzing if evidence files found on one device is also present on some other device. In that case, you would create your own hash set from interesting files.

Whitelisting can actually also be used in incident response. It can, for instance, be used to verify the integrity of system critical files. In that case, you would create hash sets of static system files. If an incident arises, you can use hash analysis to see if any of the files that should remain static was modified; a modification to a static system file, such as a DLL, could be an indication of malware. An approach similar to using hash sets is signature analysis. Signature analysis is essentially the practice of collecting signatures of illicit code and malware, and search a device to see if the signatures are present in any files. This approach is identical to how common malware analysis tools (antivirus programs) work.

9.3 Automated Analysis

Another form of forensic analysis that could be classified as triage is automated analysis. Forms of automated analysis are commonly employed to generate a quick listing of information on a device that can be swiftly sent to investigative parties while a deeper forensic analysis continues. Automated analysis relies on predetermined rules over what to analyze and in what way and is employed using some kind of script. In essence, it is a way of instructing some forensic software to go get, and preferably analyze, artifacts that are commonly interesting. A very common example is to automatically get a timeline of activity on the device during a specific time period. That can quickly answer question such as was the computer used at all?

Or was the computer used for communication? Another common example of automated analysis within law enforcement is the use of the tool Internet Evidence Finder that is a tool primarily used to automatically identify and assemble browsing and communication history. Using such a tool saves the forensic examiner from manual reconstruction and analysis of databases of such information.

The obvious benefits of using automated analysis are that it does deliver results swiftly. Also, when using automated processes that have been rigorously tested and verified, the chance of errors is generally lower than when a forensic examiner does the same task manually. However, it should be noted that automated analysis will only detect and analyze what it has been created to detect and analyze. As such, there is a fair chance that it misses something of interest. Also, if databases and services included in automated analysis change their structure, for instance, during an update, the analysis tool also needs to be updated. This leaves a possibility for a time period when an automatic analysis tool may not be able to identify data that it previously identified. While this is how stuff is rather than a drawback, it is a fact that forensic experts needs to be aware about.

9.4 Field Triage

The final flavor of triage to be discussed in this book is field triage. Field triage, as described by Rogers et al. (2006), is the process of applying forensic techniques to identify, analyze, and interpret digital evidence during a live investigation. Field triage is not, as the previous forms of triage, a mindset or a part of a standard forensic examination. Rather, it is a complement or a completely different approach to the forensic examination. The aim of field triage is to answer questions during a live investigation and should be employed whenever that is needed. As such, it can often be wise to include field triage in the live examination process. In a criminal investigation, it can be important to get evidence early on; it may be needed to put someone dangerous into custody. It is also possible that it is important to assess the level of risk that someone poses to the general public. A forensic examiner can bc involved in an ongoing murder investigation where the suspect is still on the loose.

Rogers et al. (2006) describe the key reasons for field triage to be to:

- Find important evidence immediately to give the investigators the upper hand against suspects.
- Identify possible suspects that are in acute danger. This can actually be the case in, for instance, child exploitation cases or abductions. Consider a case where a suspect abducted and locked in another person somewhere. If information on that person's location is available in a computer, it must be discovered as soon as possible.
- Use to guide the ongoing investigation by, for instance, finding links to other digital devices or perhaps contact to other individuals that should be treated as suspects.
- Identify potential charges.
- Assess if the suspect poses a risk to society.

Essentially, field triage is concerned with finding information of evidentiary value on site. As different artifacts will likely be important in different situations, it would be impossible to assemble a list of what to look for. Also, looking for everything would be too time-consuming and conflict with the reason for even doing field triage to begin with. The golden rule is to, just as with any live examination, plan carefully and look for what you want to look for in the situation at hand. Knowing what to look for comes from experience and reading, for instance, this book. While there are many reasons for performing field triage, there is a big drawback. Everything that you do on a running computer will leave traces. As such, field triage may be impossible due to legal constraints. And even if it is allowed, it will leave traces in memory, possibly erasing important other data. As such, it is necessary to prioritize if a good memory dump or field triage is more important.

9.5 Questions and Tasks

A very well-known police raid was the one against The Pirate Bay in 2006. It is safe to say that the police did not use any form of triage in that case. Since The Pirate Bay servers were hosted by a web hosting company, servers belonging to other organizations were seized as collateral damage. As a task, investigate The Pirate Bay raid and discuss how it should have been executed.

References

Gielen M (2014) Prioritizing computer forensics using triage techniques. University of Twente, Enschede

Rogers MK, Goldman J, Mislan R, Wedge T, Debrota S (2006) Computer forensics field triage process model. J Digit Forensic Secur Law 1:2

Analyzing Data and Writing Reports 10

For the final part of the theoretical section, we will discuss how to analyze data and write reports. This is the step where you work with the evidence that you collected in a sound manner in the previous step. That would, for instance, include forensic disk images and memory dumps. As a general rule of thumb, always perform your analysis on disk images rather than actual hard drives, to ensure that you do not modify the original data. However, in some cases it is not possible to get a forensic image, and in these cases you would have to analyze the actual device directly. Different regulations for how to manage these cases exist in different legislations. At the very least, make sure you document WHY you had to investigate the device directly and what you did!

Okay then, analyzing data and writing reports are processes that are tied very closely together; the analysis is what you do, and the report should describe your analysis and conclusions. While that sounds quite easy, the reality is a bit more daunting. First, there are rules and regulations that decide what you can do and how you should do it. Then, you need to consider that the audience of your report is usually not very good with computers but they still need to understand. To begin this discussion, I want to say that the rest of the chapter is written from a law enforcement perspective. This is because you are commonly more restricted when working with criminal investigation than when working with corporate investigations. Within a corporate environment, you can basically do whatever your manager tells you to (with reason of course). You should, however, keep the previous discussion on incident response in mind and follow legal practices even in corporate environments; there is a fair chance that incident response situations will be followed by legal processes.

J. Kävrestad, *Fundamentals of Digital Forensics*,
https://doi.org/10.1007/978-3-030-38954-3_10

10.1 Setting the Stage

Before we move on, there are some general guidelines that should be followed when conducting a forensic examination. These guidelines are of different importance in different legislations. Important in this case refers to what you are forced to do by law. From an ethical perspective, the following guidelines should always be followed in order to ensure a sound and fair investigation. A general rule in criminal investigations is that everyone is innocent until proven guilty and that investigations should not aim to prosecute a specific person but to uncover the truth. In the bigger picture, this is achieved in different ways including that suspects have the right to a proper defense, investigations should be unconditional and transparent, and the defense should be able to know how conclusions were reached so that they can be disputed.

In many ways, this is similar to the foundations of scientific research where it is dictated that any study should be done in an unbiased and transparent way that allows for reproduction of the study. There are even more similarities in that a forensic investigation, much like a research project, aims to provide an answer to a question, i.e., Are there any evidence of this computer being involved in an online fraud scheme?

So before we move on, we should just highlight that during the analysis and report writing, the forensic expert has to make sure that his work meets the following requirements:

Unbiased meaning that incriminating and exonerating evidence is considered and taken into account. In reality, this would mean that if you are asked to see if a computer was used during a specific period in time, you should put an equal amount of time for evidence supporting the opposite, namely, that it wasn't used. The bottom line is that it should not be important for the forensic examiner to find incriminating evidence; rather it should be important to find a correct and objective answer.

Reproducible meaning that you document the basis for your conclusions well enough for someone else to replicate your analysis. The general idea is that if someone does the same thing you have done, they will reach the same conclusion. A big part of this property is also to provide transparency, meaning that you account for all your findings as well as the methods you used. This has to, of course, be applied with sense. For instance, if the aim of your analysis is to find pictures, you may not need to account for e-mail history on the investigated device. Also, if you are asked to get a list of the files on the computer desktop, you do not need to document that you browsed your way to the desktop and wrote down the file names. However, if you were asked to see if a computer was remote-controlled and conclude that you found no such evidence, you should document how you searched for remote control software, how you analyzed firewall logs, and so on.

As a final point to discuss, I want to stress the importance of using some clear and preferably standardized way of expressing conclusions. For instance, you may do an analysis with the aim of investigating if some pictures were taken in a specific place. Depending on what information you find, it is important to express your conclusion in a way that gives a just presentation of the evidence. Consider a case where you

Table 10.1 Scale of expressions for conclusions

Expression	Explanation
The analysis shows that ... did not...	The key point here is that first "shows that" is a completely decisive expression, and combined with a negation, did not, it can be used to claim that something did not happen. This expression should be used with care since it is often hard to claim that something did not happen with absolute certainty
The analysis strongly suggests that ... did not ...	Same as above but leaving room for an alternative explanation for the found evidence. However, when saying that your analysis strongly suggests something, you are saying that you do not see any other plausible explanation for the evidence found
The analysis indicates that ... did not	"Indicates that" basically says that what you are saying is likely but it is quite possible that some other explanation is also true
The analysis is inconclusive	Inconclusive is to be used when your analysis does not really provide evidence that says anything about what you supposed to look for, or when the evidence is saying different things
The analysis indicates that	In this case, your analysis indicated that some statement was true; however, other possibilities are plausible
The analysis strongly suggests that	Your analysis shows that something is true and other explanations are possible but not plausible
The analysis shows that	Your analysis shows that something is true

manually could see that the wallpapers in the found pictures matched the place that you were asked to match the picture against. This would be an indication that the picture was from that location, but it would not be a decisive piece of information. However, if you could also find GPS coordinates, matching the location, embedded in the picture, you could go further and say that your investigation strongly suggests or even shows that the picture was taken in the suggested location. That being said I would suggest using a seven-graded scale that is heavily influenced by the one that is being used by the Swedish police. The steps of the scale and how to express them are presented in Table 10.1.

Being able to express yourself in a way that gives a just view of your analysis and that provides enough punch to the investigation can be really hard and takes practice. But when you are making your conclusions, you should try to argue with yourself and also have a colleague challenge your conclusions to make sure that they hold!

10.2 Forensic Analysis

Well then, having discussed the boundaries and requirements of a forensic analysis, it is time to get at it. First off, remember from the discussion in Chap. 1 that a forensic analysis is basically about answering question that the investigation has. To answer the question, you must analyze the data found on the forensic images you created in the "collect evidence" phase. You may also have some other data that you collected during a live investigation. As a final point, you should also be aware that it is common to include information from other sources, such as interrogations or whatever seems reasonable in your case.

Giving some attention to questions that you may be asked by the investigators, you should know that it can be about almost anything. It is often the case that the investigators do not really know what to ask for and your expertise in forensics is usually needed to clarify the purpose of the forensic investigation. Further, it should also be noted that when you report your findings in relation to one question, it is common that the investigators have follow-up questions that result in a new analysis. Also, the nature of the questions may range from "Is this picture present in the suspect's computers" to "Find all incriminating or exonerating evidence in relation to online fraud." Your task as a forensic examiner is to find the underlying questions and bring conclusions for those.

Another thing worth mentioning is whether or not to stray from the purpose of the analysis and look for "other" information. In my opinion, there are two ways you should handle this dilemma. First of all, I think that there are some basic information that you should always uncover from every computer that you investigate. What information that should be included in this basic set of information would differ from legislation to legislation as well as between departments. But one thing you should know is that you must be prepared to take the stand and be a witness under oath, in court. And in my own experience, there are some questions that are very common to get and that you would like to have answers to; thus, starting every analysis by gathering some common information is recommended! The second part of "other" information would be information that may be related to crimes but not directly to the question you are set to answer. The way you should treat this kind of information is strongly depending on your legislation and on occasions, the conditions in the search warrant. I would strongly suggest that you make notes about this type of information and discuss it with the lead investigator or prosecutor!

The discussion that we just had leads us to the process of a forensic analysis. One could just say that you should take your questions and find data that helps in answering them, but I would suggest using a more structured approach. Using a structured approach makes it easier to ensure that all evidence is treated in the same way and that all investigations are handled in a similar fashion no matter who the examiner is. In Fig. 10.1, I have tried to give a quick overview of how a forensic process could be structured. The first step would be to get an understanding of the case at hand. Getting an understanding of the case you are working with will help you get a better idea of what to look for. This step would normally include reading about how the investigation got started, what types of evidence that is present in the case, and transcripts from interrogations with suspects and witnesses in the case. All of this information is information that will help you understand the person that was supposedly using the computer you are examining and could include important information for your analysis such as the suspect's explanation for different pieces of evidence, other persons involved in the case, and how the supposed crimes were committed.

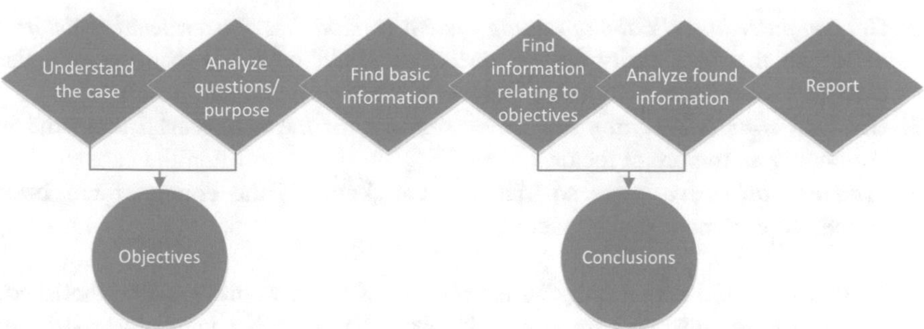

Fig. 10.1 Overview of a forensic process

The second thing that you should analyze is the questions from the investigator. They outline the actual purpose of your analysis. What you must know here is that the investigators are not always too good at asking questions or specifying a purpose; it is even common that the devices to analyze are just handed to the forensic examiner with no question or purpose at all. In these cases, I would encourage asking the investigators what they expect you to do and what outcomes they are hoping for and expecting. On the other hand, you must expect that questions will be very narrow or broad depending on the investigation. In this sense, "Find out all you can about this device in relation to this narcotic case" is a purpose that is just as legitimate as the question "Was this picture taken at the suspect's home address?" What the forensic examiner should do in this step is to use what she knows about the case and analyze the questions/purpose of the investigation to establish her own objectives for the forensic examination. This is where you use your expertise to decide what you should look for and how. Also note that depending on what you find during your analysis, you may need to add additional objectives.

When you established what to actually look for, you should go into the process of actually looking for evidence. The first thing I encourage is to find some basic information. This would be a step that you carry out for each and every one of the computers that you examine. The information you find during this step will make sure that you do not miss something fundamental and will, in my own experience, be very useful when appearing in court. Deciding what should go into the set of basic information is up to you or your manager and could be decided in legislation. However, the following list is a suggestion from me on what should, at least, be included.

1. *Account for all data* meaning that you examine the physical size of the hard drive and then look at how much of this space that is allocated to a visible partition. If a drive is able to carry 250 GB but only 200 GB are allocated to active partitions, the other 50 GB may contain a hidden or encrypted partition or something else. You will have to figure out if the data not allocated to a visible partition is of interest to your analysis.

2. *Get computer install date, operating system version, list of users, and registered owner* so that you easily answer questions about what operating system the computer used, how many users there were on the system, and so on.
3. *Get time zone information and clock settings* for the sole reason that time is commonly an important factor.
4. *Find network drive maps* so that you can know if the computer has been connected to remote storage media.

Next, you should get working on the objectives that you previously established. What you are going to do here is heavily dependent on what your objectives are. Your ability to complete these steps are of course what makes you a forensic expert, and some common objectives and tasks will be explored in the practical section of this book. However, there is one aspect that needs attention. You will surely do most of your investigative work using well-proven forensic tools. However, there may be times when you have a need to use tools you never heard about or tools that you even made yourself. To ensure that your investigation is fully transparent, it is of great importance that you document these tools. On the same topic, I want to stress, once again, that the work you do in this step should be done in an objective way. You are supposed to look for evidence that is in favor as well as in opposition to your objectives. Your aim is not to make someone committed of a crime but to provide a just view of what happened.

When you completed your investigation and used different methods to search through the data on the computer you are examining, it is time to analyze the information you found and draw conclusions. What is notable about this step is that your conclusions are reflecting the way that you interpret the data. Also, as previously discussed, it is important that you draw conclusions in a way that ensures that your conclusions are strong enough, meaning that you should not be afraid to actually make the statements that are backed up by your evidence. However, you must also make sure that you "do not claim too much" meaning that, well, your conclusions must actually be supported by your findings. A neat way to find the right balance is to debate your conclusions in a critical manner with yourself as well as with your colleagues.

When you completed your analysis, it is time for the final task of reporting your findings in a good report, and that deserves a section of its own.

10.3 Reporting

The final step in a forensic analysis is to write a report. The report basically serves two purposes. First, it is where you present your *objective* findings and then you may include your *conclusions* based on the findings. As such, it is important to understand that the conclusions will always depend on your knowledge and interpretation of your findings; thus, the conclusions are in some sense subjective. In addition to the content of the report, the reports should be written in a way that provides a *transparent* recapture of the examination. The report itself should be enough for someone else with forensic expertise to reproduce the reports. It should also be mentioned, again, that the reports should be easy to understand for persons without forensic expertise, such as judges and jurors. A very good advice is to include a vocabulary that explains terms that are not known by the general public. The content of a report will differ depending on legislation and local policies. However, it is common that all reports include:

1. Case data
2. Purpose of examination
3. Findings
4. Conclusions

The remainder of this section will describe common information and considerations found in each part of the report. A sample template report is presented in Appendix C. Note that while the template includes what should in most cases be included in a forensic report, the actual layout may differ between cases. Also note that local regulations and policies may provide additional or other requirements on the format of the report. The upcoming sections will include a sample report, using the template in Appendix C for a case with the following description. Note that Appendix C holds a report template as well as a complete report for our sample case.

In the sample case, the forensics expert was asked to conduct a forensic examination of a turned-off computer in an online fraud case. The suspected crime was as follows:

> The suspect, John Doe, was suspected of online frauds by selling goods that he did not deliver. The modus operandi was that someone had been putting ads on eBay, someone bought and payed for the product that was sold but the product was never delivered.

John Doe was interrogated and claimed that he was not guilty; he admitted to having seen the ads when browsing around the Internet and said that it could therefore be possible that the pictures in the ads were present on his computer.

The task given to the forensic examiner was to see if the pictures from the ads were present on John Doe's computer and, if possible, determine how they got there and find any circumstances that could determine how John Doe had been using the pictures.

10.3.1 Case Data

Case data, or similar in a corporate setting, is simply information that describes the investigation that the examination is part of. Case data would include the name of the person that ordered the examination, some identifier of the investigation it concerns, and information that identifies the pieces of evidence that are subject to examination. Key points here are to maintain chain of custody or similar and being able to distinguish the examination from other examinations. The exact information that should be contained in the report is heavily dependent on local regulations and legislation. For our sample case, the case data section of the report would look as follows:

Awesome police station	**Date**	**Case numer**
Forensics dept.of Skövde	2018005017	344301231017
Examinerstreet 12		

Protocol of forensic examination of computer 1234567-32
Examination data

Examination requested by:	Peregrin Took
Lead forensic investigator:	Joakim Kävrestad
Reason for examination:	Identify if pictures found in fraudulent ads can be tied to the computer and/or the suspect in the case
Time of examination	2018-05-14 to 2018-05-17
Additional information	Suspect claims that the pictures in the ads may be present on his computer due to him browsing said ads using the computer

Beginning from the top, the sample starts with addressing, the date the report was written, and the case number. Then comes a headline including an identifier for the piece of evidence. It is common for an examination to cover several pieces of evidence, and in such a case the headline may be something else, and a list of evidence can be included as a list below the table of information. Note that the identifiers for the evidence covered should always be present in the protocol in some way to provide clarity and traceability.

Moving to the table of examination data, it contains two fields of extra interest. Those are *reason for* examination where the purpose of the examination should be summarized and *additional information* where other aspects that have been taken into account during the examination should be presented. Those fields are commonly extracted and given individual sections, depending on how much information they should hold.

10.3.2 Purpose of Examination

The purpose of the examination should be expressed in the report for the reason that it presents what you have been looking for during your examination. It is unreasonable to assume that an examination of one or more computers can produce a complete overview of all data on all storage devices. Therefore, expressing the purpose of the examination describes the focus of the examination and gives the reader and understanding of what he can expect as results.

Stating the purpose begins with the question or purpose that was expressed by the one who ordered the examination. It could, however, also include any objectives that the forensic examiner identified when analyzing the case. One example of a purpose statement could be as follows:

> The purpose of this examination was to identify if documents stolen during the break-in at samplestreet 41 was present on the computer. The suspect stated, in an interrogation, that the computer was hacked. Thus, the examination also included looking for evidence of remote control software, malicious software and evidence of intrusions

It should be mentioned that the nature of the purpose statement is very versatile depending on the needs of the investigation, the nature of the examination, or the local procedures. In some cases, the forensic expert may only be tasked with gathering data from the device for someone else to analyze, in that case the problem statement could be:

> The aim of the examination was to extract all pictures from the device

In contrast, in some cases the examination that is conducted by the forensic expert is much more comprehensive. However, if the purpose of an examination becomes too widespread, it is sound to consider splitting the examination into several smaller examinations. To achieve that you could conduct one examination, or at least produce one report, for each step in the examination. For instance, it is common for examinations of computers suspected to be involved in online fraud scams to include looking for and analyzing pictures, recovering e-mails, recovering chat logs, and analyzing browsing history. Creating one report for each of those purposes would likely make the conclusions more understandable and increase the readability of the reports. In reality, it is advisable to discuss the way that the reports are created with the recipient of the report(s). In the sample report, the purpose section is combined with a summary of the report including a summary of the findings and other information that is needed for the reader in order to read the protocol. For our sample case, the summary section, including the purpose of the examination, could be expressed as follows:

Summary

The purpose of this examination was to identify if pictures used in online fraud ads were present on the computer that is the target of the examination. The pictures used in the ads were given to the examiner by the Officer Took. The examination should also attempt to determine how the pictures had been used on the computer and if they could be tied to the suspect. After the pictures had been discovered, it came of interest to analyze if the pictures had been taken with the suspect's phone, an iPhone X with serial number 123456—analyzed and presented in a separate protocol.

(continued)

Pictures that visually appeared to be the same as in the ads were found on the computer, and thus the examination came to cover analysis of the pictures. Based on the EXIF∗ data in picture, it could be determined that they were taken with an iPhone X at GPS coordinates that were in close proximity to the suspect's address.

Words marked with an asterisk (∗) are explained at the end of the protocol.

10.3.3 Findings

Presenting findings include presenting the pieces of evidence that you found during your examination. Findings should be presented in an *objective* manner, meaning that you should present the pieces of information that you found as is and not make any subjective conclusion or interpretation. In essence, you could say that you should present and describe exactly what the information you present is telling you. For instance, consider a case where the forensic examiner was asked to analyze if some pictures were taken at a suspect's apartment. To fulfill this purpose, the examiner would look for GPS coordinates in the picture metadata. As findings, the forensic examiner will present the GPS coordinates, if any are found, and possibly state if they match the coordinates of the suspect's home address or not—these are objective facts. However, stating that the picture is actually from the suspect's apartment would be a subjective conclusion that needs more information. Also, the methods used to find the findings could be included if they matter to the information related to the findings or the conclusions. In our scenario, the findings sections could look as follows:

Findings

Hash lookup∗ was used to identify if the pictures used in the ads were present on the computer. A hash∗ database containing the pictures from the ads was created and matched with a hash database containing all files on the computer. Visual inspection of the matching pictures was performed to validate the results. The hash lookup identified that all pictures used in the ads were present on the computer in a folder called "C:\PICS". The names of the found pictures were:

- Jacket.jpg
- Shoes.jpg
- Merrys awesome sword.jpg

(continued)

The pictures were extracted from the computers and delivered to Officer Took on a DVD.

EXIF data was extracted from the found pictures; the EXIF data included name of the model of the camera and GPS coordinates. The EXIF information was the same for all pictures and included the following information:

- Camera model: iPhone X.
- GPS coordinates:

° Latitude	68.27211388888889
° Longitude	23.715005555555555
° Altitude	168.26573426573427

The Windows registry∗ was examined and the key *Software\Microsoft\Windows\CurrentVersion\Explorer\RecentDocs\jpg* showed that the computer has been used to open the pictures.

10.3.4 Conclusions

The last piece of information that is commonly present in a forensic report is conclusions drawn by the forensic expert. What differ conclusions from findings is that a conclusion is made by the forensic expert based on the findings, her knowledge, and experience. That makes the conclusions *subjective*, and a very important aspect of writing a forensic report is to clearly separate objective findings from subjective conclusions. A common way to indicate the strength of the conclusions is to use a scale that is common in the organization or jurisdiction. An example of such a scale was presented in Table 10.1 earlier in this chapter. An interesting point to discuss is that the notion of including conclusions in a forensic report is something that not everyone agrees on. Some professionals think that subjective information in a forensic report is just plain wrong. However, one cannot neglect the fact that the computer forensic expert is the person that is best suited to draw conclusions from the findings of her examination. What remains certain is that conclusions must be clearly stated and separated from the *objective* findings. In cases where several forensic experts worked together on an examination, it must also be clearly stated what experts(s) that drew what conclusion. The conclusions sections for our sample case are present at the end of this sub-chapter directly followed by the word list. When writing the word list, remember that the protocol must be understandable by people with no IT expertise. Some points to make note of, as far as the conclusions go, are the following:

The first conclusion is about if the pictures found are the same as the pictures in the fraudulent ads. Looking at the pictures and visually examining the content is a good start but would not be enough to actually state they are the same pictures. However, using hash analysis makes it possible to determine that the actual data in the pictures matches exactly and that gives enough information to determine that the analysis can show that the pictures are the same.

Looking at the second conclusion, which is about meeting the suspect's claim that the pictures ended up on his computer after he browsed the ads, the first point of interest is the location of the pictures. The location of data from browsing history should be in some application specific folder and not a folder located directly under C:. Further, since the registry analysis shows that the pictures were actually used, the explanation becomes very unlikely. In this case, the expression "strongly suggests" is used instead of "shows" because it is still not totally impossible for the suspect's explanation to be true. For instance, a scenario where the suspect actually browsed the ads and the pictures were placed and later removed from a temporary storage while someone else used the same computer to create the pictures and look at them is possible, even if it would be extremely unlikely.

As for the third conclusion in relation to what camera that was used to take the pictures, it is determined that the pictures were taken close to the suspect's home address and with a camera of a telephone matching the telephone owned by the suspect. However, it must be considered plausible that the neighbor of the suspect or even a friend of the suspect owning a similar phone took the pictures. That analogy results in a conclusion that is a weak indicator that the suspect's phone was used to take the pictures.

Note that none of the conclusions are saying that the suspect did something. Rather, the conclusions express what a device was doing. Determining who the user of the computer was at a certain point in time is a very difficult task that a forensic examiner should be very careful about embarking on. Some techniques that can be used to find evidence about the computer user is discussed in Part 3.

Conclusions

The first aim of this examination was to identify if pictures used in fraudulent ads were present on the computer. Pictures that visually appear to be the same as the pictures in the ads were found in the folder "C:\PICS"; further hash lookup was used to identify the pictures and showed that the pictures in the ads matched the pictures stored on the computer exactly. In summary, the analysis shows that the pictures in the ads were present in the computer.

Further, the suspect claimed that the pictures could be stored in his computer due to him browsing the ads using a Web browser. When browsing the Internet, pictures may be downloaded to your computer and stored in predeterminable temporary folders. "C:\PICS" is not such a folder. Further, the analysis of the Windows registry shows that the pictures have been opened

(continued)

using the computer. In summary, the analysis strongly suggests that the suspect's claim cannot explain how the pictures were placed on the computer.

Looking into how the pictures ended up on the computer and where they came from, the EXIF data was examined and showed that they were taken in close proximity to the suspect's home address and with a phone of the same make and model as the suspect's phone. This indicates that the pictures were taken using the suspect's phone.

Word List

EXIF—EXIF data is data stored in an image file that provides information about the image. The data can include what camera that took the picture, GPS coordinates, and more.

Hash—A hash is a function that can create a unique alphanumeric value from a data set. The data set can be anything from a picture to a word file, and the value can be compared to a fingerprint of the input value.

Hash lookup—The process of comparing hash values for different files to determine if they are identical.

Windows registry—Data base of settings and usage information on a Windows-based computer.

10.4 Final Remarks

As a final note on the process of performing and reporting on a computer forensic analysis, it is important to mention that no examination is the same as the other. This is demonstrated by the broad range of different devices that may be subjected to a forensic examination and the broad range of questions that may be asked by the investigation. While this makes it unpractical, if not impossible to follow a common process in every single examination, the ground rules are still the same. The most important knowledge is to understand that forensic examinations must be conducted and reported on in a way that is unbiased and reproducible. This ensures transparent processes that can hold for scrutiny.

Further, claiming that there is one single tool or method that should always be followed is equally hard as determining one common process. While working as a computer forensic examiner, it becomes evident that different tools have different strengths (and weaknesses). It also becomes evident that there are cases when the most common tools are not able to do what is needed at the moment. In these cases, it is tempting to develop your own tools or use tools that are less common and that may be a feasible way to go. However, it is of utmost importance that a forensic examiner understands that the need for detailed documentation increases when you stray from the common path, all to ensure the transparency of the examination.

Something that has been touched but not fully discussed in this book is what you have the right to examine. This discussion is much up to local laws and regulations, but it should not go unnoticed that you need to know what you seized and what your warrant covers. It is very common to find references to data stored in the cloud. Cloud data would include a long list of services including online storage such as Google Drive and e-mailing services. It is a very common practice that data that is stored online is off-limits. This is due to the fact that a warrant will cover an actual computer or physical location. Thus, if you seize a computer, you get access to the data stored on that computer. A general recommendation is to never follow references that are taking you online, at least not without asking a prosecutor. However, it is often possible to find traces of cloud data that is lingering in temporary files, slack space, memory, or likewise. That information is, at least in Sweden, up for grabs.

As a final note on the theoretical section, it must be stressed, once again, that while this book presents strategies that do describe considerations and processes common to computer forensic examination, the local laws and regulations often dictate requirements that a computer forensic examiner must follow. Thus, what you read in the theoretical section is an overview of practices that you should consider. However, the actual implementation of the forensic processes is dictated by local regulations!

10.5 Questions and Tasks

Here are the questions for Chap. 10.

1. The results presented during a forensic examination should be unbiased and reproducible. What does this mean and why is it important?
2. In Fig. 10.1, an overview of a forensic process was presented. Describe all steps in brief.
3. Why is it important to report conclusions using a standardized scale?
4. Consider a case where you found references to files located at a Dropbox account. You then found the credentials to said account. Is it ok for you to download the files stored in Dropbox.

Part III

Get Practical

Following the theoretical discussions on computer concepts, forensics, and the forensic process, it is time to get practical. This part of the book introduces and demonstrates forensic tools that are commonly used in forensic examination. Furthermore, forensic artifacts are presented and explained along the way. Upon reading this part, you will have a better understanding of how to work as a forensic analyst and a toolbox that will send you along your path to become a forensic expert.

11 Collecting Data

A forensic examination or incident response process will most likely begin with collecting data. As previously discussed, you may want to collect data from different sources such as hard drives, Windows registry, and volatile sources. It is also common, especially in incident responses, to collect live data from a network and networking devices such as routers and switches. Collecting data from different sources is discussed in this chapter. As a final treat, I included a short discussion on collecting data from video surveillance systems, as this can be a tedious task that often falls into the hands of a forensic examiner, and a practical discussion on steps that can be involved in a live examination.

11.1 Imaging

Imaging is the process of copying a hard drive or other secondary storage media into a forensic image that can be used for the forensic examination. An important aspect of a forensic examination is to ensure that the actual data on the storage device that is to be examined is not compromised, and the only way to fully do that is by making a forensic image and then examining the image. Working with an image instead of examining the actual hard drive also brings other benefits; it usually enhances performance.

The best and safest way to create a forensic image is by making a physical image of a hard drive. To do this, you physically remove the hard drive from the computer and connect it to your own computer using a write blocker. A write blocker is a device that prohibits your computer from writing to the hard drive. If you are not using a write blocker, it is almost certain that your computer will write some data to the hard drive you are to examine, thus compromising the evidence. As an alternative to a physical write blocker, you can mount the examined device as read only; there are system settings or special software you can use for this purpose. When you have connected the hard drive to your computer, you can use your imaging software to create a physical disk image. Note that a physical disk image will create a copy of

J. Kävrestad, *Fundamentals of Digital Forensics*,
https://doi.org/10.1007/978-3-030-38954-3_11

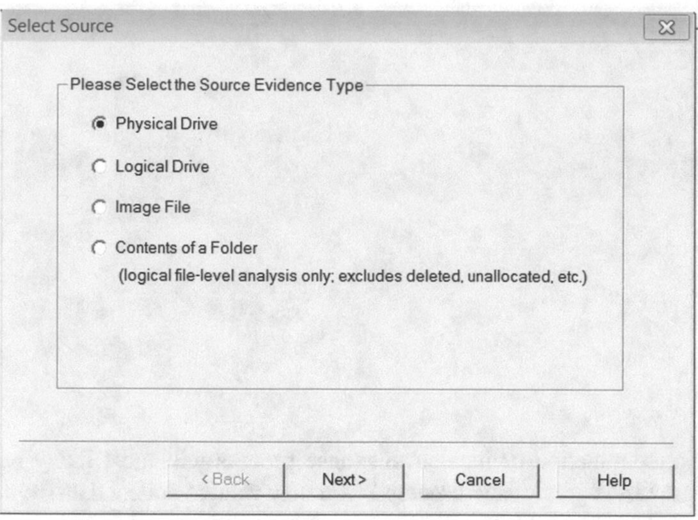

Fig. 11.1 FTK imager source selection menu

the hard drive from the first bit to the last giving you an identical copy of the hard drive that you are to examine. Also, note that even if you have to image a running computer, you may still do a physical image as long as the hard drive is not encrypted.

If the hard drive is encrypted, a physical image will do you no good because the image will also be encrypted. When this is the case, you will have to do a logical image instead. When doing a logical disk image, you image a live computer, and the resultant file will contain the data on the hard drive as seen by the computer. This gives you reduced possibilities to recover deleted files and to examine file slack, but may in some cases be your only option since encrypted devices that are currently open will result in an unencrypted image.

Well then, to make a disk image with FTK, you can use the program FTK imager. Open FTK imager and click the add new evidence button in the upper left corner, and you will get the source selection menu as shown in Fig. 11.1. In this menu, you can select to image a physical or logical drive as we just discussed. You may also select a pre-existing image file for analysis or reimaging or just select the contents of a specific folder. Selecting a single folder may be useful if you are collecting data from a large computer system such as a company file server.

If you want to import a physical device, you will get the menu shown in Fig. 11.2 where you will have to select the physical hard drive you want to image; this is what you will do if you are to collect data from a computer that is turned off or a running computer that is not encrypted. Selecting a logical device will give you the menu in Fig. 11.3, where you can select the partition you want to image; this is your best option if you are imaging a running computer with an encrypted hard drive. Imaging an encrypted computer as a physical device will cause the encryption to prevail in the disk image where a logical image will image a partition as seen by the computer,

Fig. 11.2 FTK imager physical source

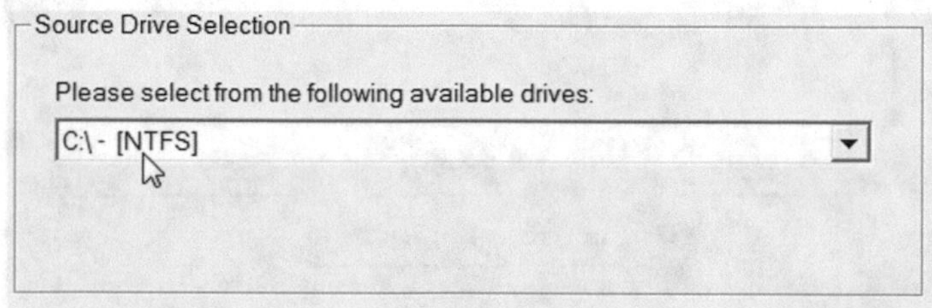

Fig. 11.3 FTK imager logical source

Fig. 11.4 FTK imager export disk image

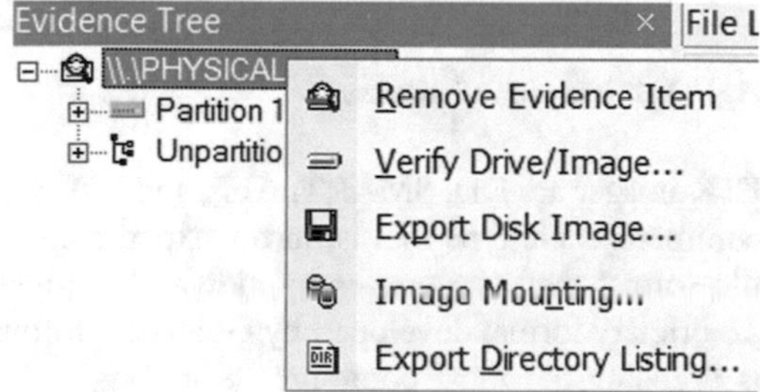

namely, decrypted. Selecting an image file or contents of a folder will let you browse for the image or folder you want to import. When you hit "Finish," the device you selected will be loaded into FTK imager, and you may verify that you loaded the correct device by browsing it using the evidence tree located on the left-hand side.

The next step is to export the evidence that you loaded into FTK imager as an image file; the process is the same regardless of what type of device you imported to FTK. Right click the device in the evidence tree, and select export disk image as shown in Fig. 11.4. This will start the image creation wizard that will begin with the menu shown in Fig. 11.5.

This dialog lets you create a new image and make several settings by pressing add. Also notice that "Verify images after they are created" is checked. This is a feature that is present in most imaging software and that uses hashing to ensure that the image is identical to the device that is being imaged. When clicking "Add," the first step is to select the file type for the output image. The file types supported by

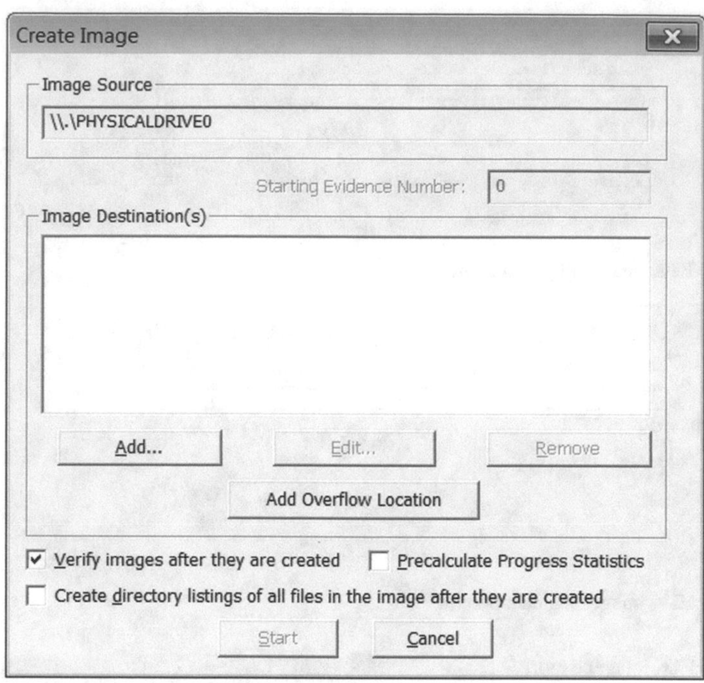

Fig. 11.5 Image creation wizard

FTK imager are DD, SMART, AFF, and E01. DD is a pure bit-stream. SMART is a commercial file type that is, in my experience, rarely used. AFF is an independent file format that supports encryption and compression of the output file. E01 is a proprietary format developed by Guidance Software, creator of EnCase forensics. It is arguably the most common file format, at least in law enforcement. E01 also supports compression (ForensicsWiki 2017). The "Select image type" menu is presented in Fig. 11.6. This demonstration will continue by discussing how to create an E01 image.

As shown in Fig. 11.7, it is common practice to include case data as metadata in an image. This data will help you distinguish what device and case you are working with at a later stage. The importance of this information should not be underestimated!

Finally, you need to give your image a name and set parameters for compression and fragmentation, as shown in Fig. 11.8. Compression allows you to use compression algorithms to compress the image that you create. This will slow down the process of creating the image but will also preserve space on the storage location. Since the hardware that will store forensic images will usually hold quite a few images, some compression is advised. The image will be separated into several files, and the fragmentation parameter decides the size of each file. Using fragmentation will make moving the image file easier on the file system and makes it easier to store the image on several different devices. This may actually be necessary in cases

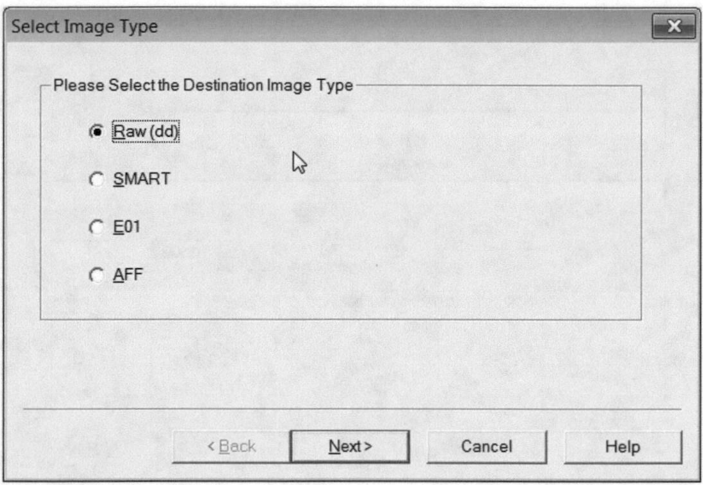

Fig. 11.6 Select image type

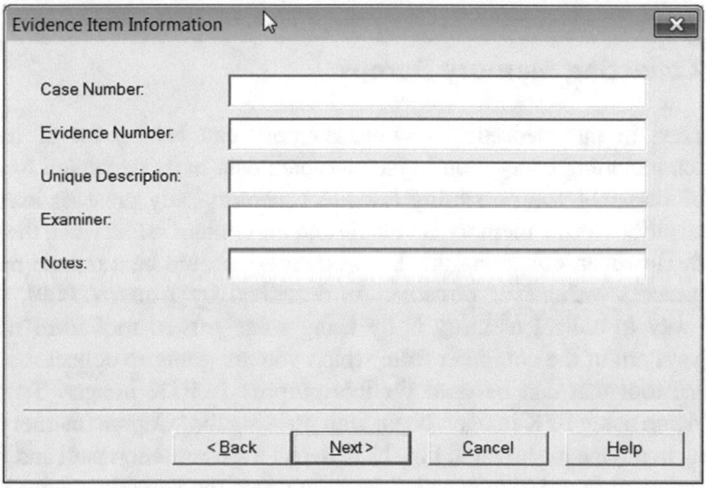

Fig. 11.7 Enter case information

where really large partitions have to be imaged. When this is done, the image is ready to be created. In FTK imager, you start the process by hitting "Start" in the create image menu, as shown in Fig. 11.5.

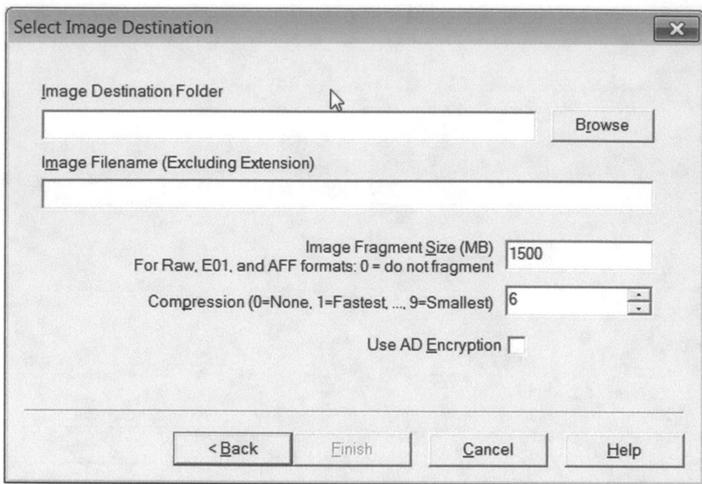

Fig. 11.8 File name, compression, and fragmentation

11.2 Collecting Memory Dumps

As discussed in the theoretical section, memory can hold a lot of interesting information including encryption keys, encrypted data in its decrypted format, and more. Unfortunately, the possibility to collect memory only presents itself during live investigations as the memory is volatile and the content is lost when the power is turned off. However, collecting the data in memory should be a natural part of the forensic process—whenever possible. As described by Amari (2009), the most common way to collect memory is by using some trusted tool from within the operating system of the computer from which you are going to collect the memory dump. One tool that can be used for this purpose is FTK imager. To collect a memory dump using FTK imager, begin with pressing the "Capture memory" button leading to the menu shown in Fig. 11.9. Select the destination path and file name and you are good to go! You can also select to dump the Pagefile, where Windows store volatile data that does not fit in memory.

Important to consider when you are collecting memory is that the memory dump is stored as one big file. This fact brings that you need to ensure that the device you use to store the memory dump on is partitioned with a file system that can support big files. This excludes FAT32 that can only store files of 4 GB of data or less. Good options are to use filesystems native to the computer you are examining, as follows:

- Windows: NTFS
- Mac OS/iOS: HFS+
- Linux: EXT4

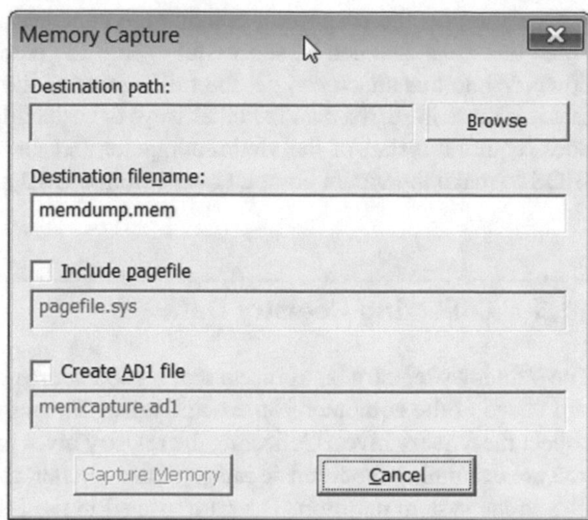

Fig. 11.9 Memory capture

In most cases, you may also use exFAT that works in most situations.

As described by Amari (2009), it is not always possible to access the operating system of the computer you are examining. This can, for instance, be the case when the computer is logged off and you cannot find or force the password. In these cases, there are other, more intrusive, attacks that you can use. Among those are direct memory access (DMA) and cold boot attacks that will be briefly presented next.

DMA attacks exploit the design of the IEEE 1394 interface (often referred to as FireWire), more specifically the part of the standard called DMA (Witherden 2010). Many different connectors, including FireWire, Thunderbolt, PC card, and other PCI express devices, use the IEEE 1394 interface and are thereby susceptible to a DMA attack. To conduct a DMA attack, you would connect your computer to the victim computer and present your computer as a SBP—2 unit directory. The victim computer will then give you Read/Write access to the lower 4 GB of its RAM, allowing you to dump it (Break & Enter 2017). One tool that allows you to do a DMA attack is Inception, a free open-source tool (Break & Enter 2017). While the DMA attack is easy to carry out and rather nonintrusive, it does suffer the drawback that you would normally only get access to the lower 4 GB of RAM, and modern computers often hold much more memory. Further, it should be noticed that operating system vendors are developing more and more defenses to the DMA attack, rendering it hard to succeed with.

Cold boot attack is an attack where you basically freeze the memory modules, reboot the victim computer, and use a USB stick to make it boot a small process designed to dump the contents of memory (Halderman et al. 2009). The attack is possible due to the fact that when a computer is rebooted or turned off, data in memory is not lost immediately. Rather, it is degrading over time and the time that the data lingers is increased if the memory modules are cooled down. That makes it possible to boot the victim computer using a USB stick containing special software that only serves the purpose of copying the contents of memory. It should also be noted that the attack can be successful even if the memory modules are not cooled down. While this attack can get the full content of the memory, it should be noted that it is more intrusive than the other ways of collecting memory. This is because it does require a restart of the victim computer and, in some cases, modifications in BIOS to make the victim computer boot from a USB stick.

11.3 Collecting Registry Data

The Windows registry is, as discussed, a good source of information about settings and usage of the computer you are analyzing. To analyze the registry, you need to collect the registry hives. Collecting the registry hives is a straightforward process. If you are examining the forensic image of a computer, the registry hives are stored as files in the system partition. They are located in the folder "C:\Windows\System32\config\." Also notice that NTUSER.dat is located in the root of each user's home directory. If you are doing a live examination, you can extract registry files using FTK imager. Begin with pressing the button looking like a yellow box, labeled "obtain protected files." This will result in the menu shown in Fig. 11.10. In this menu, you can select if you want all registry files needed for password recovery or all registry files available. In my experience, there is no reason for selecting anything other than obtaining all registry files. This is a fairly fast process. Decide where you want to store the obtained files and press "OK."

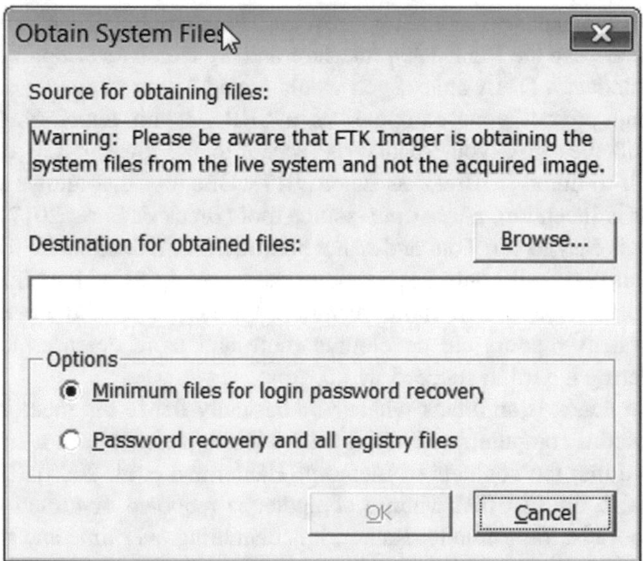

Fig. 11.10 Capture registry files

A fact to be aware of, in regard to registry data, is that some registry keys are not notified immediately. Rather, they are updated when a user logs off or when the computer is shut down. It is therefore possible that registry hives captured during a live examination do not hold the latest version of all registry data. As such, it can be a good idea to extract registry hives during live examination and then again from a captured image during the analysis step. This way, what you capture during live examination will be seen as a safeguard in case something goes wrong and you are unable to extract the registry hives later on.

While FTK imager may not be open source, it is distributed as freeware and downloadable from the AccessData Web page. In the opinion of the author, it is a very good tool, and thus no alternative for collecting images, memory, or registry files has to be discussed.

11.4 Collecting Network Data

A source of information that is sometimes important in criminal investigations and almost always important in incident response is the actual network infrastructure. By collecting data from the network and information from network devices, a computer incident response team (CIRT) or forensic examiner can get an understanding about what is actually going on the network. In incident response, a typical incident could be that some malware infected some device in the network that is now used to relay malicious e-mails to other organizations. A CIRT would be very interested in swiftly locating the infected host, and the most reasonable way to do that would be to monitor network traffic to identify the originating device or those e-mails. Collecting and analyzing network traffic can be done with a number of different tools and usually require some knowledge about data communication. While a demonstration is beyond the scope of this book, a tool that is well-known and free to use is Wireshark.[1]

While monitoring the actual traffic is powerful, network devices such as routers, switches, firewalls, and intrusion detection systems (IDS) should be given equal attention. To give a simple explanation, routers and switches are used to forward data from one location to another, while firewalls and IDS determine and monitor what type of traffic can leave and enter the network. Those devices will typically contain log files or volatile data that describes the rules that are used at the moment and how they were recently applied. This data can answer questions about who communicated with whom and what service (or at least port number) they used for communication. Considering, for instance, a very common objection to evidence found in a computer during a forensic examination in law enforcement, the computer must have been remote controlled. While it is very hard to determine if a computer was ever remote controlled, it should be possible to analyze network devices to see if a computer is currently remote controlled. Gathering data from network devices

[1]https://www.wireshark.org/#download

would be performed in different ways depending on the vendor and model of the devices. As a general rule, it would include accessing the device and downloading configuration files and log files. Also be aware that some important data may be volatile and captured in some other way. When accessing devices as part of incident response, it is likely that you have access to passwords needed to gain access. In law enforcement, that is commonly not the case. However, it is common for networking equipment to come with a pre-configured password that is never changed by the customer. It is very likely that the password is a standard password that you can find by searching for the device on the Internet or that the password is printed somewhere on the actual device.

11.5 Collecting Video from Surveillance

While not totally "on topic" for this book, collecting video from surveillance deserves a mention in this chapter because it is not as easy as you would think. What I want to mention in this brief section is that you never know what to expect when you set out to collect video from surveillance equipment. As a brief introduction to the area, know that there are loads of different manufacturers, standards, and approaches to record and store surveillance video. The lesson to learn here is to always come prepared.

In this sense, remember that some systems are only able to read FAT32-formatted memory sticks. However, other systems may store the video in files that are too big for the FAT32 file system, and, in these cases, you will need a memory stick formatted with NTFS or sometimes even ext4. Lesson here is to come prepared so that you can handle whatever situation that you encounter. In my personal experience, I collected video from devices that could just accept an external hard drive and devices that you could not export video from at all; instead, we had to make a recording of the screen. It is also common for different vendors to actually create video files in different, sometimes proprietary, formats. In these cases you need special viewers for those formats that may or may not come with extracted data. A hands-on tip is to gather viewers from different vendors whenever possible.

When you are working with video from surveillance equipment, time is usually of importance. However, you should know that it is not possible to trust the time stamp or time settings that are present in the surveillance equipment. Anyone who is used to work with surveillance video will attest to the fact that time stamps in these videos are very often way off. For that reason, you should make sure that whenever you are collecting surveillance video, note the time that is given by the surveillance gear and the current accurate time. Finally, calculate the difference if there is any.

11.6 Process of a Live Examination

As described in Chap.8, the process of a live examination is often more comprehensive than just imaging, collecting memory, and collecting registry. At a minimum, you would also like to collect information about time settings, active user, devices connected via USB, or the network and document active programs. There are also some interesting considerations that you have to remember:

- You want to capture as good information as possible, meaning that you want to do memory dumps and images as early as possible because you don't want to compromise the content.
- You want to capture what is on screen as early as possible so that it doesn't disappear.
- You want to capture information about other devices of interest early on so that they stay up if you find any.
- You really want to ensure that the computer will not go into sleep mode or be tampered with remotely.

As you surely understand, it comes down to a trade-off between all the things that you want to do first. The basic idea becomes to do tasks that are as safe as possible, meaning that you want to minimize the chance of the computer crashing while you minimize any contamination your steps may do to the data collected in later steps. You should also prioritize your steps so that you ensure collection of the data that is more relevant in your specific case.

Above all is that the computer has to stay on and preferably be removed from the network. However, network connections have to be gathered before taking the computer off the network. A simple way to achieve this is to run the script located in Appendix B to collect common information and then disable any network interfaces and configure the computer to not enter hibernation. Remember to consider whether or not you need to perform network forensics as previously described before taking the computer offline.

A reasonable next step would be to document active programs. The easiest way to do this would be to use a camera or to use a screenshot utility that can be executed without installation from a USB. In my opinion, using an external camera is the better choice as it will not compromise the data on the computer whatsoever. However, it should be noted that just copying data from the computer if you see something that is of high relevance is encouraged. In such a case, document the location of the data you copy, and remember that the metadata in the copied file may not be accurate.

Before moving on to imaging, memory capture, and registry collection, it can be useful to run a tool such as USBDevview to detect if any USB memories have been inserted into the computer. This can provide guidelines for the continued house search. Also, it is good practice to run tools that can help detect whether encryption software is running on the computer. One such tool, that is free to use, is Encrypted

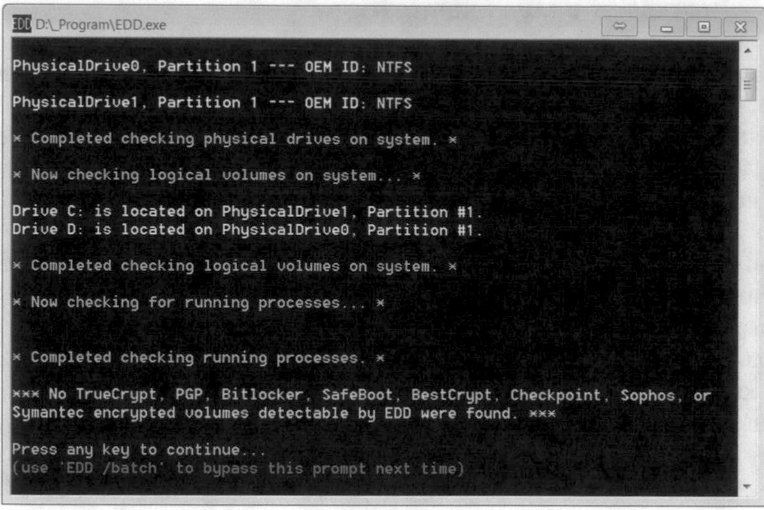

Fig. 11.11 EDD usage example

Disk Detector (EDD) by Magnet Forensics.[2] EED output is exemplified in Fig. 11.11; in the example, no encrypted data was found. However, note that a manual inspection should be conducted in addition to the tool.

As we discussed throughout this book, memory should always be collected whenever possible, and the next step is to collect memory and registry files as described earlier in this chapter. The final step of the live examination is to image the hard drive and that is commonly only done if there is a need for it; it is a very time-consuming process. The bottom line is that the hard drive should be imaged if there is any suspicion of encryption software running on the computer, and data currently readable may go into an encrypted state when the computer gets turned off. Using EDD to manually inspect the list of running and installed software would be the first step in looking for encryption software. A second step could be to load the physical drive into FTK imager; if it is readable, it should not be encrypted. Note that readable in this context means that you can actually read and understand the Master Boot Record in the beginning of the hard drive. For instance, a hard drive that appears to contain "bogus data" is likely encrypted. Analyzing such a drive in FTK imager would likely result in a scenario where FTK imager is unable to identify any partitions or other device information. The "better safe than sorry rule" applies, if there is the smallest suspicion of encryption being in use—make sure to image the computer during the live examination.

[2]https://www.magnetforensics.com/free-tool-encrypted-disk-detector/

11.7 Questions and Tasks

Here are the questions for Chap. 11.

1. Image some small device such as a USB drive. Create two different images using different compression settings. What are the results?
2. Collect memory from your own computer.
3. Collect the registry hives from your local computer.
4. Are there any case where you would, during a live investigation, want to image the computer as your first step in the process?
5. Optional: Do a cold boot attack and describe the process!

References

Amari K (2009) Techniques and tools for recovering and analyzing data from volatile memory. SANS Institute InfoSec Reading Room

Break & Enter (2017) Inception. Available online http://www.breaknenter.org/projects/inception/. Fetched June 03, 2017

ForensicsWiki (2017) Forensic File Formats. Available online http://www.forensicswiki.org/wiki/Category:Forensics_File_Formats. Fetched June 03, 2017

Halderman JA, Schoen SD, Heninger N, Clarkson W, Paul W, Calandrino JA et al (2009) Lest we remember: cold-boot attacks on encryption keys. Commun ACM 52(5):91–98

Witherden F (2010) Memory forensics over the IEEE 1394 interface. Available online https://freddie.witherden.org/pages/ieee-1394-forensics/revisions/c1c615827b7647933e5a3d00668d6183.pdf. Fetched June 03, 2017

Indexing and Searching 12

While the previous chapter described data collection, this and upcoming chapters will describe different actions and methods that are common parts of the analysis phase. The order of which steps in a forensic analysis are performed can differ from time to time, and the book tries to keep an organization that resembles the order of which things happen using common forensic tools. This chapter will describe the process and considerations that are relevant during the process of creating a text index. A text index is commonly used for two purposes; first, it is a database that allows for fast searching using keywords or regular expressions. Second, it can be extracted and used as a dictionary in password cracking attempts; essentially, it is a database that keeps track of all strings stored on the examined device and where the strings are located. After discussing how to create the index, the chapter moves on with a discussion on different types of search engines that are commonly included in forensic software followed by a more detailed discussion on regular expressions and their role in digital forensics. AccessData FTK and Autopsy are used interchangeably in this chapter, and most functions are available in both programs.

12.1 Indexing

Indexing is a technique where you create an index of a forensic disk image. When creating an index, the data on the hard drive is seen in alphanumerical form. The data is read from beginning to end, and all cohesive strings are listed in the index. You will commonly also get a listing of what strings belong to each file. The resulting index is useful in two ways; first, you can use the index to do fast searches for keywords. This is because the index contains information that states where each found string is located. Thus, if you search for a keyword, the forensic software will return all files that contains that keyword. The second use of the index is as a word list in password cracking. Since the index will contain every alphanumerical string present on the device that you are examining, there is a good chance that it will contain one or more passwords related to something on the system.

J. Kävrestad, *Fundamentals of Digital Forensics*,
https://doi.org/10.1007/978-3-030-38954-3_12

```
#·$·Ðÿ·Stretch=ÿ$·Èÿ·Center=ÿ$·Ñÿ·5¤þ··çÿè···#FF808080$·æÿ·0.5,0.75,0.5,0.75qý··
```

Fig. 12.1 Data sample

On the topic of indexes, there are some terms that you need to be familiar with: spaces, letters, and noise words. Spaces are symbols that are used to separate the data into strings, letters are the symbols that make up a string, and noise words are words that are ignored in the index because they are considered too frequent. In essence, strings are made up from character defined as letters and separated by characters defined as spaces. Noise words are usually words such as "it," "and," and "or" and are excluded from the index even if they are strings. As an example of how the indexing works, consider a case when the signs a-z are considered letters and all other signs are considered spaces. Then, look at the data sample in Fig. 12.1.

The strings that will be added to the index are the following:

1. Stretch
2. Center
3. FF

The reason is that those strings are the cohesive strings of signs defined as letters in the sample data. If numbers were to be defined as letters, the third string would be FF808080, and if Center was to be added as a noise word, it would not be added to the index. It is also common that forensic tools allow for the opportunity to limit the string length for index entries and other fine tuning. In FTK, creating an index is done during preprocessing (as described in Chap. REFTEXT) or by hitting "Evidence" and then "Additional analysis" and selecting "Search Index" under the "Index/Tools tab." Note that you may only modify letters, noise words, and such when creating the index as a preprocessing task. The index settings window is demonstrated in Fig. 12.2. To add or remove symbols of words in a section, simply use the add or remove buttons. Understanding the indexing process is crucial in order to fully be able to use the index. For instance, when using the index for password cracking, you must ensure that characters that you expect in the password are not considered spaces in the indexing process. Further, those signs must be added as letters to be added to the index.

As for indexing in Autopsy, the fine tuning you can do is more limited. Autopsy will run with predetermined options but does allow you to select what character sets to use. Selecting a character set that contains the letters and signs you want to be able to search for is therefore important. How the indexing and index actually work is similar in FTK and Autopsy.

As final notes on indexing, you should know that creating an index is a time-consuming process. However, searching for keywords with an index is much faster than searching a case without an index. Also, the index is very useful for password cracking. You should also know that the index will include words that are readable to

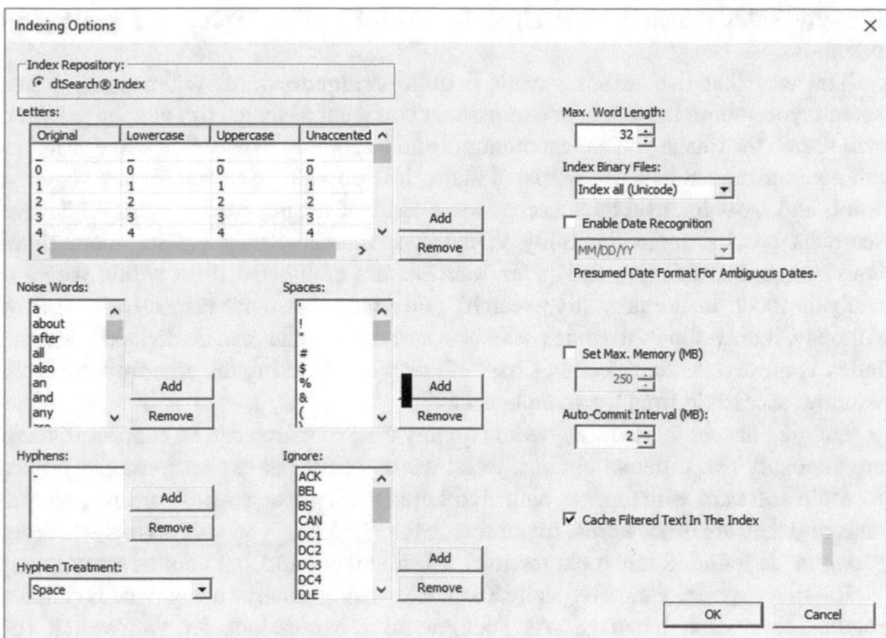

Fig. 12.2 FTK indexing options

the indexing software at the time of indexing. Consider, for instance, a case where you are examining an image that contains a compressed folder that, inturn, contains a lot of text files and you create the index before you expand the compressed folder. In this case, the text from the files in the compressed folder will not be present in the index, and this is because it was in a compressed format at the time of indexing. The same case applies to encrypted files and, while not a bug, must be understood by the forensic examiner. That being said, indexes are very useful for the forensic expert that knows how and when to use them!

12.2 Searching

A very common task during forensic examinations is to search for keywords. In my experience, searching for different keywords is of interest in almost every case. While searching is a common and important task, it can be time-consuming, and it is therefore important to get it right. Most forensic tools, including FTK, provide two different ways to conduct searches, namely, live and index searches. An index search is a search through an index. If the word you are searching for is present in the index, you will get a hit. The main advantage of the index search is that it is very fast, and you commonly get the results instantly. However, as made evident by the discussion on indexing, it is hard to find strings that contain signs that were not considered letters during the indexing process. Further, it can be difficult to find sentences even if many index search engines allow for use of regular expressions and logical operators.

The way that live searches work is quite straightforward. When doing a live search, you submit the words or expressions you want to search for, and the software will search the image you are examining, from beginning to end. Since live searches are not constrained by a precomputed index, it is possible to search for any sign you want, and most forensic tools accept some kind of regular expressions. While live searches provide more flexibility than index searches, they are far more time-consuming. In FTK, live and index searches are conducted from within the case analysis mode in the tabs "live search" and "index search," respectively. As for Autopsy, it only allows for index searches, and the searches can be defined when the index is created, as described in Chap. 17, or when working the case from a search window accessible from the main interface.

Digging deeper into how keywords for any type of search can be expressed, there are generally two different options: exact words or regular expressions; any proper forensic software will support both. Explaining what exact words are is a simple task, and they are exact words. If you search for "Joakim," you will get hits wherever "Joakim" is found. Regular expressions, on the other hand, are another story.

Regular expressions are basically about expressing patterns using what is called a regular expression language. As such, regular expressions let you search for variations of a word or patterns that will be completely made up from code. The usefulness becomes obvious when you look into some examples for what they can be used for:

- Variations in spelling. Consider a case where the word ecstasy is an interesting search term, but it appears to be spelled in different ways, as ecstasy, Xstasy and ecstazy. Using a regular expression, you could search for all terms at the same time.
- Searching for patterns. Consider a case where you want to search for all e-mail addresses. You have no clue about what e-mail addresses you need, and you just want all of them. Regular expressions can define a pattern matching any e-mail address. The same goes for phone numbers, credit card number, social security numbers, and more.

So, how would this be done? What we have to do is to express a pattern using a regular expression language. Naturally, there are several different languages and even our forensic products are using different styles. Autopsy is using the grep way of expressing regular expressions,[1] and FTK uses a flavor called dtSearch.[2] Follow the links at the bottom of the page for a reference guide to the type that you need. The chapter will continue using grep regular expressions.

[1]https://www.sleuthkit.org/autopsy/help/grep.html

[2]https://www.syntricate.com/files/Regular%20Expressions.pdf

When creating a regular expression, you are to build a pattern using some code to express what character you want and (optionally) how many times it should be repeated. Using grep regular expressions, the easiest way to express what characters should produce a match is by expressing the character range within square brackets as follows:

- [a-zA-Z] will match any upper or lowercase English letter.
- [a-z] will match lowercase letters.
- [0-9] will match numbers.
- [a-zA-Z0-9] will match any letter in any case and numbers.
- [akz] will match any of the letters a, k, and z.
- [a-g] will match any of the letters a to g.
- You may also require some part of the regular expression to be a precise match to a character by simply writing out that character, a will match a.
- . is a wildcard and will match any character.

Now that we got the hang of that, we have some quantifiers that determine how many times an expressed character can occur, and those are:

- ? says that a character is optional and can only occur once.
- * says that a character is optional but can occur several times.
- + also says that a character can occur more than once but is required to occur at last once.
- | is *or* and allows you to say this or that should be a hit. For instance, a|b would match a or b.

Knowing the basics, we can now start building regular expressions. Let us begin with building an easy expression that will match a misspelling of the name Joakim. It could be built as follows:

```
J[oa]*kim
```

Looking at the regular expression, it says that the term should begin with "j" and end with "kim." The interesting part is "[oa]*" that says that any of the letters "o" and "a" are a match, and the star says that it can be there any number of times. Thus, any of the following terms will be a match for this pattern:

- Joakim
- Jaokim
- Jkim
- Jaaaaaaaaaaaaaaaaaoooooooookim
- Tons more

Fig. 12.3 Autopsy regular expression search hits

In practice, this is displayed in Fig. 12.3 where the regular expression was used to search a text file containing Joakim and Jaokim, and both spellings of the name are highlighted as search hits.

Continuing with a more advanced example, a common way to use regular expressions would be to search for e-mail addresses. To do that, we would have to start by determining how an e-mail address would commonly look like. For instance, joakim@example.com would be an e-mail address, as would joakim.kavrestad@email.com. What is common in the format is that there are characters, followed by an "@," followed by characters, followed by a ".", and followed again by characters. Having determined the structure, we can now start building the regular expression that would look something like this when it is done:

```
[a-zA-z0-9._]+@[a-zA-Z0-9]+\.[a-zA-z0-9]+
```

Looking at this expression from left to right, it begins with expressing the starting characters as any alphanumerical character, a dot, or an underscore. Several other characters may be in an e-mail address, but let us consider this as complete. The following plus says that there can be any number of characters, but we need at least one. Then there is an @ in clear text as that is the next part of an e-mail address followed by any alphanumerical character. In this group, the dot and underscore were omitted, because they would not be seen in this part of the expression. The next character is a dot again, this time preceded by a "\". This is because when used outside of square brackets, the dot is a wildcard that will match anything, the "\" is used to escape this function, apply the actual dot in the search, and the same thing could have been expressed as [.]. The final part is alphanumerical characters again and that concludes our regular expression. As such, this would be a regular expression that can find e-mail addresses, and even if it can be perfected, more would work in many cases when using Autopsy.

12.2.1 Questions and Tasks

To stimulate learning and bringing practice to the theory, there are some questions and tasks:

1. Use Autopsy or FTK to create a text index of the image you created in the tasks for Chap. 11.
2. Do index searches, using Autopsy, for the following and analyze the hits:
   (a) Your name
   (b) Phone
   (c) Docx
3. Do index searches, using Autopsy, for the following regular expressions and describe what they mean:
   (a) [0-9]*
   (b) \.docx
   (c) [a-zA-Z][:space:][a-zA-Z]
   (d) (\.exe)|(\.bin)
4. Using FTK, index a forensic image and then search for the following keywords. Do live and index searches for all keywords. Describe the results of the searches and explain why differences may appear.
   (a) System32
   (b) .appdata
   (c) Alink.dll

13 Cracking

Cracking, usually also called hacking, intrusion or whatnot is the art of breaking something. Perhaps the most common is to break passwords or encryption to get access to data or to break authentication systems to gain access to some system. In the context of digital forensics, cracking is a common practice used to get access to data that someone made unavailable. While some theoretic background to password cracking was given in Sect. REFTEXT, this section will describe password cracking in action using AccessData Password Recovery ToolKit (PRTK) and the open-source alternative Hashcat. While both of those tools are good and flexible tools for password cracking, remember the discussion on password theory and password cracking previously presented. While good programs can make the task of cracking password easier, it is up to the forensic expert to leverage knowledge and experience about passwords to create good attacks. We will soon head over to practical password cracking, but before that, I want to describe another use of the DMA attack, namely, using it to bypass authentication mechanisms of operating systems.

Remember that the DMA attack is possible because you can connect to the Firewire port of a target computer and get Read/Write access to the lower 4 GB of memory. Most operating systems keep code that handles the log-in procedure in memory, and the code (very abstracted) says that if you submit the correct password, you are in. Else, you are out. The tool Inception, discussed in a previous section on DMA attacks, can search for this code and modify it so that you are in no matter what password you submit. Using this attack lets you log into an operating system without submitting the correct password. Thus, it is a very powerful tool to use during live investigation where you would need access to the target computer to collect volatile data. It can also be used in a similar fashion if you need elevated privileges. This is a common case when you get access to a running Linux or MacOS system; users on those systems does typically not have administrative privileges and that prevents you from doing many of the tasks a forensic examiner needs to do. Inception can help you gain those privileges and, thus, is very helpful during a forensic examination.

Using this approach to crack your way into a computer has been very successful in the past. In my own experience, it has worked wonders against Windows as well

J. Kävrestad, *Fundamentals of Digital Forensics*,
https://doi.org/10.1007/978-3-030-38954-3_13

as MAC. However, while the attack is still possible, it is less likely to succeed today. This is for two reasons. First, modern computers usually have more than 4 GB or memory, and for the attack to work, the authentication code must be present in the part of memory that Inception can access. Second, more and more protections against DMA attacks are created and implemented by operating system vendors, hardware manufacturers, and third-party developers. However, the attack remains relevant as it is often the only way to break into a live system without a reboot.

13.1 Password Cracking Using PRTK

As for password cracking using PRTK, PRTK is a tool that can crack a large number of different file types and encryption schemes. However, as discussed in the theoretical section, perhaps the most important part of password cracking is the engine for developing dictionaries. On this topic, PRTK does a good job. Another very helpful feature of PRTK is that is can analyze files and often determine the type of encryption algorithm that has been used to encrypt it. In some cases, PRTK will even be able to launch decryption attacks instead of password guessing attack and that can save you a lot of time. When you find some encrypted file or password you need to crack, you can summarize the procedure you need to follow as follows:

1. Create dictionaries.
2. Create attack profile.
3. Run the attack.

To begin, an overview of PRTK is shown in Fig. 13.1. The main left pane lists all waiting jobs, and marking a job will show details of that job in the right pane. You can also double click a job to see more detailed information and progress about it. The tools menu is used to access the dictionary tool, and the edit menu is used to access the profile creation menu.

To create dictionaries, enter the dictionary tool shown in Fig. 13.2. This is the tool you would use to import a dictionary that is in the form of a simple row-separated text file. This would be the case if you downloaded password lists from the Internet or if you exported a text index from a case. This tool also provides options to remove duplicates, remove long or short words, and choose what characters to include. When you selected your settings, hit generate to generate the list.

To create a biographical dictionary, there is a special tool accessible through the dictionary tools menu. There are also tools for passphrases and permutations of words; all three tools work in similar ways. The tool for creating biographical lists is shown in Fig. 13.3. What you should do is to input the biographical data you found. The words can be categorized according to its type, such as name, date, or plain words. When you entered all the data you found, you can go to the generator tab and hit generate. PRTK will combine the different words and dates, etc., and create a

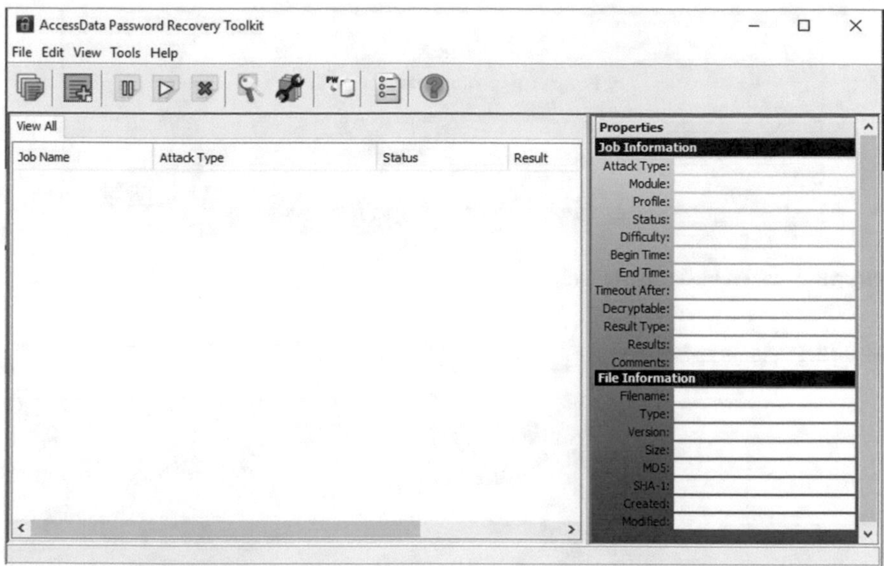

Fig. 13.1 PRTK interface overview

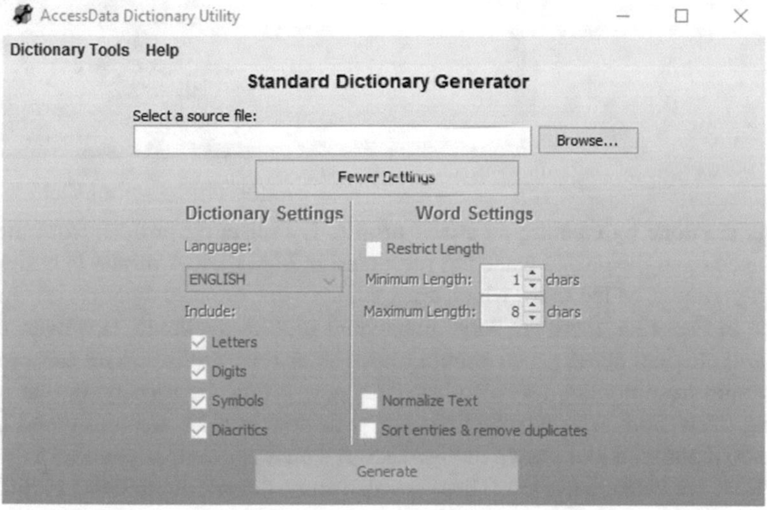

Fig. 13.2 PRTK dictionary tool

biographical dictionary for you. Note that the dictionary creation is a process that can be somewhat time-consuming. Plan your work for optimal efficiency!

The next step is to create the attack profile. PRTK allows you to run different mutation and combination algorithms on your dictionary. It can also include different brute force attacks and combinations of dictionary and brute force attacks. These

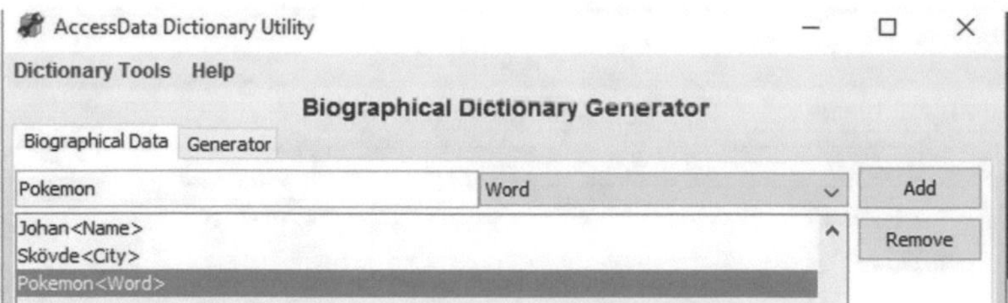

Fig. 13.3 PRTK biodictionary tool

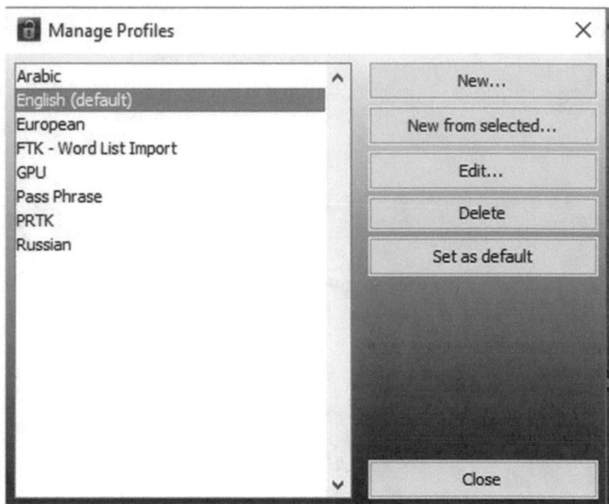

Fig. 13.4 Profile manager

settings are done by creating an attack profile. By selecting profiles from the edit menu, you open the profile manager, presented in Fig. 13.4. A profile is basically a set of algorithms, called rules, which are applied to one or more dictionaries. As you can see in Fig. 13.4, there are some precreated profiles available. However, to get good and efficient attacks, you should create your own profiles. You can create a new profile from nothing (New) or create a new profile by modifying one of the existing (New from selected). Settings for your new profiles are configured in the profile configuration tool shown in Fig. 13.5. All dictionaries that you ever imported into PRTK are listed to the left. There are also some default dictionaries in different languages. Select the dictionaries that should be used in your profile. Then hit the order tab to select the order in which the dictionaries should be applied. The available rules are listed to the right. Simply check the rules you want to use, and notice that the order they appear in is the order that they will run in. I want to mention the highlighted rule. This is the rule that tests every entry in every dictionary. There are other rules that test the word in the dictionary as uppercase or lowercase only. Also notice that the rules are marked BAS or ADV. BAS is for basic, and those rules are less time-consuming than ADV rules. The first number in the BAS and ADV

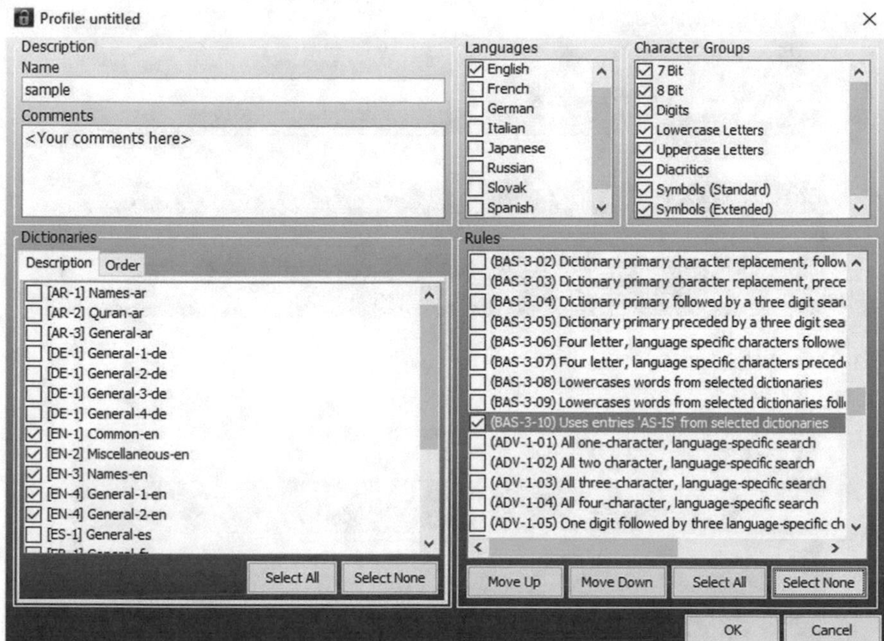

Fig. 13.5 Profile configuration dialogue

marking also indicates the complexity of a rule. As such, ADV-2-1 is more complex than ADV-1-2 and, thus, more time-consuming. When your profile is completed, select OK to save it.

The final step in the attack processes is to execute the actual attack. To begin, drop the file you want to crack into PRTK. PRTK will analyze the file and try to figure out the file type and suggest the type of attack to use. You can read about all different attack types that PRTK can execute through the user manual accessible by clicking the question mark in the main program. When the file is analyzed, PRTK will present the wizard as shown in Fig. 13.6. This is where you select the profile to use for the attack. This is done in the upper left corner. It is possible to create new profiles from here. Clicking next will take you to the list of available attacks as demonstrated in Fig. 13.7. In this case, the file to be attacked is a password-protected .rar file. It is only possible to do a dictionary attack against this type of files, but there are files that have several different attack options. Select the one you want to use and hit Finish to start the attack.

When the attack is started, you can see the status of the attack (queued, running, and finished) from the PRTK main window. If you double click an attack, you can see detailed progression statistics including what rule PRKT is currently working with and how many attempts that PRKT can make per second. Note that different file

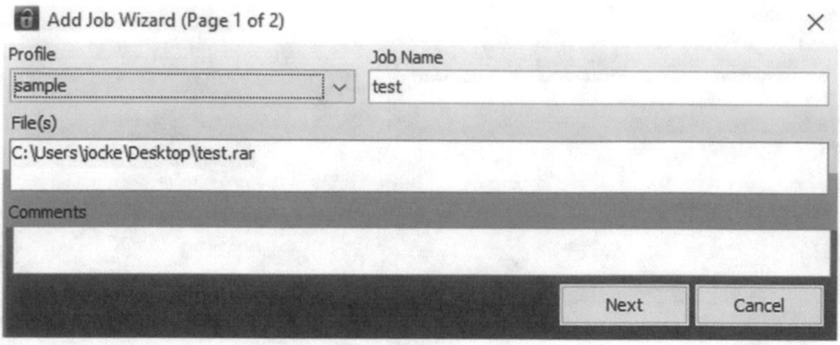

Fig. 13.6 Add job wizard

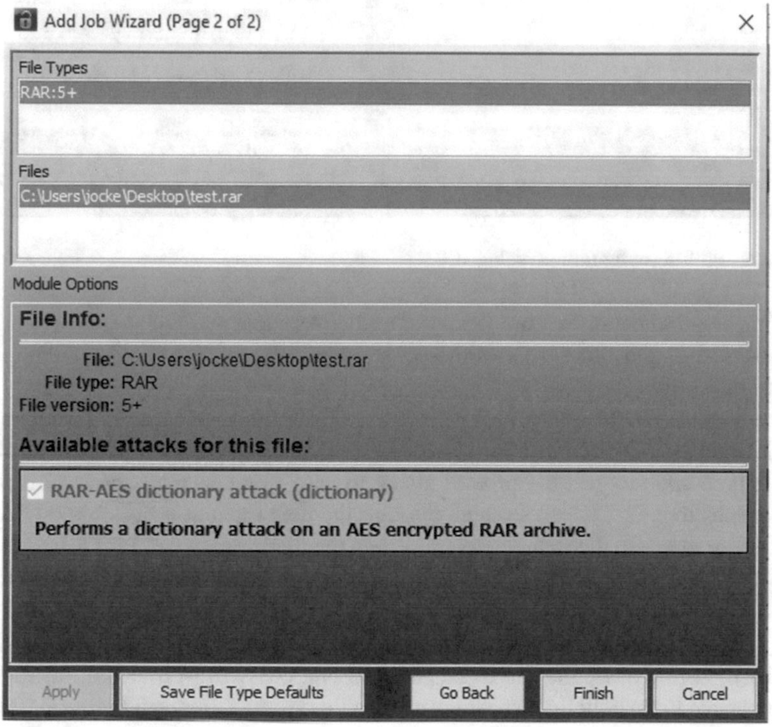

Fig. 13.7 Select attack

types have vastly different attack time. When the attack is complete, PRTK will show you the password in the right part of the main window, as demonstrated in Fig. 13.8. At times, the password is followed by an "∗". This indicates that PRTK found several passwords. You can see all of them by double clicking the attack.

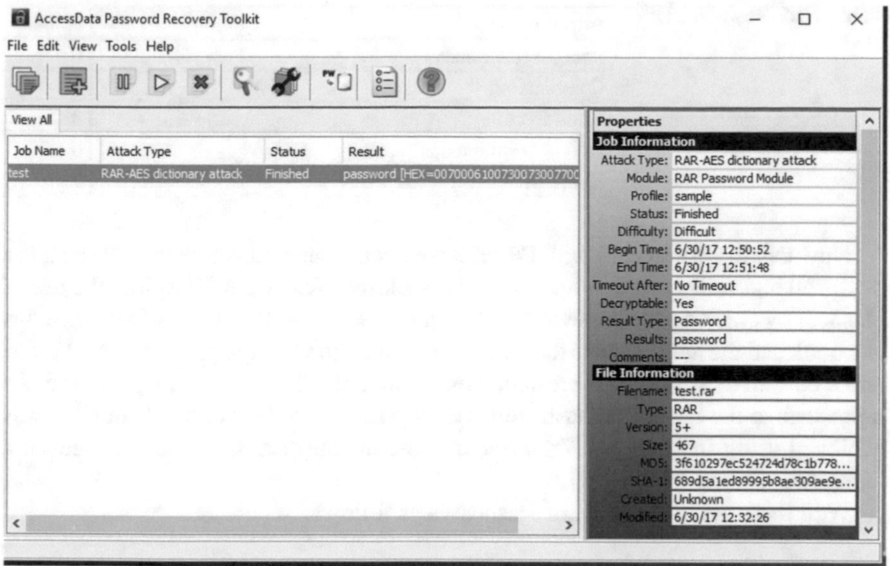

Fig. 13.8 PRTK result presentation

13.2 Password Cracking Using Hashcat

Cracking password hashes with Hashcat is a vastly different approach than using PRTK. Perhaps the most notable differences are the following:

- Hashcat expects a password hash to be cracked. Nothing else. The hash should be contained in a text document, and you may supply a number of hashes in the same file. This gives you the chance to supply a full document and hope that Hashcat finds the hash you need to crack on an individual line. However, you should expect to have to do manual extraction of the hash you need to crack and not just supply a file you need to crack.
- Hashcat is a cracking tool and not a dictionary utility. This means that you need to create dictionaries manually or find some other tool to create them. When on the topic of dictionaries, Hashcat expects dictionaries in the format of plain text files with one word on each row. The main difference here, as compared with PRTK, is the lack of a biographical dictionary generator. This can be overcome, to some extent by using rules, as will be discussed later.
- Again, Hashcat is a password cracker. As such, it supports many hash algorithms but it does not include decryption attacks.
- It is a CLI cracker, not a GUI.
- It uses the GPU to crack passwords, at least that is when it does its best job. You may need to have specific drivers for your GPU to make Hashcat work fast.

Table 13.1 Hashcat attack modes

Attack mode	Number
Straight (dictionary)	0
Combination	1
Brute force	3
Hybrid word list and mask	6
Hybrid mask and word list	7

Now that the differences with PRTK have been discussed, know that Hashcat is a powerful and well-used tool for fast GPU cracking. Next we will explore the use of Hashcat by cracking the password hash of a password-protected 7zip file. Since this is a book and the author wants the demonstration to go well, the password used is *test* and a custom dictionary was created, which conveniently contains the password. As a prestage to the attack, the hash from the 7zip file has to be extracted, and this was achieved using the free tool *7z2hashcat*.[1] The demonstration was completed on a computer running Windows 7.

Well then, the basic usage of Hashcat is as follows:

```
Hashcat64.exe --mhashtoattack --aattackmodehashesdictionary
```

What follows the –m parameter is the hash type to crack. Just issuing the command *Hashcat64.exe –help* will display the different hashes supported by Hashcat. Attack mode refers to the type of attack to use. Hashcat supports the modes listed in Table 13.1, and the attack mode should be expressed with the corresponding number.

For our sample attack, a standard dictionary attack will be used. The other attack modes will be explored in a little while. The next part of the line is for the path to the file containing the hashes to crack followed by the path to the target dictionary. In our case, the line to invoke the attack would be as follows:

```
Hashcat64.exe- -m11600- -a07zhash.txtdictionary.txt- -force
```

–force has to be used since the GPU drivers on the used computer appear to be broken. –force will tell Hashcat to continue the attack anyway. The output from Hashcat upon succeeding with the attack will look as presented in Fig. 13.9, where the password *test* is displayed.

Now, the basic usage if Hashcat has been demonstrated, using a standard dictionary attack where all passwords are tested as is. However, the real power of Hashcat lies in the possibility of using other attack modes to build more sophisticated ways of testing passwords from dictionaries. This will be described next.

The opposite of a dictionary attack would be a brute force attack where the idea is to try all possible passwords until the correct one is found. As has been previously

[1] https://github.com/philsmd/7z2hashcat

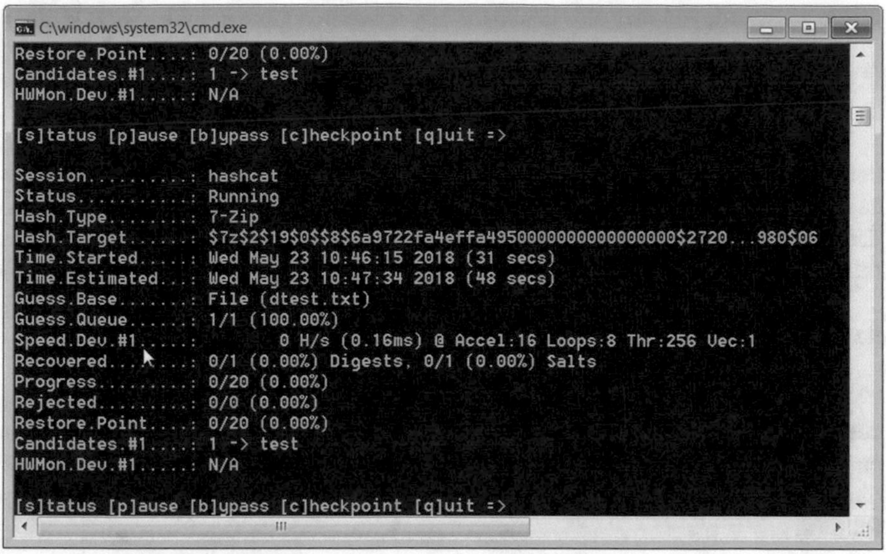

```
C:\windows\system32\cmd.exe
Restore.Point....: 0/20 (0.00%)
Candidates.#1....: 1 -> test
HWMon.Dev.#1.....: N/A

[s]tatus [p]ause [b]ypass [c]heckpoint [q]uit =>

Session..........: hashcat
Status...........: Running
Hash.Type........: 7-Zip
Hash.Target......: $7z$2$19$0$$8$6a9722fa4effa4950000000000000000$2720...980$06
Time.Started.....: Wed May 23 10:46:15 2018 (31 secs)
Time.Estimated...: Wed May 23 10:47:34 2018 (48 secs)
Guess.Base.......: File (dtest.txt)
Guess.Queue......: 1/1 (100.00%)
Speed.Dev.#1.....:        0 H/s (0.16ms) @ Accel:16 Loops:8 Thr:256 Vec:1
Recovered........: 0/1 (0.00%) Digests, 0/1 (0.00%) Salts
Progress.........: 0/20 (0.00%)
Rejected.........: 0/0 (0.00%)
Restore.Point....: 0/20 (0.00%)
Candidates.#1....: 1 -> test
HWMon.Dev.#1.....: N/A

[s]tatus [p]ause [b]ypass [c]heckpoint [q]uit =>
```

Fig. 13.9 Successful password cracking using Hashcat

Table 13.2 Masks supported in Hashcat

Mask	Contained characters
?l	abcdefghijklmnopqrstuvwxyz
?u	ABCDEFGHIJKLMNOPQRSTUVWXYZ
?d	0123456789
?s	*SPACE*!"#$%&'()*+,-./:;<=>?@[\]^_`{|}~
?a	All of the above
?H	0123456789ABCDEF
?b	0x00-0xff
?h	0123456789abcdef

described, this is very time-consuming but can, at time, be the only option. The way to implement a brute force attack in Hashcat is not actually to make a true brute force attack, but rather to build one using a mask attack, it is invoked using the attack mode 3 and supplying a mask instead of a dictionary, like so:

```
Hashcat64.exe - m11600 - a07zhash.txt?l?l?l?l - force
```

In this case, the mask dictates the key space, and what you have to do is basically to define the possible key space for your brute force attack by expressing a mask. In this case, four occurrences of ?l dictate that the attack will run through all possible, four-letter, lowercase passwords. As default, Hashcat supports the masks presented in Table 13.2. You may also add your own charsets to be used in the masks.

As such, building a brute force attack comes down to defining a mask that matches the key space you want to brute force. If you happen to know the structure of the password, you may also define the key space in a more granular way. While a full brute force attack of a six letter password would be expressed as *?u?u?u?u?u?u,* if you know that it begins with two digits and ends with a lowercase letter, the key space can be reduced by expressing the attack as *?d?d?u?u?u?l.*

Moving on to the combination attack, this is an attack where two dictionaries are combined, i.e., all words in each list are appended to all words in the other list. This can be especially useful if you believe that passwords begin or end with biographical data that you captured into a dictionary. The way to invoke the combinatory attack in our case would be:

```
Hashcat64.exe - m11600 - a07zhash.txtwlist1wlist2 - force
```

Finally, Hashcat supports what is called a hybrids attack. It is basically a combination attack where one of the dictionaries is substituted for a mask. That enables you to, for instance, run a dictionary but append a date to every word in the dictionary. Using a hybrid attack of a word list followed by a mask is invoked as follows:

```
Hashcat64.exe - m11600 - a67zhash.txtwlist?d?d - force
```

In this case, all combinations of digits will be appended to the end of every word in the supplied word list. To put the mask value in front of every word, the expression is reversed and attack mode 7 is used, like so:

```
Hashcat64.exe - m11600 - a7zhashtxt?d?dwlist - force
```

That is it for the quick description and demonstration on how to use Hashcat for password cracking. There are more advanced ways to use Hashcat and much more documentation available on the Hashcat Web site.[2] However, before moving on, it is worthwhile to mention that even if Autopsy does produce a text index for searching, there is no neat way to export is for use as a dictionary. Still getting the text index into a dictionary is of importance, and thus we will figure out a way to do it using some manual labor that will serve as an example of how to use scripting and program usage analysis to determine how program works and how to get the data you need.

By analyzing the case folder of Autopsy, it is evident that the text index is placed in thc folder *[caseroot]\ModuleOutput\keywordsearch\data\solr4_schema2.0\index.* Looking at the files, the text index is structured in the files with an extension of *.tim,* and there appears to be one file for every runtime of the keyword search ingest module.

Analyzing the files, it becomes apparent that they begin with some data describing the file, but the important thing to notice is that it appears to contain keywords for every analyzed file, and the data for every file begins with the string

[2]https://hashcat.net/hashcat/

——————METADATA——————. Basically, what we need to do is to extract the data under every such string and format it so that every string within the field is placed on a row of its own. Looking further in the file, it can be noted that there are a lot of nonstandard characters and whitespace that needs to be removed. In Appendix B, there is a script that converts the *.tim* files to dictionaries that can be used in Hashcat for password cracking.

13.3 Questions and Tasks

Here are the questions for this chapter.

1. When using Hashcat, why would you want to use masks?
2. PRTK supports various decryption attacks where Hashcat does not; what is a decryption attack?
3. Why do you sometimes need to extract a password hash from a file that you want to crack using Hashcat?
4. Download and use Inception to force a Windows logon screen. Describe your efforts and your results. If you were unsuccessful—elaborate on possible reasons for why.
5. Create a password-protected rar archive, and use your favorite password cracker to crack it open. Describe your efforts and your results.

Finding Artifacts 14

In doing a forensic examination to answer questions asked by the investigation, you need to look for evidence that you can use to draw conclusions. The pieces of evidence that you find are sometimes referred to as artifacts, and this chapter will describe how to find some artifacts that are common for a forensic examiner to look for. This chapter will also present demonstrations of how to analyze file metadata, log files, chat logs, and unorganized data such as slack. In addition to the artifacts described here, several other key artifacts were described in a more theoretical manner in Chap. 4, and even more artifacts will be described in the upcoming chapters.

14.1 Install Date

The install date for the computer can be of great importance. Consider a situation where you are looking for information about some event that took place in 2015. If the computer was installed in 2016, that information will be hard to come by and you can skip the computer in question. Further, if a suspect says that he or she just bought the computer in 2017 but it was installed in 2015, it is easy to suspect that the suspect is hiding something. Anyhow, the install date is found in Windows registry, in the SOFTWARE hive. Using AccessData Registry Viewer, the install date can be found by viewing common areas, as shown in Fig. 14.1.

As displayed, the InstallDate key holds the value describing when the system was installed. The date is expressed as a UNIX time stamp, seconds that passed since January 1, 1970, but Registry Viewer presents a translated time stamp in the bottom left pane. Note that the time stamp is reported with the local time zone and UTC. Time zones are discussed in more detail in the next section, and a complete list of time zones is available in Appendix D. The InstallDate key can also be found by browsing the registry hive to the following path: Microsoft\Windows NT \CurrentVersion.

J. Kävrestad, *Fundamentals of Digital Forensics*,
https://doi.org/10.1007/978-3-030-38954-3_14

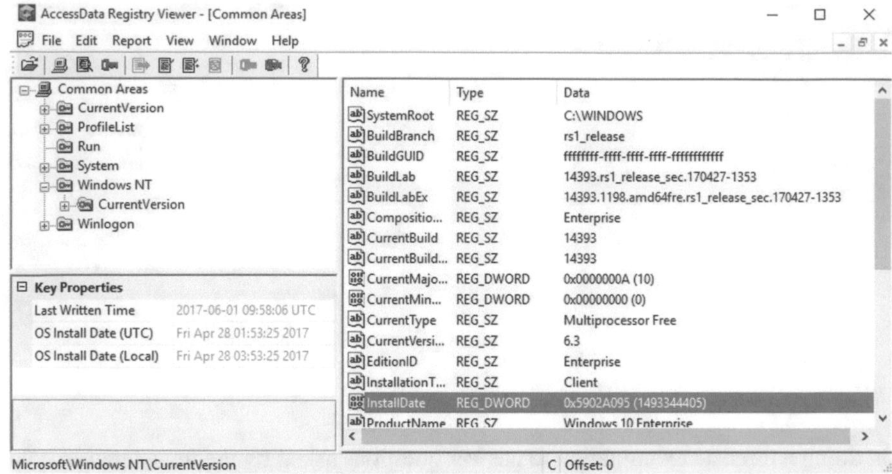

Fig. 14.1 Install date in Windows registry

14.2 Time Zone Information

As you are surely familiar with, the world is divided into time zones that make the time differ from location to location. The time zone settings on your computer will therefore affect the displayed time and the time that is noted in time stamps. For that reason, it is important to verify the time zone settings (as well as the correctness of the system clock) during a forensic examination. Basically, the time zone will create a time offset from UTC. That is, how much the system clock will differ from UTC (sometimes also called Greenwich mean time). The time zone is sometimes expressed as the name of the time zone (Pacific Standard Time) or as the offset from UTC (UTC-08:00). Time zone settings applied for a computer are found in Windows registry, in the SYSTEM hive, in the following path: ControlSet001 \Control\TimeZoneInformation. Figure 14.2 shows time zone information found with Registry Viewer common areas.

The system clock is also dependent on the daylight savings settings. Daylight savings tells you to turn the clock 1 hour back in the fall and 1 hour forward in the spring. The dates when daylight savings are applied are also found in the different keys in: ControlSet001\Control\TimeZoneInformation.

14.3 Users in the System

Finding out what users that are present in the system is a task that is sometimes overlooked. I must admit this is a task that I have personally overlooked at several occasions. The thing is that a suspect may decide to claim that some other user did

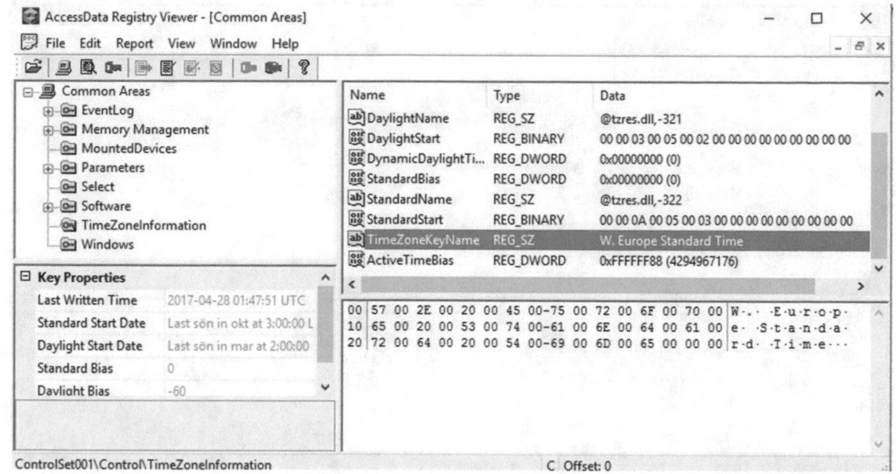

Fig. 14.2 Time zone in Registry Viewer

everything that the prosecutor claims that he did. If this statement is presented in court and the forensic examiner cannot testify to whether or not there were any other users, other than the suspect, present on the computer, this may harm the case. There are several ways to find out what users that are present in the system such as looking into what users that have home folders in the Users folder. However, it is easy to manipulate a file system. Thus, looking into the registry is a much safer way to find out the users of the system. Information about the users in the system is present in the SAM hive under the key: SAM\SAM\Domains\Account\Users. Each user gets a key of its own, and clicking each key will show you information about the user. An example is given in Fig. 14.3, showing information about the administrator user. This is a good place to describe user identifiers in Windows. Each user is given a security identifier (SID), and the last part of the SID is a numeric value called a relative identifier (RID). The RID for the built-in administrator account is always 500 and the guest account is always 501.

The user accounts added manually starts at RID 1000. Notable is that the SID and RID never change for a user account. However, it is possible to change the username. As such, it is possible to change the name of the administrator account into something else and name a normal account administrator, for the sake of confusing. However, it is the SID and not the name that is used to evaluate user permissions (Zacker 2014). Also note that users that are removed are, at least for a time, kept in registry. That being said, the SAM registry hive will tell you the users present in the systems, and AccessData Registry Viewer will evaluate the RID and username for each user. The registry will also keep track of the number of log-ins for each user, when the user last logged in, when the user last changed password, and more.

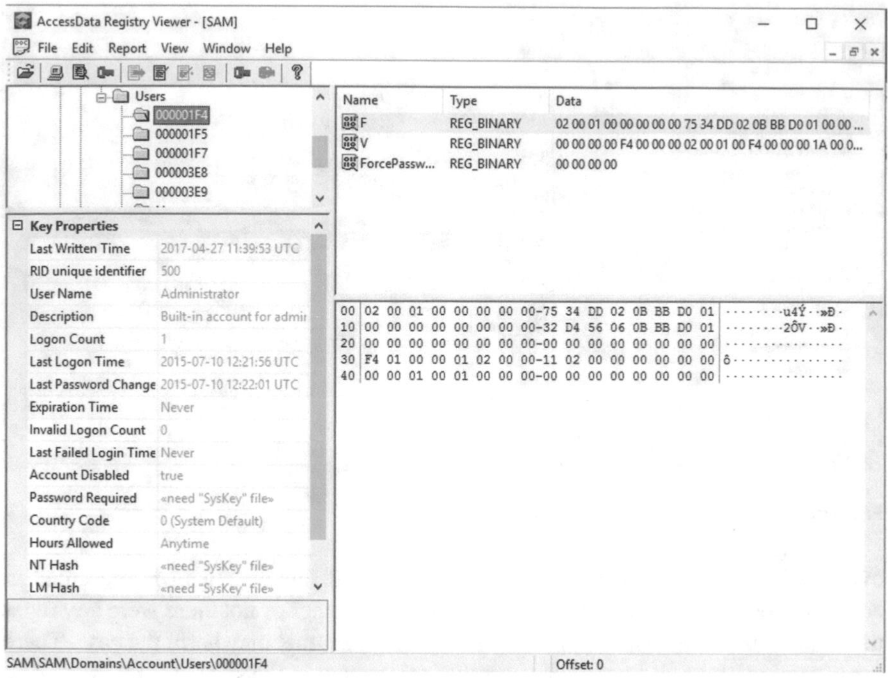

Fig. 14.3 User information in Windows registry

14.4 Registered Owner

When installing Windows, you can register a name as the registered owner of the system, and this information is kept in registry. It may seem as if someone with ill intent would make sure not to store his own name in registry, but I found the name of the suspect as the registered owner on more than one occasion. The registered owner is present in the SOFTWARE registry hive at the following path: Microsoft \Windows NT\CurrentVersion.

14.5 Partition Analysis and Recovery

As discussed, accounting for all data on a hard drive is essential and a good way to identify hidden partitions or slack space. Looking at a hard disk in FTK imager, you will see the list of partitions and "Unpartitioned space" that shows unallocated space on the hard drive. As shown in Fig. 14.4, the unallocated space is shown as a list of files. Each file contains a contiguous run of unallocated space, and the name identifies the starting sector of the free space (AccessData 2013).

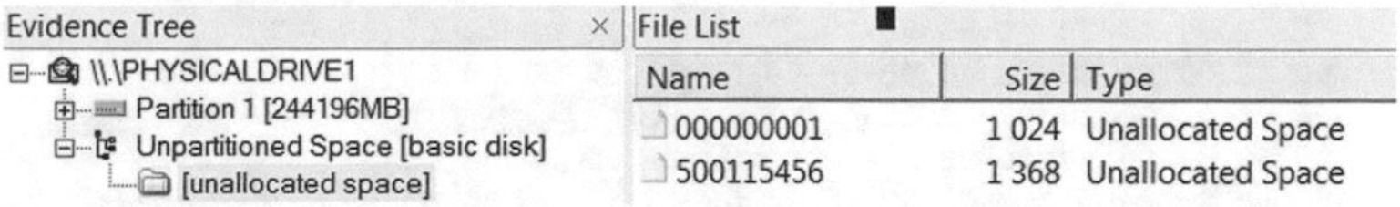

Evidence Tree	File List		
\\.\PHYSICALDRIVE1	Name	Size	Type
Partition 1 [244196MB]	000000001	1 024	Unallocated Space
Unpartitioned Space [basic disk]	500115456	1 368	Unallocated Space
[unallocated space]			

Fig. 14.4 Unallocated space shown in FTK imager

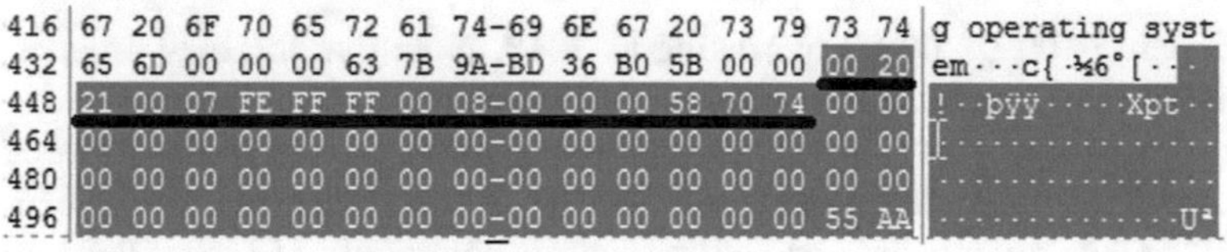

```
416 67 20 6F 70 65 72 61 74-69 6E 67 20 73 79 73 74  g operating syst
432 65 6D 00 00 00 63 7B 9A-BD 36 B0 5B 00 00 00 20  em···c{·½6°[···
448 21 00 07 FE FF FF 00 08-00 00 00 58 70 74 00 00  !··þÿÿ····Xpt··
464 00 00 00 00 00 00 00 00-00 00 00 00 00 00 00 00  ················
480 00 00 00 00 00 00 00 00-00 00 00 00 00 00 00 00  ················
496 00 00 00 00 00 00 00 00-00 00 00 00 00 00 55 AA  ··············Uª
```

Fig. 14.5 Partition table entry viewed in FTK imager

It is normal to find small pieces of unallocated space, as in this example. However, if you encounter big chunks of allocated space, it is wise to do a manual examination of the partitions on the hard disk as the chunk of unallocated space can contain a deleted or hidden partition.

When manually examining the partitions on the hard drive, we need to recall that a hard drive will, normally, contain a master boot record (MBR) containing a list of partitions. This is true for MBR-partitioned disk; in modern computing, the GPT partitioning scheme is gaining in popularity and it works a little bit different. However, while this section concerned MBR partitioning, most of the section is to a large extent applicable for GPT-partitioned disks as well.

However, the MBR is what FTK imager (and most other forensic software) will use to make out the partitions on the hard drive. The partitions are listed in the partition table that is located in offset 446 in the MBR. That means that it begins 446 bytes from the beginning of the MBR (Guidance Software 2016). The partition table continues until the MBR signature (hex 55 AA) is found, and it is 16 bytes long. Figure 14.5 shows the data representing a partition table with one entry. The marked part is the partition table, and the underlined part is the partition table entry seen by marking the entire disk in FTK imager. In FTK imager, you can jump to a sector or byte offset by right clicking in the data field and selecting the appropriate option.

What you need to know next is how to interpret the partition table entry; it is structured as follows:

- The first byte tells if the partition is bootable or not; in this case, 00 for no and 80 is yes.
- The following three bytes tells the starting sector of the partition in CHS format.
- The following byte tells the partition type; in this case, 07 for NTFS.
- The following three bytes tells the ending sector of the partition in CHS format.
- The following four bytes tells the relative sector offset; that is, how many sectors from the beginning of the disk the partition is located. The hexadecimal value in

```
EB 52 90 4E 54 46 53 20-20 20 20 00 02 08 00 00 ëR·NTFS     ·····
00 00 00 00 00 F8 00 00-3F 00 FF 00 00 08 00 00 ·····ø··?·ÿ·····
00 00 00 00 80 00 80 00-FF 57 70 74 00 00 00 00 ········ÿWpt····
00 00 0C 00 00 00 00 00-02 00 00 00 00 00 00 00 |···············
F6 00 00 00 01 00 00 00-4C 2C 09 40 32 09 40 04 ö·······L,·@2·@·
```

Fig. 14.6 Start of VBR for a NTFS partition

this case is 00 08 00 00 translating to 2048. Note that the byte order is little-endian. Note that this offset is calculated in sectors and not bytes!

- The final four bytes will tell the total numbers of sectors in the partition. The hexadecimal value in this case is 00 58 70 74 translating to 1953519616. Note that the byte order is little-endian. A sector is commonly 512 bytes large, making the size of this partition roughly 931 gigabytes.

Now when you know that, what you need to do to find disk space not included in a partition is to walk the partition table and note the starting and ending sector of each partition. Gaps that you find could be slack space but may also contain hidden partitions. To find a hidden partition, you would search the unallocated space for patterns indicating a volume boot record (VBR) that is present in the start of a partition. For instance, a VBR belonging to a NTFS partition will begin with hexadecimal EB 52 90 4E 54 46 53 as shown in Fig. 14.6.

Located at offset 40 (40 bytes from the start) of the VBR is 8 bytes indicating the size of the partition in sectors, as shown in the marked part of Fig. 14.6. The byte order is little-endian. When looking for hidden partitions, one must also remember that every NTFS partition maintains a backup VBR. The backup VBR is located at the very end of the partition. This makes for a case where it is common to find backup VBR lingering in unallocated space in a case where a partition has been deleted and replaced with a partition that is even just a little bit smaller. Thus, to evaluate if a VBR we found in unallocated space is one of a hidden partition, we need to know a bit about how to interpret some of the data in the VBR. Perhaps the easiest way to decide if the encountered VBR can be a hidden partition is to evaluate the size of the partition that the VBR belongs to. Looking to the sample in the picture, the sector size for the partition is 1953519616. Since the common sector size for an MBR-partitioned disk is 512 bytes per sector, this partition would be roughly 931 gigabytes large.

To decide if this can be a hidden partition, one would calculate the space available in the unallocated space and simply see if it fits. If it does fit, it is a candidate for a hidden partition; else it must be a lingering VBR from some old partition. When you find what could be a hidden partition, your next step is to recover it. Unfortunately, FTK does not do a good job at recovering partitions. However, EnCase forensics is great at partition recovery, and there are several free tools available including EaseUS Partition Recovery Wizard (EaseUS 2017). As a final not, in the spirit of not making things harder than they have to be, a starting point when looking for hidden or deleted partitions should perhaps be to quickly scan through the data that is contained in unallocated areas. It is quite common to see that those areas are filled with all zeroes, meaning that there is no information stored there. If the areas do not contain any data, it is pointless to go through the trouble of manually interpreting the MBR.

14.6 Deleted Files

Finding deleted files is a very common task for a computer forensic expert. In criminal investigations, deleted files are often of great importance because, well, criminals like to cover their tracks. Also, criminals, just as anyone else, delete files to keep their computers nice and clean, and the deleted files may have evidentiary value. In a corporate environment, it is also common to recover deleted files when a file is deleted by mistake or something happens to a storage media. The process of recovering deleted files is usually called data recovery and can be done in a number of different ways. The rest of this chapter will discuss data recovery in the following three ways:

- Recovering files deleted from the MFT.
- File carving.
- Recover data fragments.

Recovering data fragments is done using the approach discussed in the ending section of this chapter. The remainder of this section will introduce "Recovering files deleted from MFT" and "File carving."

14.6.1 Recovering Files Deleted from MFT

Remember that Windows systems commonly use the NTFS file system and that all files are listed in the Master File Table (MFT). What happens when a file is deleted is that the file entry in the MFT is removed, but the actual file is commonly left on the hard drive. The file is left until it is overwritten. Files deleted in this manner can be restored by searching the sectors in the partition for sectors holding files not present in the MFT. Since the file is not actually gone, the restoration process is simple. This process can be completed using tools available online and is commonly performed automatically by forensic tools. Actually, this process is completed by FTK, FTK imager, and Autopsy.

From the viewpoint of the operating system, the process just described is true. However, in modern-day computers, the reality is a little bit more complicated. This is because of the way that solid-state drives (SSDs) work. When data is to be written to a block of an SSD that already contains something, the data has to be fully deleted first. Thus, keeping remains of files that have been deleted from the MFT will degrade the performance. For that reason, the TRIM technology is commonly used on SSDs. TRIM is essentially a function that immediately wipes data that is deleted from the operating system, making restoration impossible. However, not all SSDs have TRIM enabled, and then restoration is done as just described. Also, loads of computers are still using mechanical hard drives, making this type of simple file recovery very common in practice.

14.6.2 File Carving

File carving is used to find files that cannot just be restored using the process described above. Reasons for why a file cannot be restored can be that pointers to where the file is located have been broken; the file may be partially overwritten or located in some unorganized area such as the Pagefile. As discussed in Chap. 3, different file types contain specific data that distinguish them from files of other types. It is common for a file to have a header, in the beginning of the file, containing a file signature and a trailer at the end of the file. Thus, if you find the file signature and the trailer, everything in between should be a part of the file. This is how file carving works. When carving for files, you are searching for file signatures and trailers and try to rebuild the files.

File carving is usually done using a file carver. A file carver is a tool that does the carving process. Depending on what type of material you are carving for, there are different tools of different quality. However, most forensic software includes some type of data-carving functionality. In FTK, you can do data carving during preprocessing or by hitting "Evidence" and then "Additional analysis" and selecting "Data carve." Hitting the "Carving options," you notice that there are several file types that FTK can carve for. There is also the option to create a custom carver. If you find yourself working a case with special file types, you may want to create a custom carver. In doing that, you have to determine the file signature and the offset where the file signature begins. Consider the header of a PDF file in Fig. 14.7. The file signature is "%PDF-1.4," and it is located in the beginning of the file; thus, it is located at offset 0. However, if the file signature was just "PDF-1.4," it would have been located at offset 1, one character in, counting from the beginning of the file. Note that the offset in this example is counted in bytes.

When you established a file signature, you need to decide how the file ends. Some files are fixed length and then you can state the file size. Other files may have an ending signature or tag that you can input.

When you are working with data carving, there are some things to consider. First of all, the number of false positives (found files that are not really files) is often large. This is because there can be a lot of file headers lingering in slack, Pagefile, and such. Those headers will likely result in a false result being produced. While you need to

```
000000 | 25 50 44 46 2D 31 2E 34-0D 25 E2 E3 CF D3 0D 0A | %PDF-1.4·%âãÏÓ··
000016 | 34 20 30 20 6F 62 6A 0D-3C 3C 2F 4C 69 6E 65 61 | 4 0 obj·<</Linea
000032 | 72 69 7A 65 64 20 31 2F-4C 20 35 30 31 35 32 37 | rized 1/L 501527
000048 | 2F 4F 20 36 2F 45 20 34-39 38 31 31 31 2F 4E 20 | /O 6/E 498111/N 
000064 | 31 2F 54 20 35 30 31 33-32 38 2F 48 20 5B 20 34 | 1/T 501328/H [ 4
```

Fig. 14.7 Partial header of a PDF

be aware of this issue, the risk of creating false evidence is extremely small, negligible even. For a carver to generate a file that can be used as evidence, it has to be:

1. A working complete file
2. Fitting into the active case

The chance of a file matching the above criteria being a false hit is, in my opinion, impossible.

What you also need to consider when working with data carving is that the chance of the carved files being altered is not negligible. It is very possible that some bits are missing from the original file resulting with the fact that the carved file differs from the original. A few missing bits are often not even visible but can, at times, modify important data such as time stamps. If some part of a carved file is messed up, this is commonly obvious. However, when drawing conclusions, one could argue that you should be a little bit extra careful when drawing conclusions based on carved files.

14.7 Analyzing Compound Files

Several files that can contain important data are called compound files. A compound file is basically a file that maintains its own file structure and includes file types such as compressed files and Microsoft Office files. In the case of compressed files, the file content is not readable when the file is in the compressed state. Before a proper analysis of a compound file can be conducted, it has to be unpacked or expanded. This process makes all the content of the file visible to the examiner and the forensic software.

Just to be clear, it is commonly not possible to search or analyze compound files, compressed files in particular, manually or automatically before they are unpacked. Knowing this is especially important during preprocessing tasks such as indexing, because if you do not unpack compound files during preprocessing, most preprocessing tasks will not apply to the contents of the compound files. However, expanding compound files can be a time-consuming task. To expand compound files in FTK, select "Expand compound files" during preprocessing or at a later stage as additional analysis. The same can be done in Autopsy using the ingest module "Embedded File Extractor."

14.8 Analyzing File Metadata

As has been discussed over and over again, all files contain metadata, and metadata is information about the file it regards. While it is easy to focus on the actual file content, metadata is often of equal interest to a forensic examiner. What information that is present in the metadata is highly dependent on file type. However, most file

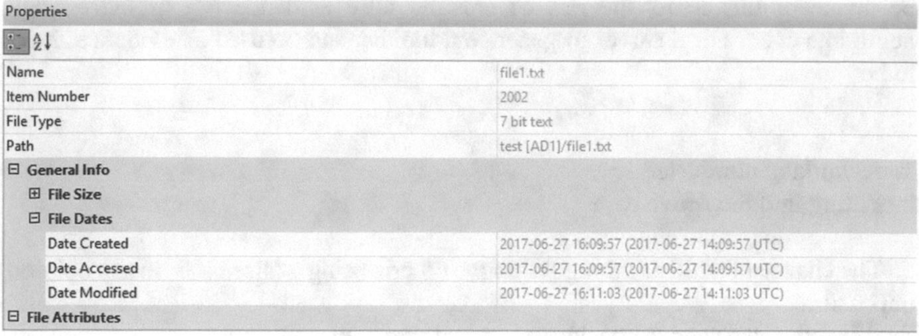

Properties	
Name	file1.txt
Item Number	2002
File Type	7 bit text
Path	test [AD1]/file1.txt
⊟ General Info	
⊞ File Size	
⊟ File Dates	
Date Created	2017-06-27 16:09:57 (2017-06-27 14:09:57 UTC)
Date Accessed	2017-06-27 16:09:57 (2017-06-27 14:09:57 UTC)
Date Modified	2017-06-27 16:11:03 (2017-06-27 14:11:03 UTC)
⊟ File Attributes	

Fig. 14.8 View metadata in FTK

systems attach some metadata, including time stamps, to all files in the file system. In FTK, you can view the metadata of a file by marking the file and then hit the properties tab in the view pane, as shown in Fig. 14.8.

The remainder of this section will discuss the following types of metadata, commonly of interest to a forensic examiner:

- NTFS time stamps
- EXIF data
- Office metadata

14.8.1 NTFS Time Stamps

All files created on an NTFS file system get time stamps, and the time stamps can tell you a fair bit about what happened to a file. The time stamps present on a file on an NTFS file system are the following (Knutson and Carbone 2016):

- Created, indicating when the file was created in the system
- Modified, indicating when the file was last modified
- Accessed, indicating when the file was last read
- MFT modified time, indicating when the file metadata was last modified

Reading the time stamps will give you a good indication of when a file was created and last accessed and modified. However, you should know that the created time stamp gets updated at every occurrence that the file is created. Created in this context includes when it is moved to a computer, when it is originally created, and if it is cut and pasted. All of those actions will also update the Accessed record. However, the Modified record seems to accurately describe when the file was last modified, meaning that the data in it actually changed. The relation of the created and modified time stamps has been of importance in several cases. Consider a case where a file that is of importance has been found on a suspect's computer. The suspect may claim that he downloaded the file from the Internet and never used it again. However, the created time stamp shows that it was created on the computer in November 2017 and the modified time stamp says that it was modified in April 2018. This would falsify the suspect's statement since the modify time stamp will prove that the file was modified after it was created on the computer.

It is also important to know that there are actually two sets of time stamps related to each file on the NTFS file system (Rusbarsky 2012). Many tools used to confuse forensic examiners will only change one set of time stamps, and that enables a forensic examiner to analyze the time stamps to find discrepancies. If there are discrepancies in the sets of time stamps, that is a sure sign that someone is trying to hide something.

14.8.2 EXIF Data

Pictures usually contain a very extensive set of metadata called EXIF (exchangeable image file format) data. EXIF data is often a very rich source of information even if the precise nature of the data is up to the camera vendor. The EXIF data can tell you a lot about a picture and how it was taken including the following:

- Name of the device taking the picture
- Serial number of the device taking the picture
- Version and model of the device taking the picture
- GPS coordinates describing where the picture was taken
- Custom tags added by the camera vendor or person taking the photo
- Much more

While FTK can be used to read EXIF data, there are several tools freely available. A personal favorite is the EXIF tool by Phil Harvey, available for download at http://www.sno.phy.queensu.ca/~phil/exiftool/. To ensure that FTK displays all EXIF data, be sure to check the "Meta carve" option during preprocessing, or hit "Evidence," then "Additional analysis," and select "Meta carve."

14.8.3 *Office* Metadata

As described by SoftXpantion (2009), Microsoft Office files come with a lot of metadata that can be of great interest to a computer forensic examiner. The office metadata holds several pieces of information including:

- Name of original author
- Name of the person who last saved the document
- Original creation date
- Last save date
- When the document was last printed
- Total time spent working on the document

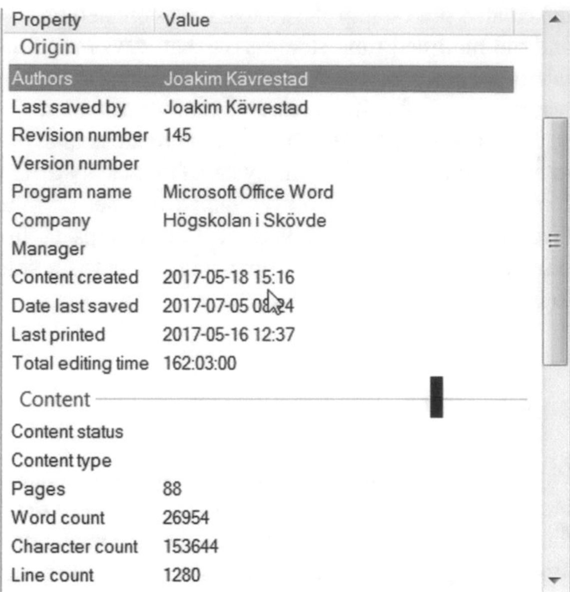

Property Value
Origin
Authors Joakim Kävrestad
Last saved by Joakim Kävrestad
Revision number 145
Version number
Program name Microsoft Office Word
Company Högskolan i Skövde
Manager
Content created 2017-05-18 15:16
Date last saved 2017-07-05 08:24
Last printed 2017-05-16 12:37
Total editing time 162:03:00
Content
Content status
Content type
Pages 88
Word count 26954
Character count 153644
Line count 1280

Fig. 14.9 Office file metadata seen in Windows

The name recorded in the office metadata is the name that the user submitted the first time that office was started. It is easy to input your real name without afterthoughts and then never think of it again; thus office metadata can be an invaluable source of information for a computer forensic expert. Office metadata can be read by right clicking a document and going to the properties tab. The metadata can also be seen in FTK, as previously described in Fig. 14.8, or by right clicking a file in Windows and selecting the details tab, as shown in Fig. 14.9.

14.9 Analyzing Log Files

In a computer forensic examination, it is common to analyze how different applications were used. This can, for instance, include messages going in and out of a chat application or analyzing transactions to and from a bit coin wallet. There are some tools available that can analyze data from some applications automatically, but it is, in my own experience, equally common that you need to manually analyze application log files in order to establish how an application was used. The rest of this section provides an example of an approach that can be used to analyze chat logs; the approach can also be applied to application logs.

Analyzing chat logs is commonly a quite straightforward process as the structure of chat logs tends to be rather obvious. As any log files, chat logs come in many different forms, and it is of high importance that you get an understanding of how the particular log file works. While it is often quite easy to figure out the structure of a chat log, there are more complicated examples, and if you do not fully understand a chat log by looking at it, it is encouraged to conduct an experiment to understand the workings of the chat program in question.

When you understand the chat log, you are commonly tasked with transferring the chat log into a format that is easier to read for the investigator. In some cases, you are asked to provide a summary including parts of the chat log, and in other cases, the investigator will want you to submit the complete chat log. To comply with transparency demand on forensic investigation, I would encourage always including the full chat log in unformatted format to the investigation. However, that does not exclude a reformatted version or a summary.

While reformatting a chat log can be done manually, it is often much more time efficient to reformat the chat log using a script. By writing a script that fetches the interesting data from each message and rewrites into a more readable format, you create a time-efficient way of working. Using a script instead of manual formatting also decreases the risk of errors and increases consistency. Also, whenever using homemade tools, be sure to mention that fact in your report to maintain transparency! This process for analyzing chat logs can be summarized as follows:

- Use your favorite forensic tool to locate chat logs. Common search terms would, for instance, include message, msg, received, or sent.
- Understand the chat log by examining it and, if needed, conduct an experiment.
- Prepare the chat log for presentation, preferably in an automatic fashion.

As an example, let's apply the process on a chat log generated by the chat client called jitsi. A snippet containing the two first messages of a jitsi chat log is presented below (a full log is presented in Appendix E).

```
<?xml version="1.0" encoding="UTF-8" standalone="no"?>
<history>
<record timestamp="2017-06-27T13:16:07.826+0200">
<dir>in</dir>
<msg><![CDATA[zup_]]></msg>
<msgTyp>text/plain</msgTyp>
<enc>UTF-8</enc>
<uid>149856217370418137890</uid>
<receivedTimestamp>2017-06-27T13:16:07.260
+0200</receivedTimestamp>
</record>
<record timestamp="2017-06-27T13:16:21.179+0200">
<dir>out</dir>
<msg><![CDATA[kollar lite affärer....sj?]]></msg>
<msgTyp>text/plain</msgTyp>
<enc>UTF-8</enc>
<uid>149856218114519064878</uid>
<receivedTimestamp>2017-06-27T13:16:21.149
+0200</receivedTimestamp>
</record>
```

Sender	Message	Timestamp
DDDUDE	zup_	2017-06-27T13:16:07.826+0200
mille	kollar lite affÃ¤rer....sj?	2017-06-27T13:16:21.179+0200
DDDUDE	samma, lurar p[vad som ar vart att sa	2017-06-27T13:16:42.293+0200
mille	hur sÃ¤krar du?	2017-06-27T13:16:52.792+0200
DDDUDE	kor engelsk dator, svart lista ut vart ja	2017-06-27T13:17:20.785+0200
mille	tror inte det funkar, ,lira tor!	2017-06-27T13:17:30.963+0200
DDDUDE	har kollat pa det, vet inte, krangligt!	2017-06-27T13:17:46.289+0200

Fig. 14.10 Formatted jitsi log

Looking at the chat log, with the intent of finding time for the message, receiving or sending users, and the message content, let's conclude the following:

- Each message begins with the tag <record> and ends with the tag </record>.
- Time of the message is included in starting record tag; there is also a received time stamp that appears to indicate when the message reached the recipient. However, concluding this without an experiment is hard, so that tag is ignored for now.
- The actual message is enclosed in <msg> tags.
- Usernames are not present; however, the direction of the message is included. In this case, you can look to other logs belonging to jitsi and conclude that the username of the local user is "DDDUDE." This particular log file is named "mille," indicating that the remote user is named "mille."

Having identified the information that is needed from the chat log, it is now possible to manually format the chat log. A more feasible option can be to create a script that automatically does the job. For the sake of this example, a script that fetches the information and presents it in a CSV file, as displayed in Fig. 14.10, was created. The script was created using PowerShell, and for simplicity, the <msg> content was stripped so that it only included the message in plaintext. The stripping was done using search and replace in a common text editor. The script is present in Appendix B.

14.10 Analyzing Unorganized Data

A hard drive will usually contain data that is best described as unorganized. This will, for instance, include slack space. There are also other sources of information that can be treated as unorganized data during a forensic examination, with great result. These sources include Pagefile and memory dumps. The Hiberfile, created when Windows is put into hibernation, can also be treated as unorganized data. Note that Pagefile, Hiberfile, and memory dumps are not really unorganized and can be analyzed in a more structured manner. An introduction to memory analysis is given in REFTEXT. Anyhow, common for these data sources is that they are not handled as the rest of the operating system, making them a source of artifacts that can be extremely good!

Pagefile and Hiberfile will usually contain the same type of information as a memory dump. The Pagefile is used by the computer when it needs to swap parts of the working memory and dump them somewhere else. The Hiberfile saves the current machine state when a Windows computer is put into hibernation as is used to enable the computer to wake up again. The information found here can commonly be very useful as it usually is information that the computer has been working with in a very near past; this is especially true for the memory dumps. Further, when a computer is viewing encrypted material or reading e-mail and likewise, this information is stored in a decrypted state in memory, and thus this type of information can be recovered from memory, Pagefile, or Hiberfile.

As for the slack space, it usually contains traces of data that used to reside on the computer. Consider a case where a file that fills up five clusters is deleted and a new file that is 4.5 clusters large takes its place. The new file will not yet have overwritten the last half cluster; that is considered file slack. The nature of slack tells us that it can contain fragments of any type of file and therefore include any sort of information.

Treating data as unorganized implies that you have no idea what to expect in term of file structures, metadata, and likewise. Thus, we are left with live searches as our means of analysis. You should know that the data sources discussed in this section are commonly quite large, and doing live searches over large data sets can be time-consuming. However, the nature of these data sources makes it possible to find extremely useful information, and the effort is therefore often worthwhile. In my own experience, key evidence has been found using live searches in especially memory dumps and Pagefiles at several occasions. At one time, I was able to recover several decrypted versions of several encrypted e-mails from a Web-based e-mail service. The e-mails recovered could tie the suspect to an alias used to sell a lot of drugs online and landed the suspect several years of jail time.

Well then, analyzing unorganized data comes down to two things: searching and making something of the results. Searching is usually done using keywords and using regular expressions that are used to search for patterns. Depending on what you are looking for, you will have to figure out appropriate search terms. A tip is to collect search terms that were successful so that you do not need to reinvent the search terms every time. One way to figure out search terms is to analyze raw data of information that is similar to the information you are looking for. That is, if you are looking for e-mail, you should analyze how e-mails are usually stored on disk and create your search terms based on that analysis. You could also include terms related to the case you are working on in your searches.

At this point, I want to stress the usefulness of building regular expressions to search for patterns instead of just using precise keywords. Regular expressions allow you to do searches for patterns, such as telephone numbers, e-mail addresses, or credit card numbers, and to include several spellings of a term in one search word. For instance, we all know that an e-mail address is made up from some signs, followed by a "@" followed by some signs, a dot, and top domain. Using regular

```
················FILE0···k-··········8···h··················;%··2···········`···
········H·······A·ç·OïÒ·1·ø·OïÒ·1·ø·OïÒ·A·ç·OïÒ· ····························
@4¸v····0···p··········T·······¾·······A·ç·OïÒ·A·ç·OïÒ·A·ç·OïÒ·A·ç·OïÒ········
········ ·······|·f·i·l·e·3·.·t·x·t·····@···(··················ôÿ,··Tç··Ï·PV°éÎ
····0··················username is wild-man····ÿÿÿÿ·yG···N·e·w· ·T·e·x·t· ·D·o·
c·u·m·e·n·t·.·t·x·t························ÿÿÿÿ·yG·······················
·····························································································
```

Fig. 14.11 Result after a keyword search

expressions, as implemented by FTK, we can express an e-mail address as follows (note that a perfect expression would have to be much longer): [A-Za-z0-9]+@ [A-Za-z0-9]+\. [A-Za-z]{2}.

The first brackets tell the expression to look for any of the letters a–z or numbers 0–9, then the + says that this can be repeated one or more times. The next part of the expression is a "@" stating that the next part of the pattern is a "@." Then we have a series of a–z and 0–9 again followed by a dot. The dot in regular expressions means "any character," but in this case a backslash is put in front of the dot. A backslash in front of a symbol that has a meaning forces the regular expression to interpret the symbol literally. The final bracket is used to match top domains; therefore, the brackets say to look for the letters a–z. The "2" in the curly brackets states that the letter should be repeated twice. Searching for this regular expression would include all e-mail addresses that are complete matches to the expression.

After doing a search, you need to interpret the results. A common way to interpret results of a search in unorganized data is to look at the data surrounding the search hit. Consider the following example of when the term "wild-man" was used to search in a memory dump. One of the hits and surrounding data is presented in Fig. 14.11.

Looking at the data, you can see that the hit is from the string "username is wild-man." Adjacent to the string, you can see the data "New Text document.txt" and "file 3.txt". This could be interpreted as a trace of a text file containing the information "username is wild-man." Another conclusion could be that the text file was likely named file 3.txt.

Analyzing unorganized data is, like much other things in digital forensics, about understanding how the data you are looking for may be represented and being able to interpret data that seems unstructured and sometimes strange. It should also be stressed that being successful in this kind of searches is to a large extent down to experience—knowing what you look for and what you can usually find. That being said, unorganized data sources are a great source of evidence that should not be overlooked.

14.11 Analyzing SQLite Databases

SQLite databases were mentioned in Part 1 as a common database type used to store application data. This is due to the portable and easy to implement nature of the database format and makes SQLite databases a common occurrence for forensic experts that dig deep. This section will provide a brief introduction to analysis of

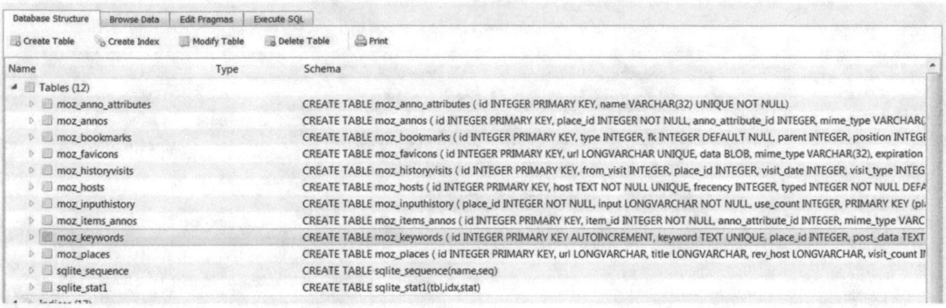

Database Structure | Browse Data | Edit Pragmas | Execute SQL

Create Table | Create Index | Modify Table | Delete Table | Print

Name	Type	Schema
Tables (12)		
moz_anno_attributes		CREATE TABLE moz_anno_attributes (id INTEGER PRIMARY KEY, name VARCHAR(32) UNIQUE NOT NULL)
moz_annos		CREATE TABLE moz_annos (id INTEGER PRIMARY KEY, place_id INTEGER NOT NULL, anno_attribute_id INTEGER, mime_type VARCHAR(
moz_bookmarks		CREATE TABLE moz_bookmarks (id INTEGER PRIMARY KEY, type INTEGER, fk INTEGER DEFAULT NULL, parent INTEGER, position INTEGE
moz_favicons		CREATE TABLE moz_favicons (id INTEGER PRIMARY KEY, url LONGVARCHAR UNIQUE, data BLOB, mime_type VARCHAR(32), expiration
moz_historyvisits		CREATE TABLE moz_historyvisits (id INTEGER PRIMARY KEY, from_visit INTEGER, place_id INTEGER, visit_date INTEGER, visit_type INTEG
moz_hosts		CREATE TABLE moz_hosts (id INTEGER PRIMARY KEY, host TEXT NOT NULL UNIQUE, frecency INTEGER, typed INTEGER NOT NULL DEFA
moz_inputhistory		CREATE TABLE moz_inputhistory (place_id INTEGER NOT NULL, input LONGVARCHAR NOT NULL, use_count INTEGER, PRIMARY KEY (pl
moz_items_annos		CREATE TABLE moz_items_annos (id INTEGER PRIMARY KEY, item_id INTEGER NOT NULL, anno_attribute_id INTEGER, mime_type VARC
moz_keywords		CREATE TABLE moz_keywords (id INTEGER PRIMARY KEY AUTOINCREMENT, keyword TEXT UNIQUE, place_id INTEGER, post_data TEXT
moz_places		CREATE TABLE moz_places (id INTEGER PRIMARY KEY, url LONGVARCHAR, title LONGVARCHAR, rev_host LONGVARCHAR, visit_count I
sqlite_sequence		CREATE TABLE sqlite_sequence(name,seq)
sqlite_stat1		CREATE TABLE sqlite_stat1(tbl,idx,stat)

Fig. 14.12 *places.sqlite*, list of tables

SQLite databases. The authors' personal tool of choice for this task is called DB browser of SQLite and can be downloaded for free.[1] Before we begin, it should be mentioned that SQLite is a database format that implements an SQL database engine; as such it can be seen as a language for data storage, and there are many different ways of structuring a SQLite database. As such, there is not a golden rule for how to interpret a specific database found. Nevertheless this database type is used for many different purposes including chat history, SMS storage in cell phones, and, as in this example, Firefox browsing history. Firefox browsing history is used in this example and located in a file called *places.sqlite* stored in *[userhomefolder]\AppData\Roaming\Mozilla\Firefox\Profiles\[something].default.*

At a very basic level, a database is made up from a structure that defines tables and relations between the tables. As such, a forensic examiner should care about the database structure and the tables. Figure 14.12 shows the structure of the database *places.sqlite.*

Figure 14.12 lists the different tables contained in the database and the columns for each table. Every column must have a data type that is also listed in Fig. 14.12; for instance, we can tell that *moz_anno_attributes* contains two columns; the first one is named *id* that is the tables' primary key and of the data type integer. The second is called name, is of type VARCHAR (32); it must be unique and is not allowed to be null. INTEGER PRIMARY KEY is interesting as it is commonly used as a row identifier. Also, unless the value for data of this type is explicitly set, it will automatically be set, usually to a number that is one higher than the highest used number. When this is true, the values in a column that is an INTEGER PRIMARY KEY will act as a counter that describes in which order the rows were written to the database. Note though that this behavior is common, but not enforced. Thus, research or experiments need to be undertaken to analyze the behavior of the database you are analyzing.

While the database structure can be a good place to get an understanding of the database that is to be analyzed, the actual good stuff is usually in the tables. Note that it may not always be easy to determine what data that is contained in which table, but

[1]https://sqlitebrowser.org/dl/

	id	url	visit_count	typed	last_visit_date
	Filter	Filter	Filter	Filter	Filter
18747	22722	http://his.diva-portal.org/smash/resultList.jsf?dswid=8558&af=%5B%2...	1	0	1561705181378000
18748	22723	http://his.diva-portal.org/smash/resultList.jsf?dswid=8558&language=s...	1	0	1561705189185000
18749	22724	http://his.diva-portal.org/smash/get/diva2:1327738/FULLTEXT01.pdf	0	0	1561705228620000
18750	22725	http://his.diva-portal.org/smash/resultList.jsf?dswid=8558&language=s...	1	0	1561705239362000
18751	22726	https://www.researchgate.net/profile/Joakim_Kaevrestad?ev=hdr_xprf	1	0	1561719847807000
18752	22727	https://www.researchgate.net/profile/Joakim_Kaevrestad	1	0	1561719852605000
18753	22728	https://www.researchgate.net/publication/333715012_Understanding_p...	1	0	1561719901895000
18754	22729	http://iodesk.net/	1	1	1561970606343000
18755	22730	http://iodesk.net/Contact	1	0	1561970612159000
18756	22731	http://www.xenolith.se/	1	0	1561970622831000
18757	22732	https://www.iodesk.net/	1	0	1561970623240000

18747 - 18757 of 18848 Go to: 1

Fig. 14.13 moz_places

some digging will usually reveal that. Let's, as one example, have a look at the table called *moz_places*; a sample of that table is presented in Fig. 14.13; however, columns that will not be discussed are omitted.

The first column named *id* is an INTEGER PRIMARY KEY and, thus, tells us in which order the different rows were written to the database. You validate that this is true by looking to the column named *last_visit_date* that holds the date of the last visit, as epoch time, padded with three trailing zeroes. The second column holds a URL, namely, a URL that was visited using the computer. The final interesting columns in this case are *visit_count* and *typed*. Visit count describes how many times the URL has been visited; in the sample data, it is 0 at one row, and this seems a bit strange. Zero seems to mean that the URL was used in somewhat by the browser but not actually visited by the user. The URL with a visit count of zero in the example is the result of a file download. Finally the typed describes if the URL was typed by the user (1) or not (0). In summary, or analysis concludes what URLs that the computer was visiting using Firefox and when the last visit to each URL occurred, and it will serve as an example of how you may analyze SQLite databases.

14.12 Questions and Tasks

Here are the questions for this chapter.

1. What is the install date of the computer you are working on?
2. What is the name of the time zone your computer is configured to use and when is the computer set to adjust time for daylight savings?
3. What is the username and RID of the default administrators account on your computer?
4. What is the starting sector and size, in gigabytes, of your system partition?
5. A file deleted from a computer can often be recovered with ease, explain why!
6. What is needed to make the content of a ZIP archive part of an index?

7. What is EXIF data and why is it relevant in digital forensics?
8. If you are asked to look for hidden partitions in unallocated space, what would you do?

References

AccessData (2013) AccessData forensics. AccessData group

EaseUS (2017) EaseUs partition recovery wizard. Available online: https://www.easeus.com/partition-recovery/. Fetched: July 01, 2017

Guidance Software (2016) EnCase computer forensics II. Guidance Software

Knutson T, Carbone R (2016) Filesystem timestamps: what makes them tick? GIAC GCFA Gold Certification

Rusbarsky KL (2012) A forensic comparison of NTFS and FAT32 file systems. Available online: http://www.marshall.edu/forensics/files/RusbarskyKelsey_Research-Paper-Summer-2012.pdf. Fetched: July 06, 2017

Softxpantion (2009) Metadata in microsoft office and in PDF documents. Available online: https://www.soft-xpansion.eu/files/cc/Metadata.pdf. Fetched: July 06, 2017

Zacker (2014) Installing and configuring windows server 2012 R2. Wiley, Hoboken

Some Common Questions and Tasks

15

The aim of this chapter is to discuss some questions and tasks that are common for a computer forensic examiner to be tasked with. The intent is not to provide a precise guideline that will work every time. Rather, the chapter presents an approach that can be used to tackle the questions. The answers and tasks are based on the author's own experience of answering these questions and defending the conclusions in court and are intended to present some more artifacts in a manner that exemplifies forensic methodology. Note that you can roughly categorize questions as "yes/no" or exploratory questions. Questions that can be answered yes or no are quite troublesome. The reason is that you may find what you are looking for and answer yes. However, not finding what you are looking does not really mean that you should answer no. Consider a case where you are asked if a picture was ever present on a cell phone. Finding the picture or traces of it would definitely be a strong yes. However, not finding the picture does not mean that the picture was never on the phone; it does not even mean that it is not on the phone right now. As such, answering such a question with a strong no is plain wrong. A better answer would be that the picture could not be found during the examination. You may stretch to make the conclusion that it indicates that the picture was never present on the phone.

15.1 Was the Computer Remote Controlled?

When you are able to present evidence found at a suspect's computer, a common objection is that the computer must have been remote controlled leading to a need to investigate if the computer was remote controlled or not. This is a perfect example of a "yes/no" question where answering no is troublesome. However, based on the author's experience, there are three good approaches on how to handle this question, namely:

- Analysis of applications
- Scenario testing
- Timelining

J. Kävrestad, *Fundamentals of Digital Forensics*,
https://doi.org/10.1007/978-3-030-38954-3_15

Application analysis and scenario testing will be described in the rest of this section. Timelining is good for determining the user of the computer and will be described in the next section.

15.1.1 Analysis of Applications

Analysis of applications is an approach that attempts to look for all possible evidences of remote control software or malware and, if any is encountered, analyze that software. The aim is to analyze if the computer contain any software that can be used to remote controlling the computer. This is an approach that is quite troublesome for several reasons including the following:

- It is common for a computer to contain remote controlling software, making it very troublesome to report a no and defend that in court.
- Best possible result is that the computer does not contain any remote controlling software at the moment.

Even if application analysis for this particular question is hard to do, it is a quite common approach used by forensic experts. While this approach is discouraged by the author, a brief description of it seems necessary. To follow this approach, you will need a fair bit of knowledge into what remote controlling software exists. Among the most common are:

- Remote desktop built into Windows, standard port number 3389
- Different implementations of VPN, protocol- and application-dependent port numbers
- Different implementations of SSH, standard port number 22
- TeamViewer, standard port number 5938

An examination would include looking for those programs among the software installed or, if possible, has been installed on the computer. This is done by looking into, for instance, the list of active processes, the program and program files' folders, and the ".appdata" folder for each user. Since remote controlling software's are communicating using port numbers that are not commonly open in the firewall, analysis of the firewall rules is also a part of this approach, how to analyze the Windows firewall will be explained in the end of this chapter. If you find any remote controlling software among installed applications, the next step is to analyze the log files of the application to see if it has actually been used and how. If you find that the ports belonging to remote controlling applications are closed, this is further evidence in favor of the statement that the computer was not remote controlled. However, if you find that the ports are open, you are forced to report that the computer was likely remote controlled—or at least that it was possible to remote control the computer.

To summarize, following this approach will lead, most likely, to one of the following results and conclusions:

- No traces of remote controlling software or open ports relating to remote controlling software leading to the conclusion that the computer does not currently contain remote controlling software indicating that it has not been remote controlled.
- Traces of remote controlling software exist, but analysis of those applications reveals that they were never used leading to the conclusion that the computer does not currently contain remote controlling software indicating that it has not been remote controlled.
- No traces of remote controlling software exist, but open ports relating to remote controlling software were found leading to inconclusive conclusions since it is not possible to tell why the ports are open.
- Traces of remote controlling software exist, and analysis of those applications reveals that they were used leading to the conclusion that the computer has been remote controlled.

When following this approach, it is also essential to exclude malware as a source of remote controlling. To do this, it is suggested to search the computer for malware using at least two different antivirus programs. Any malware found should be further analyzed to exclude them as sources of remote control.

15.1.2 Scenario Testing

Another approach, for handling the issue of remote controlling, is to test if a scenario is possible or not. While this method is easier to use, it does require that it is possible to establish a scenario that can be tested. To establish a scenario, the suspect pleading that his computer was remote controlled should be asked how. The suspect often answers with a scenario that can be tested. For instance, the suspect may say that the evidence is the result of malware or that Windows remote desktop is enabled and must have been used. Given this information you can, instead of scanning for all possible traces of remote controlling software, analyze if the suspect's claim holds true.

For instance, if the suspect does indeed state that Windows remote desktop is enabled on his computer and may even say that he has seen the mouse move around from time to time, then you should investigate Windows remote desktop. To begin, remote desktop requires that there are rules added to the Windows firewall to allow remote desktop connections. Also, remote desktop has to be configured to allow incoming connections. If those settings are not present, that is a sign that the suspect's statement is false. Moreover, you can often find log entries in Event Viewer that shows if anyone logged on to the computer using remote desktop. The

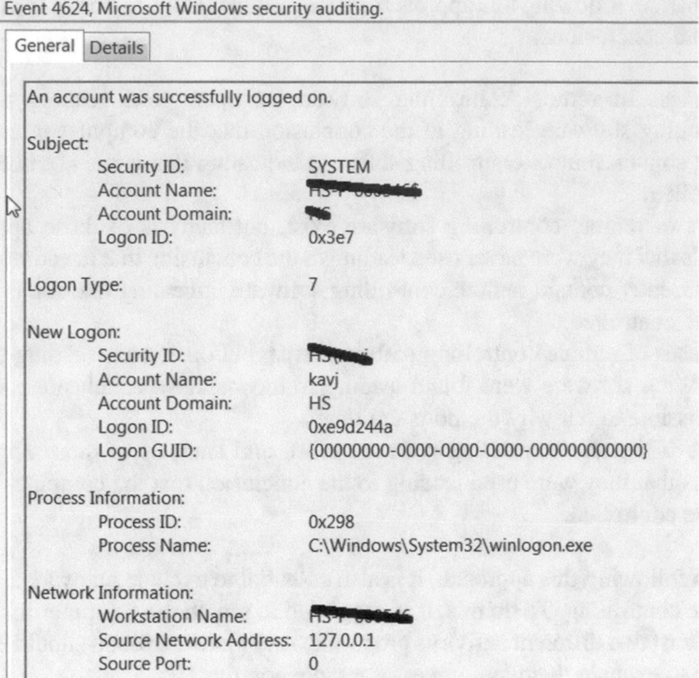

Fig. 15.1 Windows remote desktop log entry from log-on

best way to analyze Windows log files is to extract the log files from the image you are examining and analyze them in Windows Event Viewer. In this case, the log entry would be found in the security log located at the path: C:\Windows\System32\winevt\Logs\Security.evtx.

Each type of event has a unique event ID, and the event ID for remote desktop log-ons is "4624." Searching for the event ID will return any log entries related to log-ins over remote desktop; an example of such entry is provided in Fig. 15.1.

Finding log entries and finding remote desktop to be enabled or firewall rules that permit remote desktop connections will render you unable to disprove the suspect's claim. However, if neither is present, that is a strong sign that the suspect's claim is wrong. Not only will that disprove that the computer was remote controlled; it may also help diminish the suspect's credibility.

15.2 Who Was Using the Computer?

While an investigation, criminal or corporate, is interested in finding out who that did something, computer forensics is commonly limited to describing what a computer was doing. Deciding who was behind the keyboard is sometimes seen as impossible, and even if it is not impossible, it is definitely a difficult task. The troubles that arise

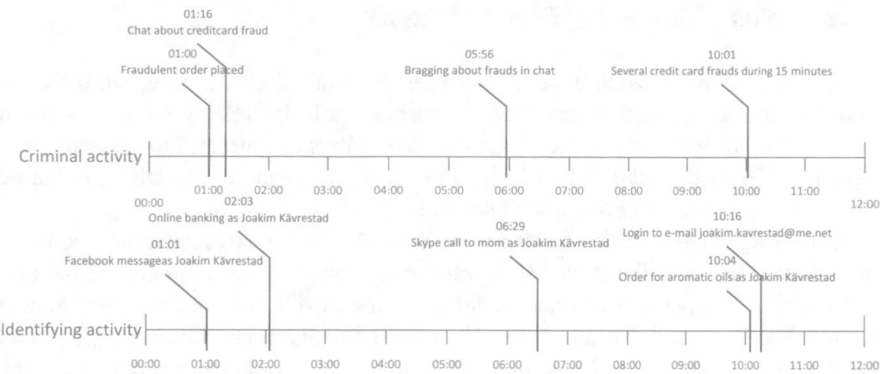

Fig. 15.2 Sample timeline

are that it is indeed impossible to tell the identity of the users that made the computer commit a certain action. The discussion on remote controlling software and the possibility of several persons having access to the same computer testify to that.

While it is impossible (and infeasible) to determine the identity of the person using the computer in general, it can be possible to determine the computer user, with some certainty, at specific times. For instance, analyzing chat log, online banking log-ins, and other pieces of information can tell you who used the computer at a certain time. Also, in a default Windows environment, it is only possible for one graphical session at the time, bringing the fact that if you can identify one user, you can also be quite sure that she is the only user. This knowledge allows us to attempt to determine the identity of a user using Timelining.

Timelining is an approach where you attempt to make it unreasonable to believe that someone else than a specific person committed actions, usually a crime, using the computer that is target for examination. The idea with timelining is that you find events relating to criminal activity and plot them on a timeline. You then look for artifacts that identify the user of the computer and plot those events on the same timeline. Identifying events can include filling out forms online, chat messages, online banking log-ins, and social media events. What you are looking for is overlaps between criminal and identifying events or at least events in close proximity to each other. Consider the sample timeline in Fig. 15.2.

As you can see in the sample timeline, the computer was used at three periods during a 12-h period. Some actions related to frauds are committed at each period and overlapping with events where the user is presenting himself as Joakim Kävrestad. While you can never neglect the possibility that the criminal is posing as someone else to obfuscate an investigation, a timeline like this does indicate that the person committing the fraudulent activities is indeed Joakim Kävrestad. The more overlaps you can identify and the longer the period containing the overlaps, the stronger indication of who the actual user is. However, make sure to fully understand the time stamps of the events you are using in your timelining!

15.3 Was This Device Ever at Site X?

So far we mostly discussed the evidence contained in a digital device, but there are times when the physical location of a device is more interesting than the data in it. This can, for instance, be the case in investigations of murder, rape, assault, and likewise. If a suspect claims that he was never on the scene of the crime, it can be possible to prove or disprove that statement.

Analyzing where a device has been can basically be done by analyzing two types of artifacts, GPS coordinates and network connections. GPS coordinates are put into many different types of events, depending on the device settings, and can include photos, Facebook activity, and tweets. Thus, if someone is committing a crime and takes a photo, updates Facebook, or sends a tweet during or in close proximity to the crime, it can be possible to position the device and thus providing an indication of the suspect's position. In FTK, it is possible to do a meta carve, as previously discussed, to uncover GPS coordinates in file metadata. You could also use a regular expression to do a live search for GPS coordinates. Since it is common for activity in Web browsers to end up in some unorganized data, a search is suggested. The search will also cover GPS coordinates found in files.

Another way to go is to analyze if the device has been connected to any network close to the crime scene. Depending on the type of device, this information is located in different places. However, a good suggestion is to collect information about wireless networks close to the crime scene and then use the network names as search terms. A drawback of looking for connections instead of GPS coordinates is that the connection information is seldom time-stamped, meaning that your best collusion will often be that device was at the crime scene at some time. GPS coordinates are commonly found in data that also contains a time stamp; this information enables you to say that the device was at a particular site at a particular time.

15.4 What Device Took the Picture and Where?

In modern-day forensics, pictures appear to play a big role. The role of pictures can be important in many types of cases where pictures are a very important part of the modus used by the criminal; this will be the case in investigations concerning, for instance:

- Child exploitation cases where pictures are often the crime itself
- Online fraud where someone is selling something that is then not delivered
- Online selling of narcotics that usually include having pictures of the goods
- Different types of harassment cases where someone is harassing someone else by sending pictures

And even if pictures are not a direct part of a crime, they tend to have a place in many investigations for the sole reason that criminals sometimes take pictures of what they did or that they are important for positioning a person at some place.

When pictures are of importance, it is not uncommon that being able to determine where and when a picture was taken as well at what device that was used to take the picture is of interest. Imagine someone selling ecstasy and is posting pictures of her pills online. When someone is arrested for the action and the pictures used in the ads are found in her computer, the prosecutor will claim that the pictures are hers. However, a common counterclaim would be that the pictures were just downloaded from the Internet. Being able to say that the pictures were taken at the suspect's home using her camera would make the evidentiary value of the pictures that much greater.

The best way to accomplish this is by doing three things:

- Hash lookup
- Visual inspection
- EXIF analysis

Doing a hash lookup is possible if you have access to the pictures found on the suspect's computer and the pictures used for the crime, in our example, the ads for ecstasy. Calculating hash values for the pictures will tell you if they are identical, and the conclusion from that can be that the pictures in the computer are the same as the pictures found in the ads. Note that many Web sites where crimes are committed are using obfuscating techniques that makes hash analysis impossible. However, even if the hash values do not match, you can still do a visual inspection of the pictures to see if they appear to be the same.

While a hash analysis can tell you if two or more pictures are exact replicas of each other, a visual inspection of pictures should not be underestimated. What a visual inspection, in contrast to a hash analysis, can give clues about is where a picture was taken. Depending on what a picture depicts, it can be possible to extract visual information about where it was taken, namely, the surroundings. Consider an example where the pictures of ecstasy were taken using a bed as a background and showing the bed linen and a portion of a window that made the outside area visible. That information can be used to match against the reality. Say that the bed, bed linen, and outside area appear to be the same as the bedroom at the suspect's home address, that is, at least an indication that says that the picture was indeed taken in that place.

Moving on to one of the most valuable areas of image analysis, the EXIF information is made out from metadata generated by the device that took the image. As we previously discussed, EXIF data can store loads of information and is created by the device that takes the picture. There are two gold mines in the EXIF data, GPS coordinates and camera serial number. If you find GPS coordinates, it is very possible to decide the precise location where the picture was taken, and serial number of the camera will tell you what camera that took the picture. If you have access to a camera owned by the suspect, the rest is down to matching. One should note, however, that the EXIF information may not always be 100% accurate and a sanity check is encouraged. If GPS coordinates say that a picture of snow was taken in the Sahara desert, there are good reasons for doubt.

Well, on the topic of EXIF information, there are two caveats:

- It does not always contain the exact information that we need.
- Many Web sites strip EXIF information when publishing images online.

The first caveat is, well, unfortunate. If GPS coordinates are not present, GPS location is impossible and that is it. However, in attempt to decide what device that was used to take a picture, the race is not over. While the serial number is an easy and convenient way to decide what camera that took a picture, it is not always printed in the EXIF information. For instance, that is the case with Apple iPhone using an updated IOS at the time of writing this book. However, there are other parts of the EXIF data that can be used for identification. In the case of an iPhone, the telephone model name is saved with the EXIF data. While this does not single out a single device, it can work as an indicator. What if the suspect owns a telephone of the same make and model as the one that was used to take the pictures of ecstasy? Combined with the visual inspection as described above, this is a very good indication of that the pictures were actually taken with the suspect's telephone.

As for the problem with Web sites removing the EXIF information, well, if the picture from the Web site is all you got, then the race is lost at this time. However, if you can do hash analysis or visual inspection to find a copy of the picture in question, then you can examine the EXIF information of that version of the picture.

15.5 Where Were the Documents Created?

Summing up this chapter on some common question during forensic examination is a question that will be explored in a corporate setting. The question of where a document was created. This is a question of great importance because a common claim by someone suspected of doing something bad relating to a document found on a device owned by him is, as always, that he got if from somewhere else or downloaded it online.

Consider a case where a company files a nice idea for patenting and realizes that someone else already registered the same patent. Turns out that the registration was filed by some employee that in turn claims that the idea was his all along. In this specific case, the information relevant for the patent is contained in an office word document that is present on the company file server and on the employee's home computer. The company would say that the document is theirs because it is on their file server, and the employee will make the same statement referencing his own computer. Our task would begin with analyzing the employee's computer to look into this matter.

There would be several ways to tackle this issue, but perhaps the first would be to look at the file metadata. Analyzing time stamps in the file metadata can provide good hints as to whether or not it was created on the computer where it currently is located. The first place to go would be the NTFS time stamps, namely, the following:

- Created that dictates then a file was created
- Modified that dictates then it was last modified
- Accessed that dictates when it was last modified

Depending on how the time stamps relate to each other, a fair deal can be said. First, the created time stamp will be updated when the file is created; even if it is just moved, it will be considered created in the new location. However, the modified date will only be updated when the content is actually updated; changing the title is not enough. Thus, if the modification date is before the creation date, the conclusion is that the file is not in its original position. Saying that this is the case in our example, it would be an indicator of the company being right in the argument. However, the employee can just have moved the file from one location to another and that could explain the time stamps.

A good next step would be to turn to the metadata that is specific to Microsoft Office. This includes information about the original author of the file and who last saved it. This information is taken from information that is entered into Microsoft Office the first time it is started. One should note, however, that this information can be changed. Would the office metadata include any information identifying the company as original author, the case would be closed to the advantage of the company. However, if the information says that the employee created the document, further analysis is required. In this case, it would be interesting to analyze the office metadata on the company server. If it matches the metadata on the employee's version of the file, it is likely that whatever is written in the metadata is correct and the case is closed. However, if there are differences in the metadata, some side of the argument must have modified it, and further examination is needed.

The next step would be to turn to the .lnk files on the employee's computer. Remember that an .lnk file is created when a user is accessing a file. Looking for the name of the file as an .lnk file could tell us two things:

- Did the user ever open it?
- Was it ever opened from another device?

The lack of .lnk files would indicate that is was never opened from the employee's computer and would be in favor of the companies claim. Also, there could be .lnk files showing that the file has been located at some external device and that can also be in favor of the companies claim. However, even if no .lnk files were located, this should be validated by looking at MRU objects for office files in the registry of the computer.

As a final step in deciding if the document was created on the employee's computer or not, it is wise to do a text search for the name of the document. This can reveal if it has been downloaded from an e-mail or the Internet or possibly other circumstances relating to the document.

15.6 Application Analysis: The Windows Firewall

Determining whit whom and in what way a computer has communicated can be important and interesting in several types of examinations. As previously discussed, it can be an important part of analyzing if and how a computer has been remote controlled. It can also be a good way to determine if a computer has been compromised or infected with malware. If a computer is compromised and controlled remotely by a rouge user, that user needs to have an established connection to the computer. Further, many types of malware are used to steal and send information to someone or simply needs to be connected with a so-called "command and control" server that can control its behavior. A common denominator for everything that needs to communicate is that it has to pass through the firewall. For those of you that are not networking gurus; a firewall is a software or device that act as a gatekeeper and decides what traffic that is allowed to enter and leave a computer or network. It will often also log historic connections. Luckily, the windows operating systems comes shipped with a firewall utility called Windows Firewall.

In essence, a normal firewall uses IP addresses and port numbers to make decisions on what traffic that is allowed to enter and leave a computer. Traffic that is determined to be good is allowed to pass, and traffic that is deemed bad will be blocked. IP addresses are the addresses used by computers to communicate over the Internet, and port numbers are used to address traffic to a certain service. As previously described, many services are assigned specific port numbers to use for communication. Thus, if a port number assigned to a certain service, say the remote control software TeamViewer, is allowed in the firewall, there is a fair chance that that TeamViewer is or has been installed on the computer. Likewise, some malware is known to use some specific port number, and thus, if a port number associated with malware is identified, a strong indication of infection is found. You may also analyze the firewall log to see what IP addresses a computer has been communicating with. This information can tell you if the computer has been in touch with someone that it should not be in touch with and possibly assist in identifying an intrusion.

When analyzing the Windows Firewall, there are essentially two main pieces of information to care about. The first is the current settings; it describes what ports and IP addresses that are allowed or blocked at the moment. The other is the firewall log files that provide historic data over previous connections; logging is unfortunately not enabled by default, but it is worth looking for the log file since it will provide a lot of information if it is present. Starting with the current rules, they are located in the Windows registry in the SYSTEM hive under the following key: \CurrentControlSet\services\SharedAccess\Parameters\FirewallPolicy \FirewallRules. The data looks as presented in Fig. 15.3.

As previously described, the firewall rules decide that traffic is allowed to enter or leave the computer. Each registry value is one rule, and the general structure is $attribute_1$ | $attribute_2$ | . . .| $attribute_e$. Let's zoom in on the first underlined rule to see how the rules are structured. The rule begins with

```
v2.10|Action=Block|Active=TRUE|Dir=In
```

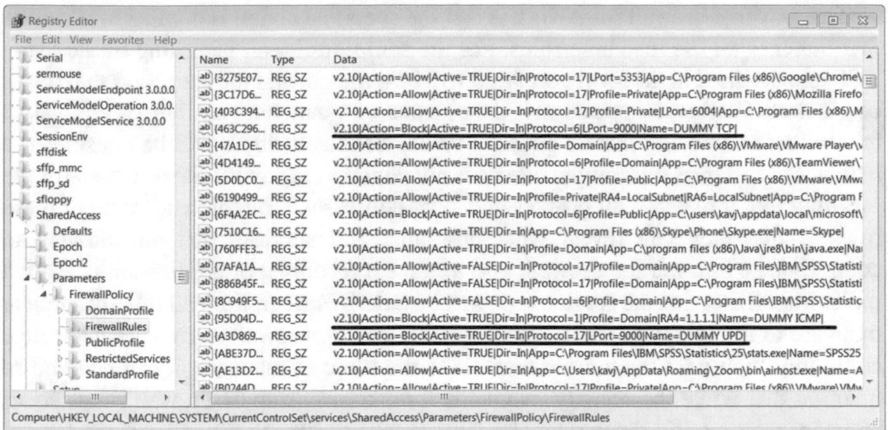

Fig. 15.3 Firewall rules in registry

The very first attribute is a version number that we do not need to care about. The second attribute describes the action of the rule, if it allows or blocks traffic. The third attribute decides if the rule is active or not, and the fourth attribute describes the traffic direction the rule is concerned with. If it says in, the rule is applied to incoming traffic, and if it spells out, the rule is applied to traffic leaving the computer. The remainder of the rule is the actual matching rules. The matching rules decide what traffic the rule matches, and the specified action is applied to all traffic that match the matching rules. The matching rules can include a number of different attributes; the most important for forensic purposes are:

- Protocol that decides what protocol the rule should match. A small experiment performed by the author revealed that 6 is TCP, 17 is UPD, and 1 is ICMP.
- Lport that decides the local port.
- Rport representing the port of the remote computer.
- LA4 or LA6 that represent the local IPv4 or IPv6 address.
- RA4 or RA6 that represent the remote IPv4 or IPv6 address.
- App that represents that application the rule should match making it possible to have application specific rules. For instance, Firefox may be able to communicate using port 80 (used for web traffic) while Skype may not.
- Name that is just a name given to the rule.
- Profile that determines under which firewall profile the rule is applied. The Windows Firewall has three different profiles (Domain, Private, and Public), and a network connection will be assigned a profile. Usually, when a computer is connected to a new network, the user is asked what profile to apply to the connecting.

The way that firewall rules work is that the specified action is applied to all traffic that matches all the matching rules. For the sample rule, all incoming traffic using TCP and destined to the local port 9000 will be a match, and the actin says that it will be blocked. Further, it appears as if the absence of a matching attribute is equivalent to a wildcard meaning that all possible values of that attribute will be considered a match. For instance, our sample rule does not contain the any Profile or LA4 attribute meaning that it matches all profiles and IPv4 addresses. The forensic value of these rules is that they can reveal what programs and services that are allowed to communicate through the firewall, and a rule for a service or application is a good indication saying that the service is or was installed. Further, firewall rules can reveal malware or intrusions as those are sometimes adding firewall rules to enable rouge communication with the outside world. On the topic of malware, it can be good to mention that while the registry maintains the current setup of firewall rules, smart malware may modify those rules. Luckily, modifications to the registry are logged with event viewer, with event IDs 2004 and 2006. Complementing the analysis of the registry with a check for those events is a good practice.

The second artifact of importance when analyzing the Windows Firewall is the traffic log. This log file tracks how the rules have been applied and describes what traffic that was allowed through or blocked by the firewall. The log file is called *pfirewall.log* and located in *[systemroot]\Windows\System32\LogFiles\Firewall*. There can also be a file called *pfirewall.log.old* that contains historical data. Unfortunately, it appears as if the logs default behavior is to only keep data one or a few days old. Anyhow, the snipped below is a part of a firewall log file and each row is one piece of traffic.

```
#Version: 1.5
#Software: Microsoft Windows Firewall
#Time Format: Local
#Fields: date time action protocol src-ip dst-ip src-port dst-port
size tcpflags tcpsyn tcpack tcpwin icmptype icmpcode info path
2019-07-03 12:35:26 ALLOW UDP 212.25.129.46 172.217.22.174 54662
443 0 - - - - - - - SEND
2019-07-03 12:35:26 ALLOW TCP 212.25.129.46 31.13.72.12 56088
443 0 - 0 0 0 - - - SEND
2019-07-03 12:35:26 DROP UDP 212.25.128.85 255.255.255.255 17500
17500 172 - - - - - - - RECEIVE
```

Looking at the first row beginning with a date, the date is followed with an action, in this case allow meaning that the traffic was allowed. Next is the protocol, usually TCP or UDP followed by the source IP and destination IP. In this file, source IP is the local computer's IP address, and remote is the remote party, the computer the local computer is communicating with. The next two values are source and destination port number. The next interesting part is the final word in the line, send or receive, that shows if the traffic was sent from or received by the local computer. In this case, the full row is interpreted as follows: UDP traffic sent from the local computer to the IP 172.217.22.174 using port number 443 was allowed. This log file can show what remote IP addresses the local computer has communicated with, and the port numbers can provide information about what services have been used during communication. As such, it can be used to find remote connection, malware, and intrusions.

15.7 Questions and Tasks

Here are some questions and tasks relating to this chapter.

1. Proving that something did not happen on a computer is very hard to do. Elaborate on why it is hard to conclude that a computer was never remote controlled.
2. Timelining is an approach where you attempt to tie certain actions to a person rather than the whole computer. Elaborate on how and why this approach can be useful.
3. What is scenario testing and what is the benefits of scenario testing over application analysis?
4. The task for this chapter is for you to examine your own computer in an attempt to prove that you are the user of your computer and that your computer has been at your home.

16 FTK Specifics

This is a chapter that is 100% devoted to describing how to use AccessData FTK and AccessData Registry Viewer and was written using FTK version 6. It is intentionally placed close to the end, but those of you who are FTK users could benefit from reading it at the beginning of the practical section. As most software vendors do, AccessData submits user manuals with their product, and while this book does not intend to provide a complete user manual, the aim of this chapter is to provide enough knowledge about the covered products to enable the reader to get a smooth start on your forensic experience. In addition to overviews of FTK and Registry Viewer, an overview of PRTK was presented in Chap. 13, and FTK imager was presented in Chap. 11. Since this chapter does not introduce any new forensic knowledge, there are no questions or tasks in the end of this chapter.

16.1 FTK: Create a Case

When you installed FTK and logged on to your instance of FTK for the very first time, you are basically faced with a database interface that is empty. The interface is presented in Fig. 16.1.

Starting with the top menu bar, the different menus have the following uses:

- File: No other use than to close FTK.
- Database: Tasks related to managing users of the database and configuration of the actual database.
- Case: Tasks related to specific cases, this section will end with a description of those.
- Tools: Tasks related to configuring FTK, for instance, if you want to use distributed case processing.
- Manage: In this menu, you can edit different tasks related to case analysis; for instance, you can manage and create signatures for data carving.

J. Kävrestad, *Fundamentals of Digital Forensics*,
https://doi.org/10.1007/978-3-030-38954-3_16

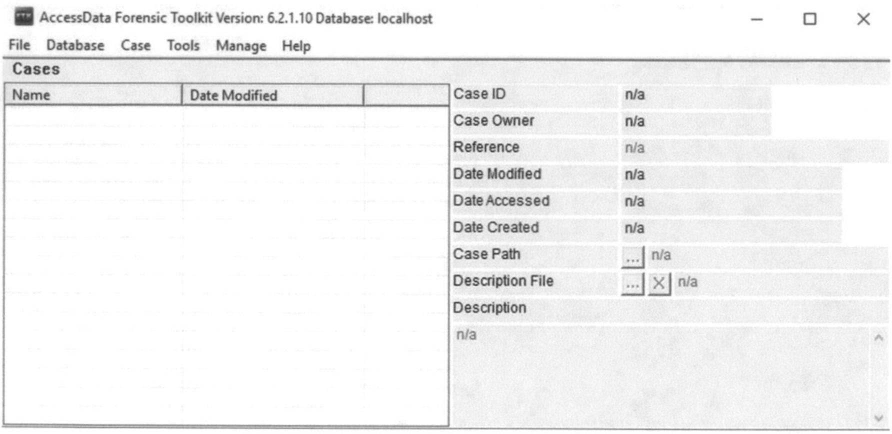

Fig. 16.1 FTK database interface

- Help: One would think that this menu contains a help section or use manual, but it only contains some licensing information.

Next, the cases pane will list the cases in your database, and the right pane will show you information about the marked case. To create a new case, hit the case menu and select New. This will take you to the dialogue shown in Fig. 16.2.

The first two parts are the case name and description. Input whatever is enforced by your organization or otherwise reasonable. The next part is the case folder; this is where your case will be stored. Next, select where the database related to the case will be stored; it is common to store it in the case folder. Note that the case database and amount of case data can be rather large and be intensively used by FTK. It is therefore a good idea to have a dedicated hard drive or storage server for FTK cases. Before you hit OK to create the case, you need to decide on, and possibly modify, a processing profile. To modify or review the processing profile, hit Customize. This will be your preprocessing settings, depicting the processes that will be done to every piece of evidence you add to the case. Preprocessing is discussed in greater detail in the next section.

Upon hitting OK, FTK will as default open the case and prompt you to add some evidence. In this case, the "Open the case" checkbox was checked out so that the case could be reviewed in the database interface. As shown in Fig. 16.3, the newly created case appeared in the case list. Also, some information about the case is listed in the right pane. From this interface, it is possible to back up and restore cases. Note the two types of backup: backup and archive. Backup is meant to be used for backups during the lifetime of the case, and archive is used to archive the case for storing after it is completed. Archive and detach will create a case archive and remove the case from the case list and thus the database.

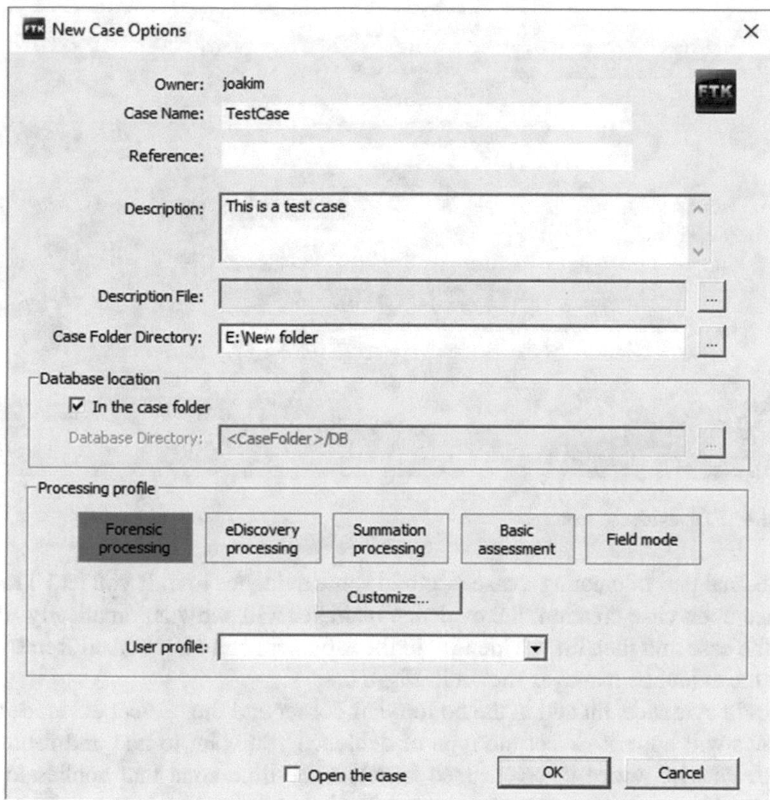

Fig. 16.2 Add a new case

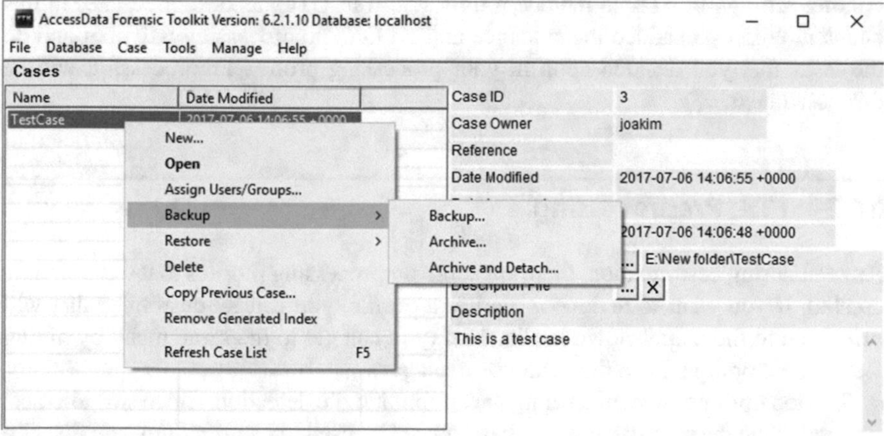

Fig. 16.3 Case options in the FTK database interface

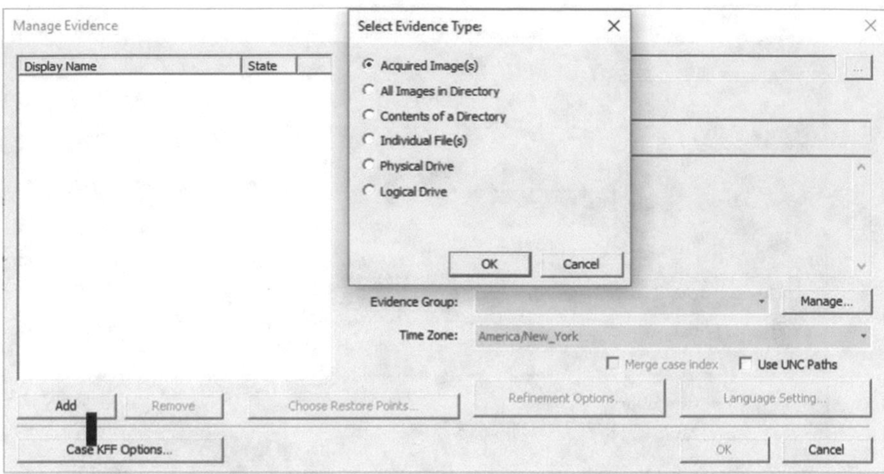

Fig. 16.4 FTK evidence manager

The final part of creating a case is to add some evidence to it. If you let FTK open the case upon case creation, the evidence manager will show automatically. If not, open the case and then hit "Evidence" in the top menu and select "Add/Remove" to get to the evidence manager shown in Fig. 16.4.

To add evidence, hit add in the bottom left corner and the "Select evidence type" windows will appear. Select the type of evidence you want to add and follow the wizard. Finally, notice that you need to select the time zone that applies to your evidence. If you are unsure, make a guess. Note that the setting here will be applied to your case and all time stamps viewed in the case will be updated to match the time zone you selected. A way to ensure that you see the correct data is to modify the column settings in FTK to include a time stamp in UTC, as described later in this chapter. When you added the evidence and hit OK, preprocessing will start and do the tasks that you decided upon in your processing profile. Preprocessing will be discussed next.

16.2 FTK: Preprocessing

As seen during case creation, there are some preprocessing profiles that were already created. If you want to review or modify a profile, you can hit customize that will bring you to the menu shown in Fig. 16.5 (you can get to the same menu by hitting Refinement options from the evidence manager).

The top options concern hashing and automatic file detection. Since two identical files will have the same hash value, hashing can be used to identify duplicate files. To generate file hashes, check the boxes that correspond to the hash algorithms you want to use. *Flag duplicate files* is used to, well, flag duplicate files based on evaluation of hash values. Known File Filter (*KFF*) can be described as an add-on

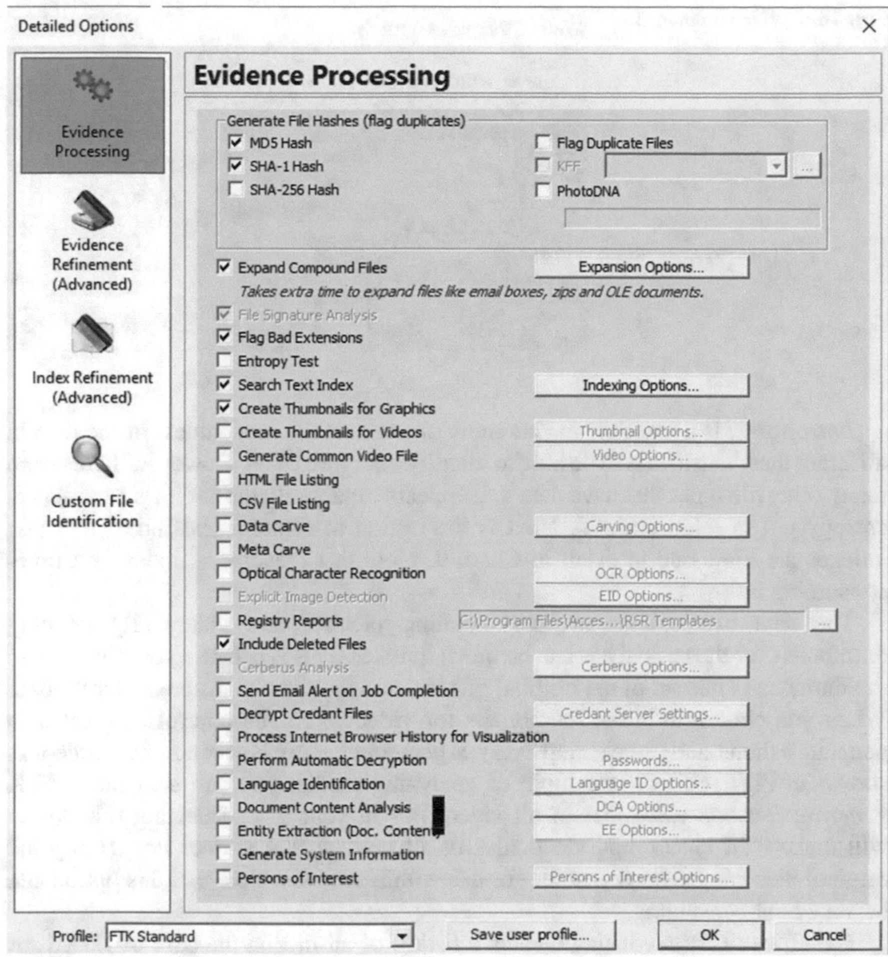

Fig. 16.5 Review and modified processing profile

that has to be installed separately. KFF allows you to use a list containing hashes of known files, such as installers, Windows files, and other files that are seldom of interest. FTK will evaluate all files in the case against the hashes in KFF and flag those that are included in KFF. The advantage here is that you do not need to spend time analyzing uninteresting files. The last option in the top box is *PhotoDNA* that can be used to identify identical or similar pictures.

Expand compound files is used to expand compound files, as discussed in Chap. 8. *File signature analysis* is a function that looks at file signatures and file extensions and flags all files where the file signature and file extension do not match. This allows you to identify files where the file type has been changed, possibly indicating an attempt to hide information.

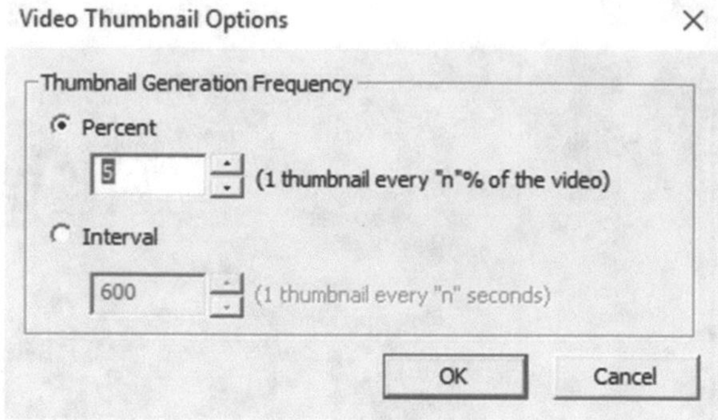

Fig. 16.6 Video thumbnail options

Entropy test is a function that attempts to evaluate the randomness of the data in different files. The idea is to be able to identify encrypted data. However, there are so many other file types that have data that appears random. In the author's experience, entropy test is seldom useful. Next is the option to create a text index, and text indexes are discussed in detail in Chap. 9. Note that creating an index is a time-consuming task.

The next two options are for handling pictures and videos. By creating thumbnails for those, analysis can be much quicker. This is because you can analyze the thumbnails instead of the original picture, and the thumbnails are faster to load. When you choose to create thumbnails for videos, you can control how often to generate a thumbnail by selecting every X percent or every X second of the video, as shown in Fig. 16.6. On the topic of analyzing media, you can also make FTK *generate common video files* of all video files in your case. Selecting this option will make FTK create mp4 video files of all your videos; it does not modify the original files but creates a new file for use within the case. Note that this option can be very time-consuming.

HTML and CSV file listing creates a listing of all files in the case of HTML or CSV. The next option is *data carving* that was discussed in the file carving section of Chap. 11. *Meta carve* will carve for metadata and for deleted directories. This is the only way to recover deleted directories using FTK.

The next option is *optical character recognition* (OCR). OCR is used to identify text in images and PDF files; it works surprisingly well. When you use OCR, it is possible to search for text content in pictures and add text from pictures to the case index. The options you can use for OCR can be seen in Fig. 16.7. In short, you can select what file types to apply OCR to and choose to exclude files based on size. Note that OCR is a very time-consuming task.

Explicit image detection is an add-on that can be used to identify explicit images, such as child exploitation. Next, the *registry report* option can be used to automatically create a report on registry data based on templates and *include deleted files* is used to make FTK consider deleted files for all processing options.

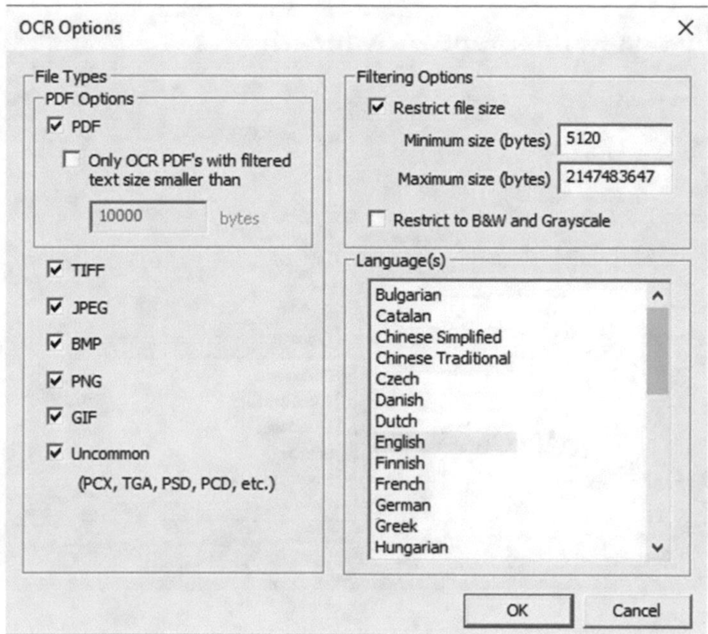

Fig. 16.7 OCR options

Cerberus analysis is another add-on; this one is used for malware analysis. Next, you can make FTK send an e-mail when a job is complete and analyze and *decrypt credant files*. In the author's experience, encryption using credant is not common.

Process Internet browser history for visualization is an option that will process browsing history so that you can view the history in a timeline. *Perform automatic* decryption is not as magical as it sounds, but can be used to automatically decrypt several encrypted file types. It does, however, require you to submit the password. *Language identification* will make FTK analyze the beginning of each document in an attempt to identify the language in which it is written.

Document content analysis attempts to group documents based on their content, and *entity extraction* can extract specific information such as credit card numbers from documents. *Generate system information* is a very useful feature that collects system information such as owner information and users on the system. Finally, the *persons of interest* is a feature designed to show connections between phone and e-mail evidence in a case.

As a final touch, you can limit what files are added to the case and considered for the index by index and case refinement in the right pane. This can be useful if you have a search warrant that is limited to some files or to a certain time span or what to analyze specific files for some other reason. The evidence refinement options are shown in Fig. 16.8.

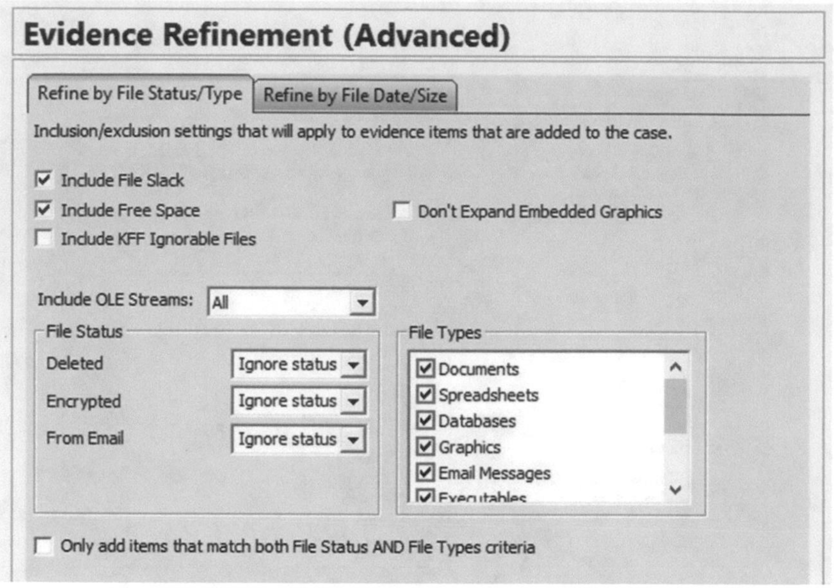

Fig. 16.8 Evidence refinement option

16.3 FTK: Overview

The final part of the FTK introduction is an overview of the actual FTK interface. This overview shows some of the views and features of FTK but is in no way exhaustive and attempts to present some of the more common areas and some less obvious but good features. An overview of the interface is presented in Fig. 16.9, and the different panes and menus are denoted in the picture.

Looking at the top menu, some of the drop-downs deserves to be mentioned. First, the file drop-down is where you find some good features including options to export system information and a word list. The word list is based on your index and can be imported into PRTK. The file drop-down is shown in Fig. 16.10.

The edit and view drop-downs are quite self-explaining and best discovered by testing, leading to the important evidence tab. The evidence drop-down is where you can reach the evidence managed, by pressing "Add/Remove." If you notice that the processes you ran during preprocessing were not enough, you can run more processing by hitting additional analysis. You can also use the evidence drop-down to import a memory dump into FTK. The evidence drop-down is presented in Fig. 16.11.

The final drop-down that is highlighted in this chapter is manage. The manage drop-down contains options that can be used to change settings related to KFF and PhotoDNA as well as a means of configuring your own file carvers. However,

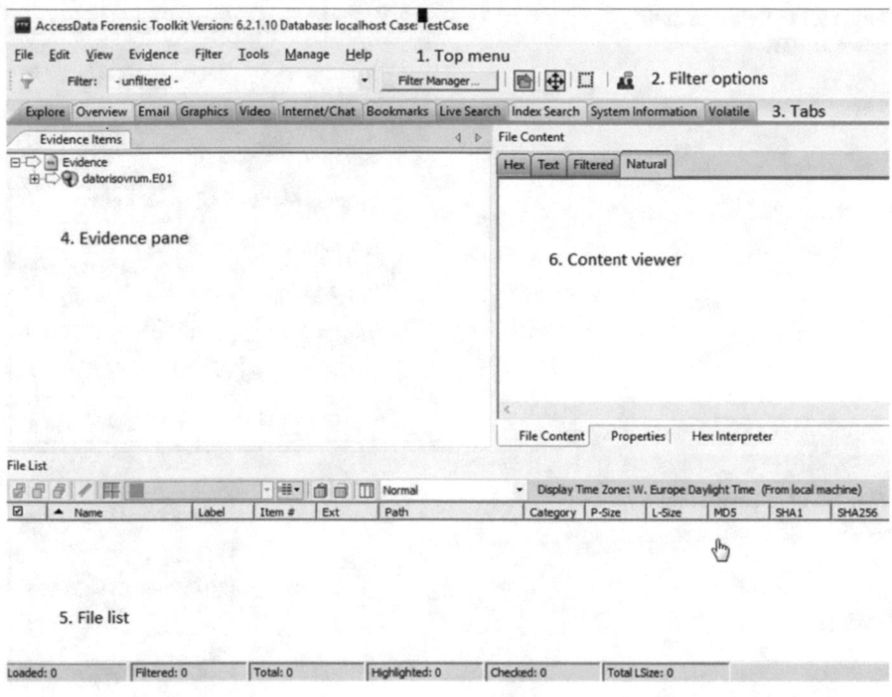

Fig. 16.9 FTK overview

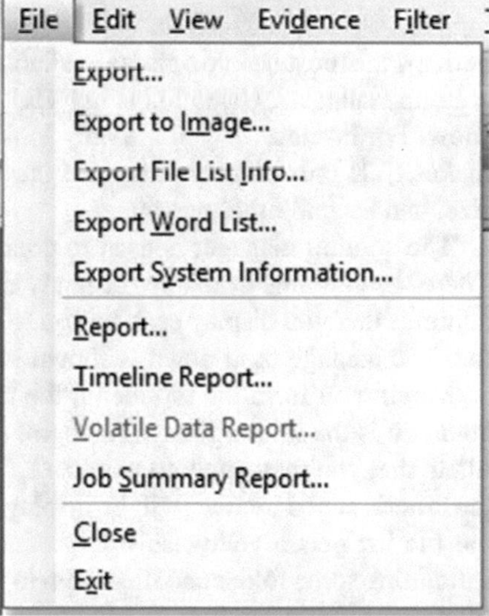

Fig. 16.10 File options in FTK

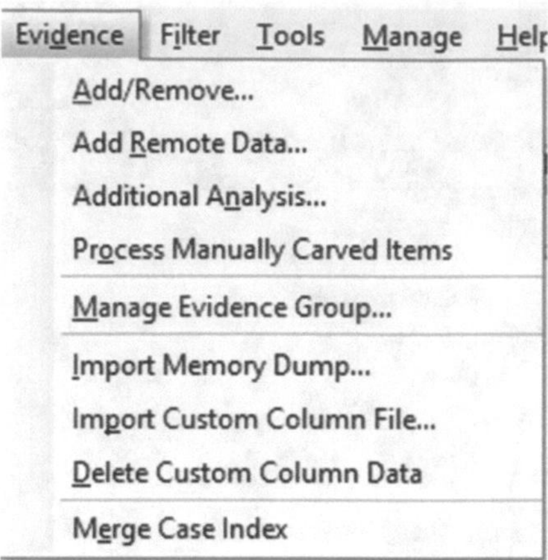

Fig. 16.11 Evidence drop-down in FTK

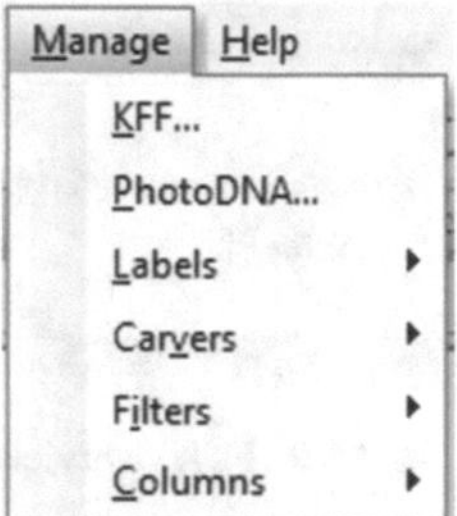

Fig. 16.12 Manage drop-down

perhaps the most usable options available in the manage drop-down are the filter and column managers. Using filters in FTK, you can decide on what content you want to show. For instance, if you are only looking for pictures, you can apply a filter that makes FTK only display pictures. Likewise, you can filter on file creation date, file size, and several other parameters.

The column manager is used to control what columns to display in the file list. There are columns available for many different types of data, and controlling what columns that you display enables you to control what data you want to see in the file list. The manage drop-down is shown in Fig. 16.12.

Moving on from the top menu, the next part of the FTK interface that deserves attention is the filter options. To begin, the filter option contains a drop-down of all filters that you may apply to your case. When you apply a filter, only files that meet the criteria stated by filter will be displayed by FTK. To indicate that a filter is active, the file list gets a yellowish background. As a tip from the real world, if you are examining some folder and files seem to be missing, it is likely that you forgot to turn filtering off. You can turn filtering off by hitting the icon that looks like a funnel, at the far left of the filter options. As is displayed in Fig. 16.13, FTK comes with a bunch of precreated filters that you use, but you can also create your own filters in the filter manager that you access by hitting filter manager.

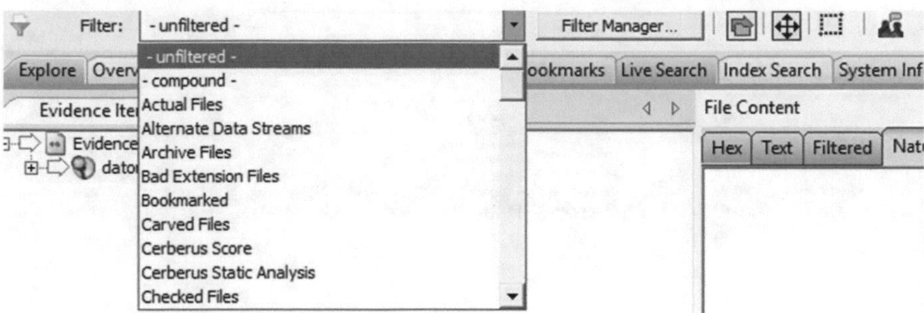

Fig. 16.13 Filter options in FTK

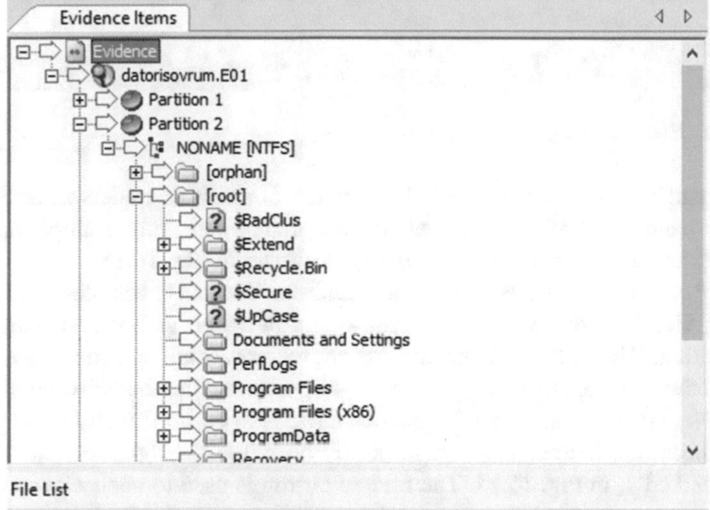

Fig. 16.14 Evidence pane in FTK

Next, there is the evidence pane. The evidence pane shows the evidence items you included in your case as a browsable tree structure. Marking a folder in the evidence pane will make FTK list the content of that folder in the file list. A very useful function in the evidence pane is "Quick picks." "Quick picks" is a function that lets you choose a folder, and FTK will display the content of that folder and all of its sub-folders in the file view. You can enable "Quick picks" for several folders at once. Note that marking a folder in the evidence pane will have no effect when "Quick picks" is active. The evidence pane is displayed in Fig. 16.14. Enable "Quick picks" for a folder by hitting the arrow in front of the folder.

Note the options [root] and [orphan] under the file system for Partition 2. [root] denotes the root of the file system, and [orphan] lists orphan files. Orphan files are files that do not appear to have a parent folder.

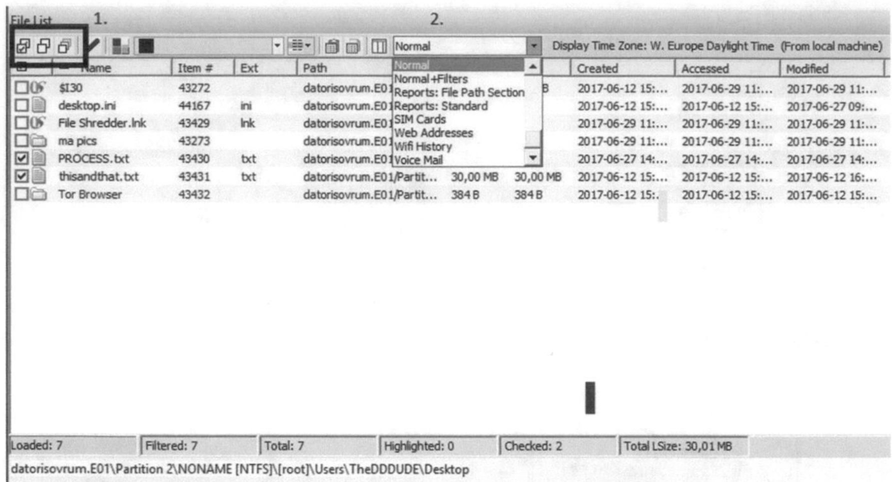

Fig. 16.15 FTK file listing

Next part to discuss is the file list where the contents of folders selected in the evidence pane are displayed. As default, file name, path, time stamps, and some more data are shown in different columns, as shown in Fig. 16.15.

Before each item in the list, there is a checkbox. You can check files as a means of selecting files that you want to perform a certain action to, such as searching or bookmarking. The bottom of the file list shows you some statistics such as how many checked files are there in your case and how many files that are currently in the file list. Note that the only way to uncheck a file is to do it manually or by pressing the "uncheck all" button. The "uncheck all" button is the rightmost button in the square marked 1, in Fig. 16.15. The middle button is used to uncheck any checked items in the current file list, and the leftmost button will check all currently listed items. For each file, information such as name, path, size, and time stamps is shown as the default FTK behavior. You can control what information is displayed by changing column settings; this is done in the drop-down denoted by 2.

When you mark a file in the file list, it will be displayed in the content viewer, as shown in Fig. 16.16. The bar above the content viewer decides how to view the file data. The natural view tries to display the file as it is intended to be viewed: a picture as a picture, a word document as a word document, and so on. FTK can view a large number of different file types. The filtered view displays the file as ASCII data, but excludes the data that FTK does not deem as interesting. The text view shows the file as plain text if applicable, and finally the hex view shows the file data in hexadecimal and ASCII.

The bar below the viewer decides what to show, file content will show the actual file, and properties will show the file metadata. Finally, the hex interpreter will try to interpret and report certain hexadecimal values that may be present in the viewed file.

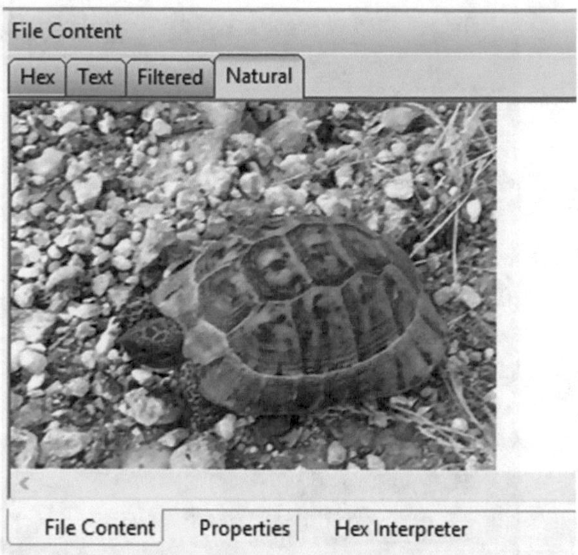

Fig. 16.16 FTK content viewer

One of the most wonderful functions of FTK is that it groups all files in a case by category. By going to the overview tab, you can browse the data in the case by file category or file extension instead of looking through the folder structure. If you know that you are looking for a document but have no clue about its whereabouts, the overview tab can be a great help. The overview tab is demonstrated in Fig. 16.17. The rest of the tabs have quite self-explaining names. Explore them on your own!

The final thing presented about FTK in this book is what you can do to a file. Naturally, when you find a file, you need to do something to it. To apply some action to a file in FTK, simply right click it, and you will be presented with the options displayed in Fig. 16.18. Figure 16.18 also shows an example of "Quick picks" in action. In the picture, "Quick picks" was applied to the "Desktop" folder. Note the yellow mark on the parent folder, THEDDDUDE, which denotes that "Quick pics" was applied to a sub-folder. Well then, highlighting some of the options available when you right click a file, the options begin with Open that opens the file in the default viewer for that file type in Windows. Using Open with, you can open it in Windows using some other application. Next is the options used to bookmark the file. You can add the file to an existing bookmark or create a new bookmark. The bookmarked files will appear under the bookmark tab.

The next option of interest is Visualize browser history that you can click if you selected to complete the appropriate process, as previously discussed. Then, you may export the file or export the file to an image. Exporting files to an image is useful when you are to send some files to someone else for further analysis. That concludes the introduction to FTK; hopefully, you have now seen enough to enable you to start working with FTK on your own.

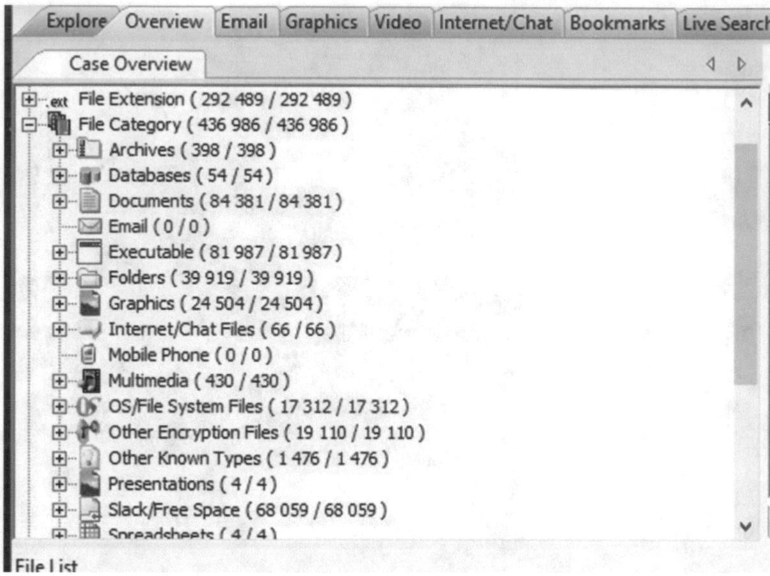

Fig. 16.17 Overview tab

16.4 Registry Viewer: Overview

This section presents an overview of Registry Viewer that is used to analyze registry hives. Working with Registry Viewer, you can analyze one hive at the time, and if you need to extract data, you would do that in a report. The main benefit of using Registry Viewer over regedit is, in the author's opinion, better search utilities and that Registry Viewer interprets values that are written in formats that are hard to understand. Well, let us get at it by examining the Registry Viewer interface presented in Fig. 16.19.

Starting from the top, there is a top menu and then a menu with buttons, and the important parts of those sections will be discussed next. Then, the top left pane shows the registry hive you are currently examining as a browsable tree-structure. The right view shows keys and their values, and the bottom left pane shows properties for the key you are currently working on. Next, have a closer look at the buttons in the button menu. The button menu in Registry Viewer provides a quick way to use the features that you will use most of the time. The button menu is displayed in Fig. 16.20.

Going from left to right, the purpose of each button is as follows:

- Open a registry hive in Registry Viewer; you can only analyze one hive at the time.
- Get to full registry view, as opposed to common areas.

Fig. 16.18 FTK file options

- Enter report view to see what keys that are added to the report.
- View common areas; pressing this button will make Registry Viewer show you the registry keys that are added to common areas. This function can be seen as a shortcut to information that is commonly of interest.
- Generate report.
- Add to report, used to add a key and its values to the report.
- Add to report with children, used to add a key and its sub-keys with corresponding values to the report.
- Add to common areas, used to add a key to common areas for quick access in future examinations.
- Remove from common areas.
- View help.

Fig. 16.19 Registry Viewer overview

Fig. 16.20 Button menu in Registry Viewer

While browsing the hive you are examining or using, common areas are common ways to examine a registry hive; there are times when you want to do a keyword search. A great way to do keyword searches is by advanced find, reachable by hitting edit in the top menu. Advanced find is displayed in Fig. 16.21.

As you can see in Fig. 16.21, this search function allows you to search for keywords present in keys or values and will display all search hits as a list. There is also a button that allows you to add search hits to the report. Our next topic of discussion is the properties pane, displayed in Fig. 16.22.

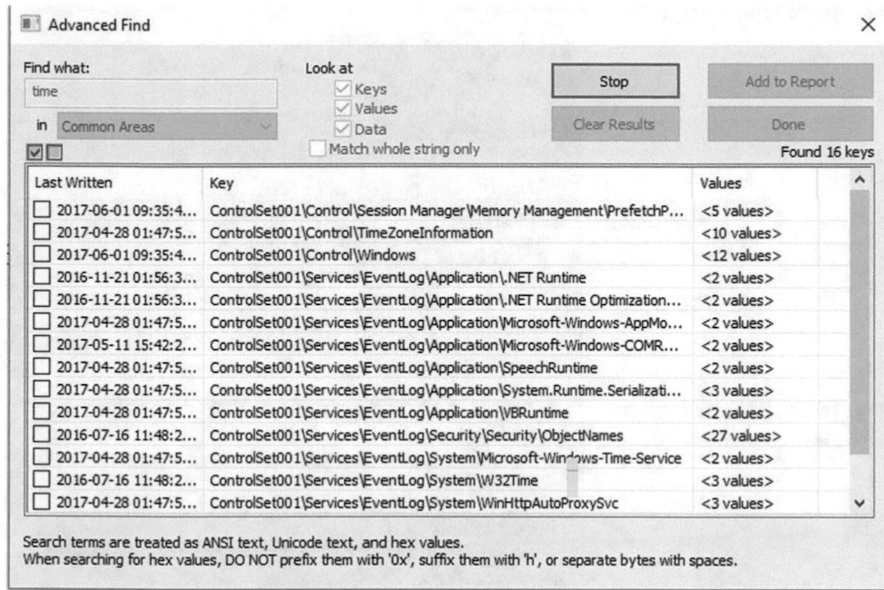

Fig. 16.21 Advanced find in Registry Viewer

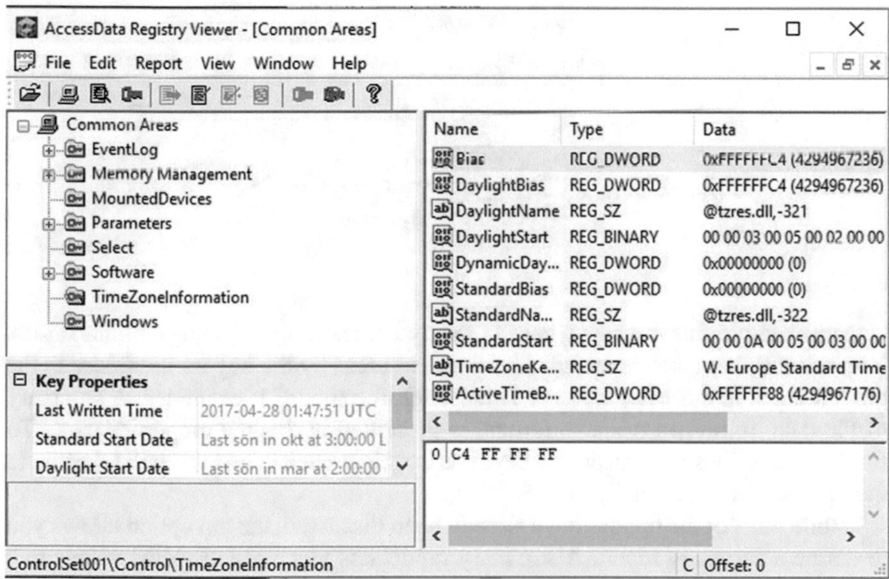

Fig. 16.22 Key properties

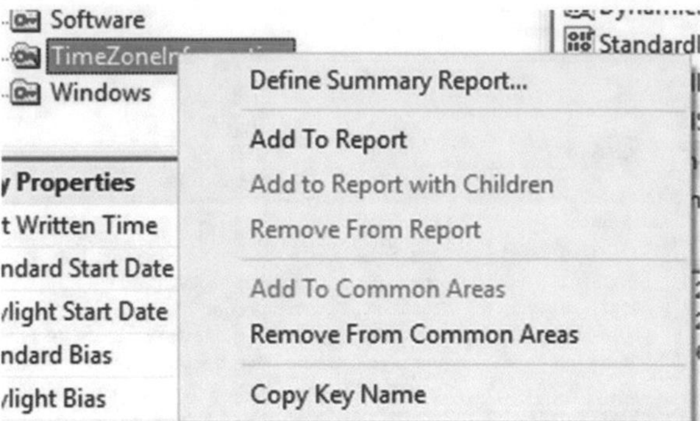

Fig. 16.23 Key options

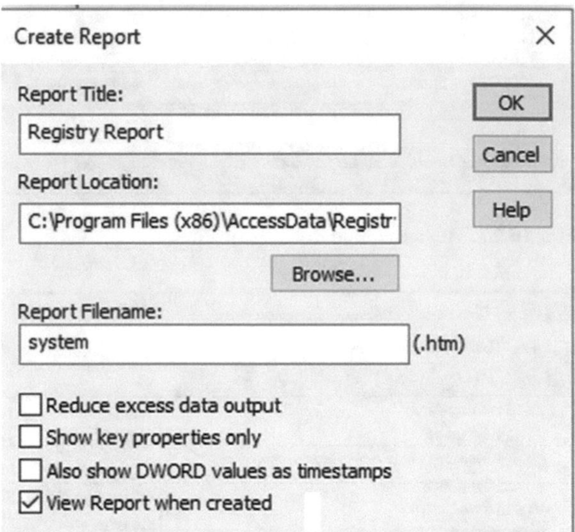

Fig. 16.24 Registry creation dialogue

The example shows a case where a registry hive is analyzed using common areas. You can tell that a key is included in common areas by the key on the folder in the top left pane. In this case, the key "TimeZoneInformation" is examined. A summary of the data, in human readable format, is presented in the key properties pane. To reach most actions you can do to a key, you can right click it, and this will take you to the options displayed in Fig. 16.23.

While most of the options have already been discussed, the top option allows you to define a summary report. A summary report lets you add individual values to a report, and a normal report requires you to include all values of a key to the report. To grasp the difference, try it yourself!

To give you an idea of how to create a report, the final part of this chapter will show you how to create a short registry report. The process begins with adding some registry key(s) to the report and starting the report generation from the button menu. The report creation dialogue is presented in Fig. 16.24. What you need to do is select

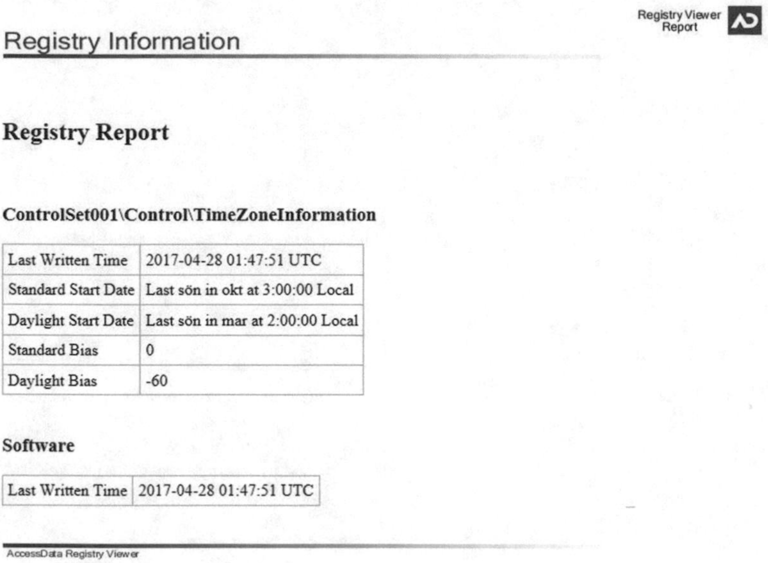

Registry Viewer Report

Registry Information

Registry Report

ControlSet001\Control\TimeZoneInformation

Last Written Time	2017-04-28 01:47:51 UTC
Standard Start Date	Last sön in okt at 3:00:00 Local
Daylight Start Date	Last sön in mar at 2:00:00 Local
Standard Bias	0
Daylight Bias	-60

Software

Last Written Time	2017-04-28 01:47:51 UTC

AccessData Registry Viewer

Fig. 16.25 Registry Viewer report sample

a title and output path. Another great option is the option to reduce excess output. This option will reduce how much information is displayed in raw data format. You may also make the report only include what is displayed in the key properties pane, by checking show key properties only. Note that the report is created as an HTML package. Finally, a sample report is displayed in Fig. 16.25. This sample shows a report including time zone information using the option to only display key properties. Note that the report also includes the last written time for the registry hive.

Open-Source or Freeware Tools 17

This chapter introduces and provides links to tools that are useful during forensic examinations and that are available for download and use, as open source or with some other freeware licensing. Some tools have been used in the previous chapters of the book, and some are just listed here because they appear good to know about, from the author's point of view. Remember that tools get updated, renewed, and deprecated and the usage of any tool requires that the forensic expert understands the output. Just as for the previous chapter, this is a demonstrating chapter and no end of chapter tasks is given. Instead, you are encouraged to download and play with the tools presented.

17.1 Prefetch Parser by Erik Zimmerman

Erik Zimmerman created a command line parser for prefetch files that takes one or more files as input and parses the data in it and reports last runtime, total amount of runs, and more for a prefetch file. What you must know about this tool is that it outputs time in UTC time; thus, you need to adjust times to match the time zone settings of the computer you are examining. The tool is available at https://ericzimmerman.github.io/ and is called PECmd. The version used in this book was 0.9.2.0. An output sample of PECmd is shown in Fig. 17.1.

17.2 Shellbags Explorer by Erik Zimmerman

Shellbags can be a good artifact for forensic experts to analyze; however, the format is binary and hard to manually interpret. One tool that does a great job at interpreting shellbags is Shellbags Explorer, written by Erik Zimmerman and available for download at https://ericzimmerman.github.io/. The tool will take a registry hive as input and parse it for shellbag data that will be presented in a readable format, as shown in Fig. 17.2.

J. Kävrestad, *Fundamentals of Digital Forensics*,
https://doi.org/10.1007/978-3-030-38954-3_17

```
PS C:\Users\joaki\Downloads\PECmd> .\PECmd.exe -f .\CMD.EXE-4A81B364.pf
PECmd version 0.9.2.0

Author: Eric Zimmerman (saericzimmerman@gmail.com)
https://github.com/EricZimmerman/PECmd

Command line: -f .\CMD.EXE-4A81B364.pf

Keywords: temp, tmp

Processing '.\CMD.EXE-4A81B364.pf'

Created on: 2018-03-14 11:12:48
Modified on: 2018-03-14 11:09:56
Last accessed on: 2018-03-14 11:12:48

Executable name: CMD.EXE
Hash: 4A81B364
File size (bytes): 6 292
Version: Windows 10

Run count: 2
Last run: 2018-03-14 11:09:56
Other run times: 2018-03-14 11:09:56

Volume information:

#0: Name: \VOLUME{01d3bb8869f25d67-5c6a9abc} Serial: 5C6A9ABC Created: 2018-03-14 11:34:29
 Directories: 3 File references: 11

Directories referenced: 3

0: \VOLUME{01d3bb8869f25d67-5c6a9abc}\WINDOWS
1: \VOLUME{01d3bb8869f25d67-5c6a9abc}\WINDOWS\SYSTEM~2
2: \VOLUME{01d3bb8869f25d67-5c6a9abc}\WINDOWS\SYSTEM 2\EN-US

Files referenced: 8

0: \VOLUME{01d3bb8869f25d67-5c6a9abc}\WINDOWS\SYSTEM32\NTDLL.DLL
1: \VOLUME{01d3bb8869f25d67-5c6a9abc}\WINDOWS\SYSTEM32\CMD.EXE
2: \VOLUME{01d3bb8869f25d67-5c6a9abc}\WINDOWS\SYSTEM32\KERNEL32.DLL
3: \VOLUME{01d3bb8869f25d67-5c6a9abc}\WINDOWS\SYSTEM32\KERNELBASE.DLL
4: \VOLUME{01d3bb8869f25d67-5c6a9abc}\WINDOWS\SYSTEM32\LOCALE.NLS
5: \VOLUME{01d3bb8869f25d67-5c6a9abc}\WINDOWS\SYSTEM32\MSVCRT.DLL
6: \VOLUME{01d3bb8869f25d67-5c6a9abc}\WINDOWS\SYSTEM32\EN-US\CMD.EXE.MUI
7: \VOLUME{01d3bb8869f25d67-5c6a9abc}\WINDOWS\SYSTEM32\EN-US\KERNELBASE.DLL.MUI

---------- Processed '.\CMD.EXE-4A81B364.pf' in 0,03577850 seconds ----------
```

Fig. 17.1 PECmd output sample

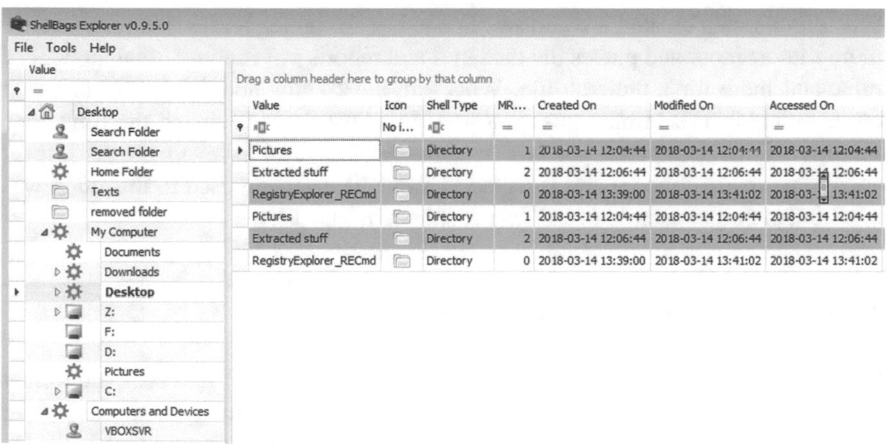

Fig. 17.2 Sample output from Shellbags Explorer

The left pane shows the root folders that were visited by a certain user, and the right pane shows deeper information about sub-folders. This information includes time stamps revealing when the folder was first visited (created on) and then the latest update of folder viewing preferences took place (modified on). The version used in this book was 0.9.5.0.

17.3 .lnk File Parser by Erik Zimmerman

Yet another tool created by Erik Zimmerman is LECmd, a command line tool used to parse .lnk files. It is very much the same as the prefetch file parser but takes .lnk files as inputs and produces a report including the following information:

- The location of the file referenced in the .lnk file (the target file).
- The time the link was created and last updated, meaning when the target file was first and last accessed.
- Information about the device where the target file is stored. If this is a local device, the volume serial number and type will be included. If the device was a remote device, the name of the share will be included.

Note that the time stamps reported are reported in UTC time; thus, adjustments according to the examined computer's time zone have to be done. Sample output from LECmd is shown in Fig. 17.3. The version used in this book was 0.9.8.0 downloaded from https://ericzimmerman.github.io/.

17.4 Thumbcache Viewer

A neat tool that can be used to parse thumbnails from thumbcache databases is Thumbcache Viewer. The tool is also capable of parsing the Windows search database in order to attempt to map the files in the thumbcache to its actual path. Thumbcache Viewer can be downloaded from https://thumbcacheviewer.github.io/ and is demonstrated in Fig. 17.4.

To map the thumbnails in the Thumbcache database, hit tools → map file paths → Load ESE Database and select the extracted Windows.edb file as shown in Fig. 17.5.

17.5 USBDevview by NirSoft

One tool that deserves a presentation is one that is most useful during live examinations, namely, USBDevview by NirSoft. It is essentially a tool that collects information about USB devices that are or have been connected to the computer. Further, it groups the devices based on type, indicates if they are currently connected, and tries to deduce the serial number of the devices. It will also describe

```
PS C:\Users\joaki\Downloads\LECmd> .\LECmd.exe -f .\remotetest.txt.lnk
LECmd version 0.9.8.0

Author: Eric Zimmerman (saericzimmerman@gmail.com)
https://github.com/EricZimmerman/LECmd

Command line: -f .\remotetest.txt.lnk

Processing '.\remotetest.txt.lnk'

Source file: C:\Users\joaki\Downloads\LECmd\remotetest.txt.lnk
  Source created:  2018-03-22 14:17:51
  Source modified: 2018-03-22 14:17:07
  Source accessed: 2018-03-22 14:17:51

--- Header ---
  Target created:  2018-03-22 14:17:03
  Target modified: 2018-03-22 14:17:03
  Target accessed: 2018-03-22 14:17:03

  File size: 0
  Flags: HasTargetIdList, HasLinkInfo, HasWorkingDir, IsUnicode, DisableKnownFolderTrackin
g
  File attributes: FileAttributeArchive
  Icon index: 0
  Show window: SwNormal (Activates and displays the window. The window is restored to its
original size and position if the window is minimized or maximized.)

Working Directory: E:\

--- Link information ---
Flags: CommonNetworkRelativeLinkAndPathSuffix

  Network share information
    Device name: E:
    Share name: \\vboxsrv\VMDShare
    Provider type: WnncNetRdr2Sample
    Share flags: 3

  Common path: remotetest.txt
```

Fig. 17.3 Sample output from LECmd

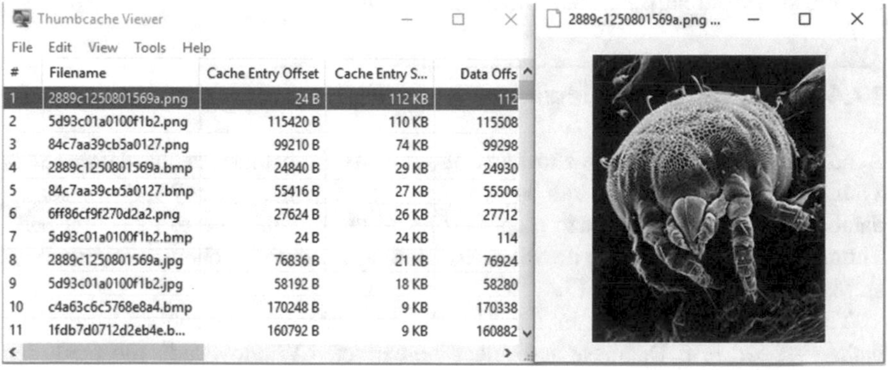

Thumbcache Viewer

File Edit View Tools Help

#	Filename	Cache Entry Offset	Cache Entry S...	Data Offs
1	2889c1250801569a.png	24 B	112 KB	112
2	5d93c01a0100f1b2.png	115420 B	110 KB	115508
3	84c7aa39cb5a0127.png	99210 B	74 KB	99298
4	2889c1250801569a.bmp	24840 B	29 KB	24930
5	84c7aa39cb5a0127.bmp	55416 B	27 KB	55506
6	6ff86cf9f270d2a2.png	27624 B	26 KB	27712
7	5d93c01a0100f1b2.bmp	24 B	24 KB	114
8	2889c1250801569a.jpg	76836 B	21 KB	76924
9	5d93c01a0100f1b2.jpg	58192 B	18 KB	58280
10	c4a63c6c5768e8a4.bmp	170248 B	9 KB	170338
11	1fdb7d0712d2eb4e.b...	160792 B	9 KB	160882

2889c1250801569a.png ...

Fig. 17.4 Thumbcache Viewer sample

when a device was first and last used. Because of the information it provides, it is great for live examinations during house searches as it can provide information that indicates if the house search team should look for USB storage devices. This tool can be downloaded from https://www.nirsoft.net/utils/usb_devices_view.html. Sample output from USBDevview is shown in Fig. 17.6.

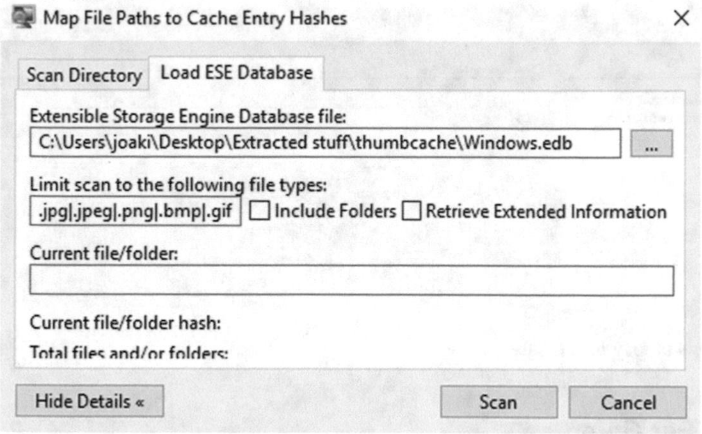

Fig. 17.5 Thumbcache Viewer—map file paths

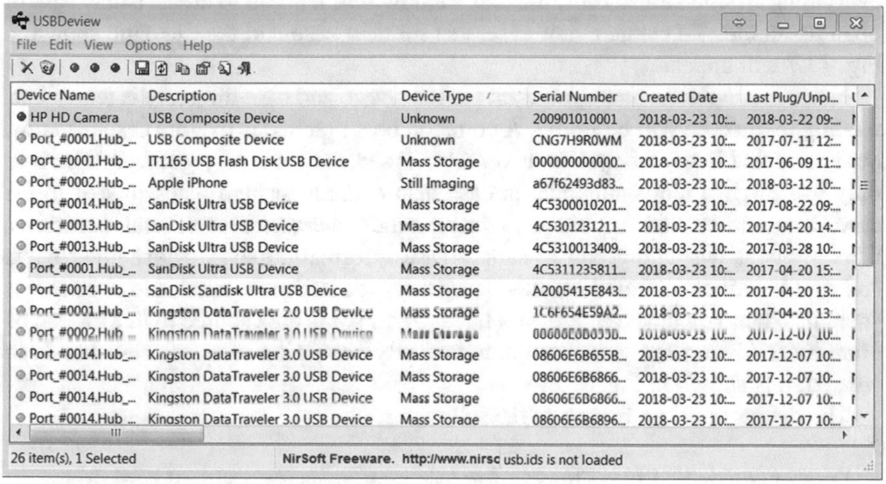

Device Name	Description	Device Type	Serial Number	Created Date	Last Plug/Unpl...
HP HD Camera	USB Composite Device	Unknown	200901010001	2018-03-23 10:...	2018-03-22 09:...
Port_#0001.Hub_...	USB Composite Device	Unknown	CNG7H9R0WM	2018-03-23 10:...	2017-07-11 12:...
Port_#0001.Hub_...	IT1165 USB Flash Disk USB Device	Mass Storage	000000000000...	2018-03-23 10:...	2017-06-09 11:...
Port_#0002.Hub_...	Apple iPhone	Still Imaging	a67f62493d83...	2018-03-23 10:...	2018-03-12 10:...
Port_#0014.Hub_...	SanDisk Ultra USB Device	Mass Storage	4C5300010201...	2018-03-23 10:...	2017-08-22 09:...
Port_#0013.Hub_...	SanDisk Ultra USB Device	Mass Storage	4C5301231211...	2018-03-23 10:...	2017-04-20 14:...
Port_#0013.Hub_...	SanDisk Ultra USB Device	Mass Storage	4C5310013409...	2018-03-23 10:...	2017-03-28 10:...
Port_#0001.Hub_...	SanDisk Ultra USB Device	Mass Storage	4C5311235811...	2018-03-23 10:...	2017-04-20 15:...
Port_#0014.Hub_...	SanDisk Sandisk Ultra USB Device	Mass Storage	A2005415E843...	2018-03-23 10:...	2017-04-20 13:...
Port_#0001.Hub_...	Kingston DataTraveler 2.0 USB Device	Mass Storage	1C6F654E59A2...	2018-03-23 10:...	2017-04-20 13:...
Port_#0002.Hub_...	Kingston DataTraveler 3.0 USB Device	Mass Storage	0060E0B033D...	2018-03-23 10:...	2017-12-07 10:...
Port_#0014.Hub_...	Kingston DataTraveler 3.0 USB Device	Mass Storage	08606E6B655B...	2018-03-23 10:...	2017-12-07 10:...
Port_#0014.Hub_...	Kingston DataTraveler 3.0 USB Device	Mass Storage	08606E6B6866...	2018-03-23 10:...	2017-12-07 10:...
Port_#0014.Hub_...	Kingston DataTraveler 3.0 USB Device	Mass Storage	08606E6B6866...	2018-03-23 10:...	2017-12-07 10:...
Port_#0014.Hub_...	Kingston DataTraveler 3.0 USB Device	Mass Storage	08606E6B6896...	2018-03-23 10:...	2017-12-07 10:...

Fig. 17.6 USBDevview sample output

17.6 Autopsy

Autopsy is an open-source forensic platform that is, in this book, presented as an alternative to FTK. It can run on Windows and Linux, and this chapter will present an overview of the version that is designed for Windows and is most current at the time of writing (4.7.0). As has been stated, Autopsy is open source and can be downloaded free of charge from https://www.sleuthkit.org/autopsy/download.php.

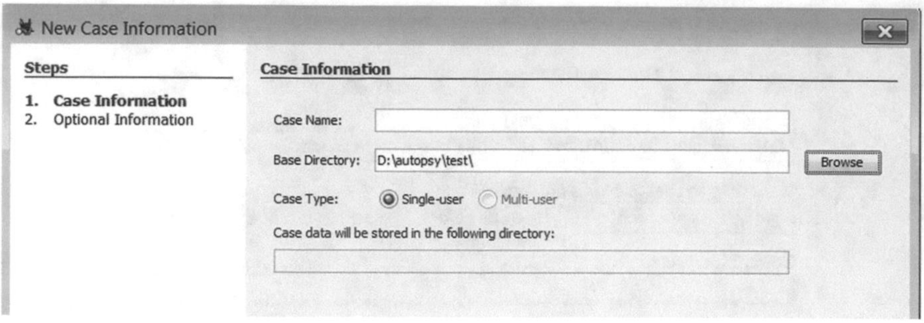

Fig. 17.7 Autopsy create case

17.6.1 Get Going

After installing Autopsy and starting it, you should know that Autopsy arranges everything around cases. Thus, the first window will tell you to create a new case or open up an old. To create a new case, just hit new case and the dialogue shown in Fig. 17.7 will appear.

Name is simply the name you want for your case, and base directory is where data relating to the case will be stored. A common best practice is to store case data on a hard drive that is not the system drive. Also, it seems as if a very good practice is to only use English alphanumerical in case data and file system paths related to the case. The author had trouble with using other characters at several occasions. Clicking next will allow you to supply case information such as examiner name and case identification number; after doing that, you can press finish and your case is created. When you create a case, you have to add some data source to it. This can be done by following the guide that automatically shows up after the case has been created; it is shown in Fig. 17.8.

The data source can be one of the following:

- Disk image or VM file: This is a forensic disk image or a virtual hard drive.
- Local disk: This is a running disk connected to the computer running Autopsy.
- Logical files: This is just plain files or folders.
- Unallocated space image file: This is some file that contains unstructured data. This alternative could be used to analyze a memory dump in Autopsy.

After selecting the type of data source to use, you are to click next to select the actual data source and then click next again to reach the ingest modules, as shown in Fig. 17.9.

Ingest modules can be compared to preprocessing in FTK. They are basically modules of code designed to do automatic analysis of the case data. Before moving

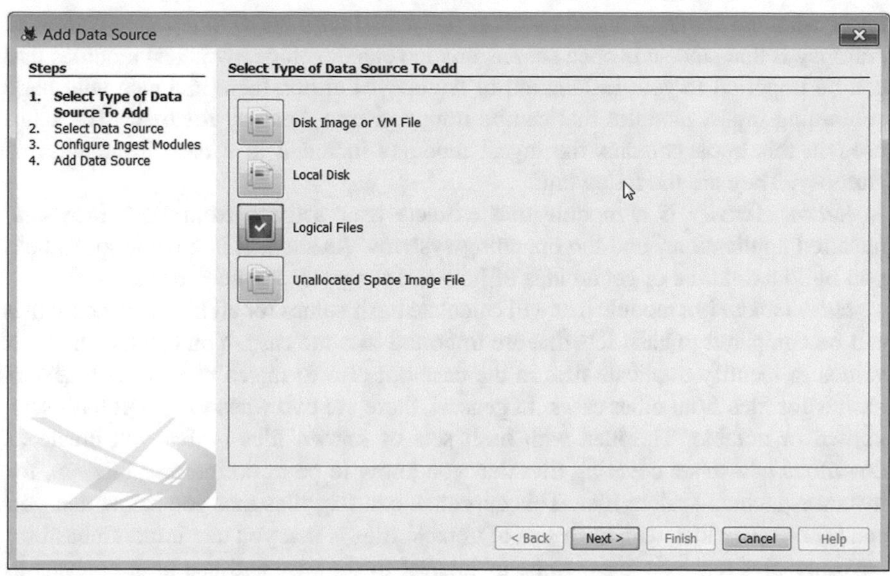

Fig. 17.8 Autopsy Add Data Source

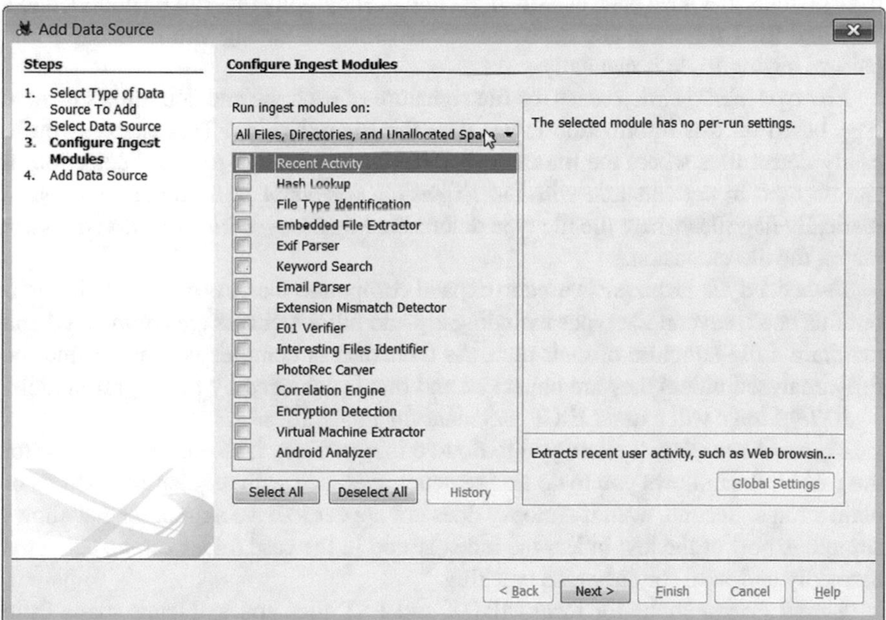

Fig. 17.9 Autopsy ingest modules

on to what the standard ingest modules do, you should know that a nice feature of Autopsy is that since it is open source, anyone can develop new ingest modules that can be imported to your installation of Autopsy. Further, there is a nice wiki page containing ingest modules that can be imported into Autopsy for free.[1] The setup used in this book contains the ingest modules included in a base installation of Autopsy. They are the following:

Recent Activity is a module that extracts user activity from Web browsers, installed applications, and the operating systems. As such, it is a nice tool to help you build a timeline or get an idea of how the computer has been used.

Hash lookup is a module that will calculate hash values for all files in the case that can be compared to hash sets that are imported into the case. You can use the hash values to identify duplicate files in the case but also to match against hash sets of hashes for files from other cases. In general, there are two ways to import hash sets, known or notable. The idea with hash sets of known files is that you create or download a hash set covering files that you know to be of no interest; this can, for instance, include system files. This approach can flag files that you know that you can ignore. The idea with hash sets of notable files is that you can import a hash set covering files that you know to be of interest to the case and use hash analysis to identify if any files of interest are present on the computer you are analyzing. This is a common approach when working child exploitation cases. There are huge hash sets over pictures that have been classified as child pornography that can be imported to a case and used for automatic detection of such images, saving you the trouble and pain of having to do it manually.

File type identification reads the file signature of each file and determines its field type based on this information rather than the file extension. This enables you to easily detect files where the file extension has been modified to avoid detection. It can be used in combination with the *Extension Mismatch Detector* that will automatically flag files where the file type determined by *file type identification* does not match the file extension.

Embedded file extractor is used to expand compound files. As described throughout this book, several file types including zip and other archives are compressed and maintain a file structure of their own. As their data is compressed, they cannot be fully analyzed unless they are unpacked and that is achieved by this ingest module.

EXIF parser will extract EXIF metadata for image files.

Keyword search will allow you to do two things. First, it creates a text index for the case. It then allows you to do text searches specified with regular expressions or plain strings. Second, even if Autopsy does not appear to have a function that allows smooth export of the text index, the index stored in the case folder can be extracted manually and used for password cracking.

E-mail Parser looks for local MBOX and PST files and extracts e-mails from them. This module would, for instance, be able to extract e-mails from Outlook and Thunderbird that are stored locally on the computer being examined.

[1]https://wiki.sleuthkit.org/index.php?title=Autopsy_3rd_Party_Modules

E01 verifier uses hash sums to detect corrupted E01 forensic images.

Interesting files identifier is an ingest module that lets you specify files or folders that you are interested in and then receive an alert if any files matching your criteria is found. You can specify criteria by file or path name, file size, last modified date, and file type.

PhotoRec carver is the file carver included in Autopsy; it will search unallocated space and attempt to find and rebuild files. This ingest module will recognize loads of file types and, in contrast to the name, not only pictures. The full list of known file types can be found online[2] and includes common (and uncommon) file formats for pictures, documents, compound files, and more.

Correlation engine lets you set up a database common to different cases that can be used to correlate data between cases and images. The idea is to provide an easy way to see if data existing in one case or forensic image is also present in another.

Encryption detector is an ingest module that attempts to identify files that could be encrypted based on an entropy test. An entropy test is basically a test of randomness and can detect encrypted files as they will appear to have random data. However, an entropy test will usually generate a number of false positives as other file types, such as compressed files, also tend to appear random.

Virtual machine extractor attempts to locate and extract virtual machine files.

Android Analyzer can extract data from a physical dump of an android device including text messages and call logs. Mobile forensics is, as you surely noted by now, not a primary target of this book, and this module is therefore not covered.

After selecting the ingest modules to run at case creation, the selected evidence will be added to the case, and ingest modules will be executed. Note that this process can be time-consuming, and in forensics, time-consuming means that some can take hours or even days to complete depending on the size of the evidence. When the selected ingest modules are completed, it is time to start analyzing the case using Autopsy.

17.6.2 Autopsy Overview

This section will present an overview of the Autopsy interface. Note that, just as with the FTK overview, the intention is to present enough to get you going rather than a comprehensive guide. The interface is shown in Fig. 17.10.

As shown in Fig. 17.10, the left pane in Autopsy resembles a file browser. This is where you can browse the contents of your data source in a couple of different ways.

- A1 is your common file browser where you can browse the folders and files in the data source you are examining; files and folders are structured as they are structured on the computer you are analyzing. Above that, note that there can

[2] https://www.cgsecurity.org/wiki/File_Formats_Recovered_By_PhotoRec

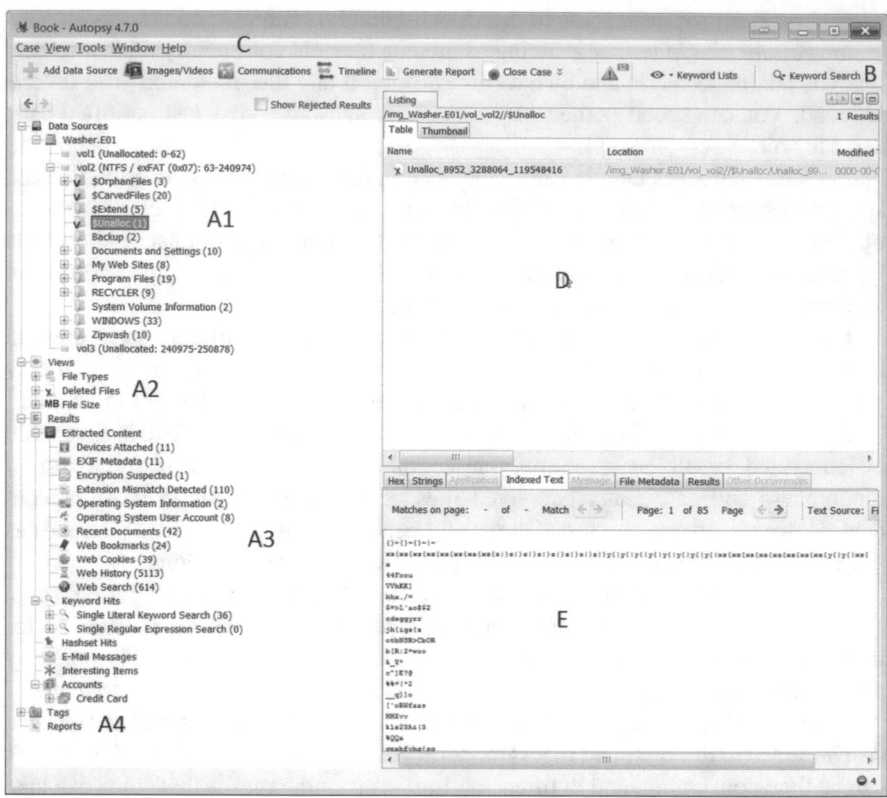

Fig. 17.10 Autopsy interface

be red crosses on some of the files and folders in the structure. This indicates a deleted file or folder that has been recovered.

- A2 provides you with an alternative way of browsing files. In A2, you can list files based on file type (extension or signature), file size, or single out deleted files that have been recovered.
- A3 is where the results of ingest modules are presented. In the sample case, there are quite a few results here since all ingest modules were executed. A3 is also where you will find search hits from text and regular expression searches.
- A4 is where you will find files that you tagged and reports that you generated, more on that soon.

Moving on to the top pane denoted B in Fig. 17.10, this pane has a number of useful buttons starting with *Add Data Source* that allows you to add another data source to the case. This will take you to the same dialogue that was presented before where you can select a data source for your case and configure what ingest modules to run. The next button *images/videos* will take you to the built-in image and video gallery that can be used for analysis and categorization of such files. This is a feature

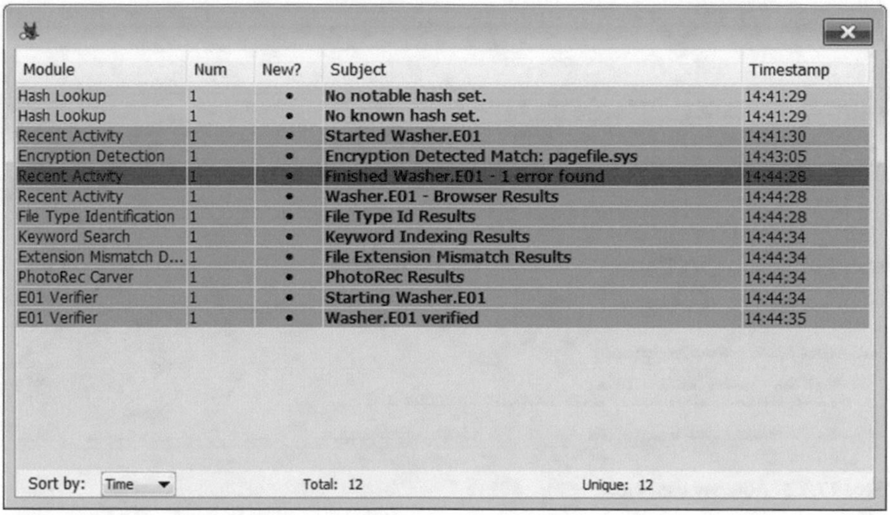

Module	Num	New?	Subject	Timestamp
Hash Lookup	1	•	No notable hash set.	14:41:29
Hash Lookup	1	•	No known hash set.	14:41:29
Recent Activity	1	•	Started Washer.E01	14:41:30
Encryption Detection	1	•	Encryption Detected Match: pagefile.sys	14:43:05
Recent Activity	1	•	Finished Washer.E01 - 1 error found	14:44:28
Recent Activity	1	•	Washer.E01 - Browser Results	14:44:28
File Type Identification	1	•	File Type Id Results	14:44:28
Keyword Search	1	•	Keyword Indexing Results	14:44:34
Extension Mismatch D...	1	•	File Extension Mismatch Results	14:44:34
PhotoRec Carver	1	•	PhotoRec Results	14:44:34
E01 Verifier	1	•	Starting Washer.E01	14:44:34
E01 Verifier	1	•	Washer.E01 verified	14:44:35

Sort by: Time Total: 12 Unique: 12

Fig. 17.11 Autopsy summary of ingest results

that is extremely useful in several cases, not least child exploitation cases. The next button *communications* will open an interface where communication data from e-mail, social media, and chat applications will be parsed out for analysis. Continuing on, the *timeline* button allows you to organize and see events based on when they occurred and can be used for timelining as described in Chap. 12. There are three sub-interfaces that will be further described at the end of this section on Autopsy. The final buttons in the B pane are *Generate report* and *Close case* that let you generate reports and close the case. Report generation is left for you to discover on your own.

Moving on in the B pane, the next point of interest is the yellow triangle. It does not provide warnings; instead, it provides a summary of the results from ingest modules. The Windows that appears upon clicking the triangle is shown in Fig. 17.11.

Ending the B pane is *keyword list* and *keyword search* that provide a quick way to search using lists of keywords or individual keywords.

Looking at the top menu denoted C in Fig. 17.10, it contains the following menus:

- Case that allows you to open, close, and delete cases as well as create new cases. There is also a selection for adding a new data source to the current case.
- View contains options that can modify the layout of Autopsy.
- Tools contain another way to reach the interfaces reachable by the B pane; above that, it contains some other useful features. First, there is the feature *file search by attribute* that lets you filter out files based on attributes such as name, size, and date. Then, there is *run ingest modules* that let you rerun ingest modules or run ingest modules that have not been run yet. The remaining options in the *Tools*

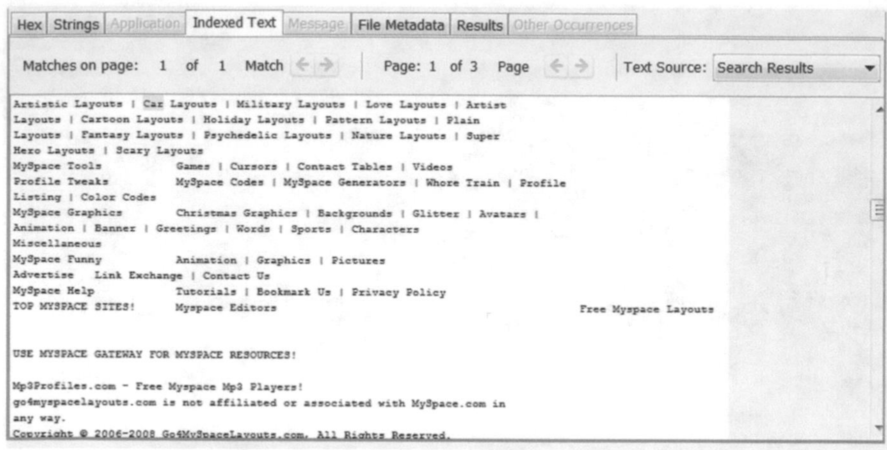

Fig. 17.12 Autopsy data view

menu let you add and manage plugins. As described before, there are several third-party modules available for download, and you may also write your own. Finally, the *Tools* menu also contains the *options* menu that lets you configure global options for Autopsy.
- Windows provides yet more options on how to organize the Autopsy interface.
- Help provides a help section including diagnostic information and links to online and offline help manuals.

Looking at the pane denoted D in Fig. 17.10, this is your file listing pane where the content of whatever is marked in the A pane will be displayed. Note that this pane contains a tab called *thumbnails* that can be used to display thumbnails of pictures in the folder marked in the A pane. This is actually a very useful way to single out the pictures in a folder that you are analyzing.

Finalizing the interface overview, we will look to the pane denoted E in Fig. 17.10. This is the actual data pane, and it is shown in greater detail in Fig. 17.12.

This pane provides you with different ways of viewing the data of whatever is marked in the D pane. When you mark a file in the D pane, the default behaviors of Autopsy are to display it using the *application* tab. This tab will present the file you are viewing as it is supposed to be viewed, i.e., pictures will be viewed as pictures. The other tabs, from left to right, work as follows:

- Hex will present the actual data of a file, presented in hexadecimal and including the file offset.
- Strings will attempt to parse out individual strings in the file data.
- Indexed text will basically provide the same interface as *strings,* but any hits from text or regular expressions will be marked in yellow.
- Messages should attempt to parse out individual messages in a file.
- File metadata will display metadata relating to a file.

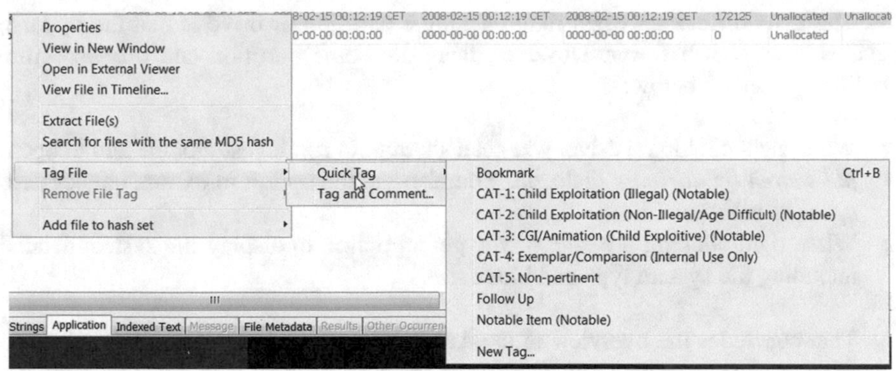

Fig. 17.13 Right click menu for a file

- Results will present an overview of results from ingest modules that are relevant for the file marked in the D pane.
- Other occurrences will display information generated by the *correlation engine* ingest module.

Knowing how the interface of Autopsy is structured, analyzing evidence comes down to using different views, searches, and ingest modules to look at and identify data that is of interest. However, when finding something of interest, you may want to do something to that. By right clicking an object, you can display a selection of tasks that you can do to a specific partition, drive, file, or folder. Depending on what type of object you are selecting, there will be some differences in the options available. The options for files are shown in Fig. 17.13.

The options available for a file or folder, from the right click menu, are described below:

- Properties will show the file metadata and other information about the file that has been extracted by Autopsy using ingest modules, for instance, hash values.
- View in new Windows will create a new data pane showing the file.
- Open in external viewer will open the file with the system default application for the file type.
- View file in timeline will open the timeline feature and show the point in time relating to one of the time stamps for the file.
- Extract file will let you extract the file to your computer.
- Search for files with the same MD5 hash will search for other files with the same hash value as the file you are examining.
- Tag file will let you bookmark or tag the file, there are several precreated tags, you may also create your own tags, and you may remove the tag with the remove file tag selection.
- Add file to hash set allows you to add the file to a hash list that has been included in the case.

The main difference when right clicking a partition or drive is that the options available are much fewer. However, there are some partition and drive-specific options presented below:

- When right clicking a drive, you get a shortcut to run ingest module and to open *file search by attribute* dialogue. You also get the option to extract unallocated space as individual files.
- When right clicking a partition, you get an option to display file system details including file system type and block size.

That concludes the overview of the Autopsy interface, but before the section on Autopsy is ended, the views available from the pane denoted B in Fig. 17.10 will be explained.

17.6.3 The Image Gallery

The image gallery is a feature of Autopsy that can be used for image analysis. It is a special interface where you can view images and videos in a quick way and also categorize them. It is intended for use with the ingest modules *hash lookup, file type identification*, and *EXIF parser*. Using *hash lookup,* Autopsy will automatically categorize images by supplying hash sets of known files. This can be used to automatically exclude images that are known to not have evidentiary values or to automatically categorize images that are known to have evidentiary values, for example, child abuse images. The *EXIF parser* will parse out EXIF information from images that can be displayed within the image gallery, and *file type identification* can help identify images where the file extension has been modified so that they are not missed in the examination.

When the task of an examination is to analyze images, there are three more reasons why using the image gallery is a smooth approach. First, thumbnails are used rather than the actual images, reducing the time needed to load the images. When scrolling through loads of images, this approach will heavily improve the loading speed of images and, thus, the time needed for the examination. The second benefit is that all images in the case can be presented in one listing; thus, no images will be missed by accident. The third benefit is that it supports categorization, meaning that there are built-in categories, designed for child exploitation cases, and you can just press a number corresponding to a category in order to categorize a picture. Videos will be shown as a number of frames that allow for quick analysis of those as well. The image gallery interface is shown in Fig. 17.14.

The following is an explanation of the marked areas of Fig. 17.14:

- A is the listing where you browse and select what you want to view. The default setting groups images by folders and let you browse the folder structure of the computer.

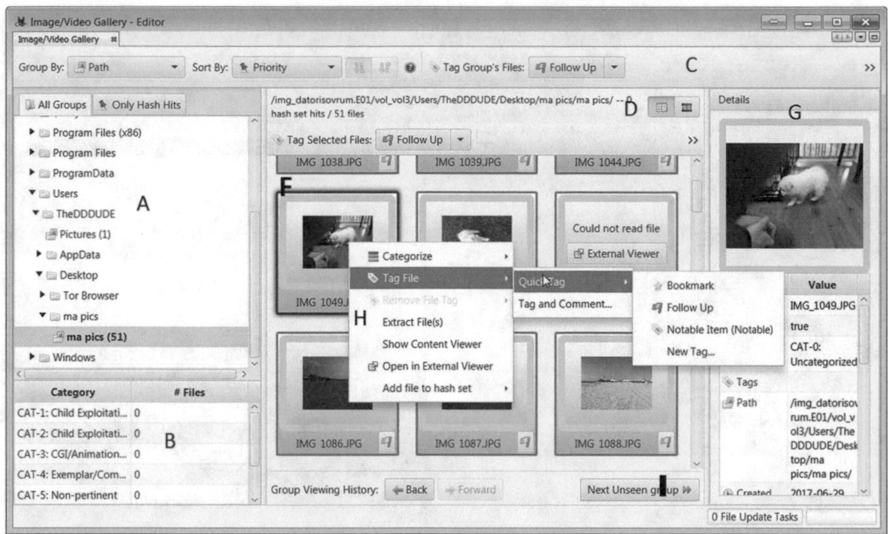

Fig. 17.14 Autopsy image gallery

- B is a listing of the categories that are available and counters that describe how many images have been categorized into each category.
- C is where you mainly control how to group images for the listing in A. You can group by folder location, file type, category, tag, camera make and model, or hash set if *hash lookup* using hash sets has been used. C also contains a zoom function that allows you to control the size of the thumbnails listed.
- D is a toolbar that lets you tag or categorize files and change from thumbnail view to viewing individual images listed in F.
- F is where files in the group selected in A are listed.
- G is a pane where more information including metadata about the image marked in F is found. This pane will include EXIF data if *EXIF parser* has been used.
- Finally, H is the menu that is opened if you right click an image. What you can do here is categorization and tagging, but you can also extract an image or open in the system default viewer. Finally, you can also select to add the image hash value to an existing hash set.

17.6.4 Communications

The communications feature is a feature that provides a swift interface to communication data that has been detected by Autopsy. This would include e-mail messages, chat, and calls. However, note that Autopsy is not able to parse out all types of communication from all types of communicating applications. Thus, while

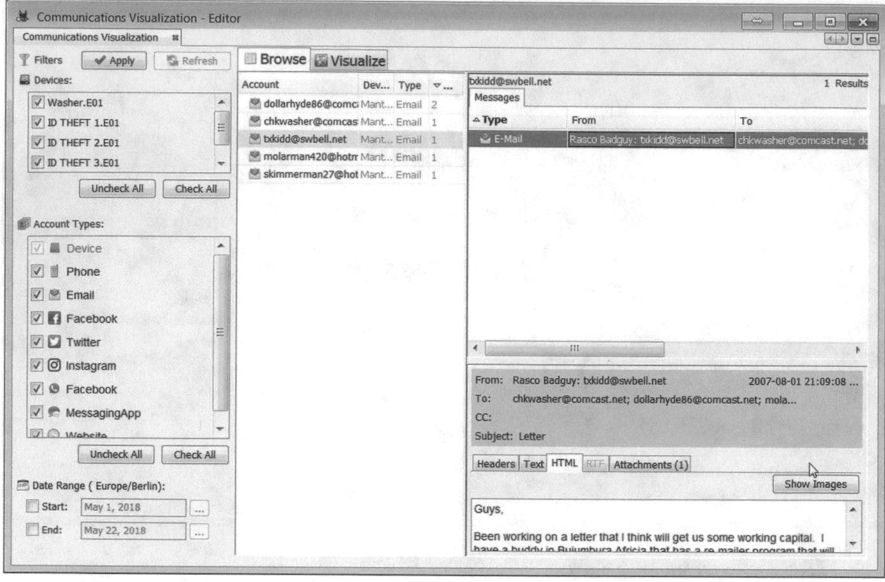

Fig. 17.15 Autopsy communications overview

providing a neat interface to analyzing communications, this feature should not be considered an alternative to manual examination. The default view of the communications feature is shown in Fig. 17.15.

As shown in Fig. 17.15, the communications feature comes with three different panes. The orientation of data in the communications feature is around accounts, and you can use the leftmost pane to filter out accounts depending on the data source where they are located and what type of account they are. The middle pane will display a listing of the accounts, and the right pane will show the data in the account marked in the middle pane. Further, it is possible to right click an account and visualize its communications. This provides a visual interface that displays whom the selected account has been communicating with, as displayed in Fig. 17.16.

17.6.5 Timeline

Now, it is time to sum up the overview of the tool Autopsy. This will be done by looking at the timeline feature. In essence, this feature provides an interface where you can see events on the computer you are examining on a timeline and is great for cases where activities around a specific time are of importance or if the timelining technique is to be used. Note that a timeline can be very full of data as all events containing a time stamp are included. One way to remove unimportant data is to use *hash lookup* to detect files that are irrelevant to the case and exclude them from the analysis. The interface of the timeline feature is shown in Fig. 17.17.

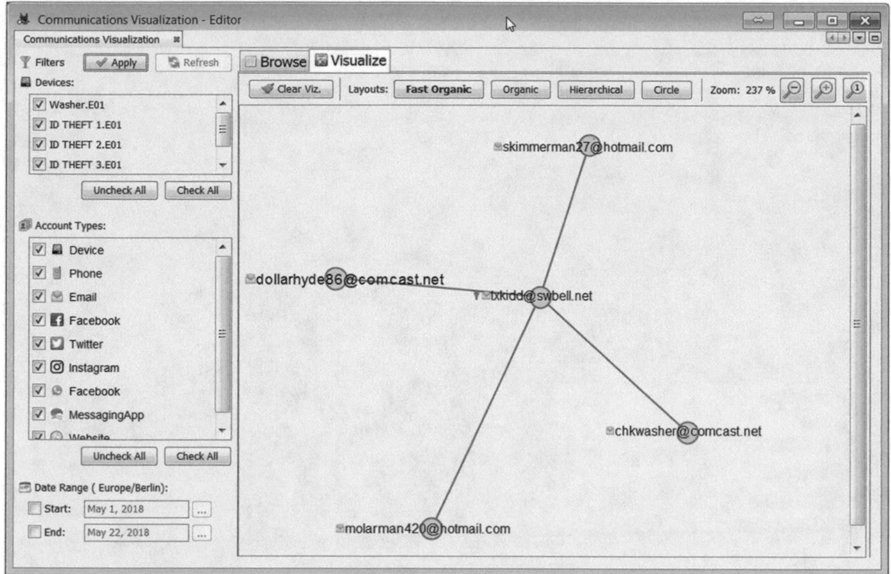

Fig. 17.16 Autopsy communications visualization

In essence, the timeline feature contains four panes that work as follows:

- A will let you select how you want to view and filter events. You can select to group events in terms of years, days, or minutes. Further, you can filter events on several properties including event time as parsed by Autopsy, events matching a hash set, or tags defined by you.
- The B pane will display the events and let you zoom into a specific date range. The default view will present events as a diagram, but you can also select to display them in a list or more detailed view. By hitting the arrows to the right in this pane, you may save the current view as a snapshot.
- The C pane will display the individual events in a group that you marked in the B pane.
- The D pane will show granular information about a single event marked in the C pane.

17.7 Registry Explorer

A good open-source alternative for registry analysis is the Registry Explorer created by Erik Zimmerman. This section is dedicated to describe how it can be used for analysis of registry hives. The version Registry Explorer used in this book is 0.9.0.0, and it was downloaded from https://ericzimmerman.github.io/. Compared to

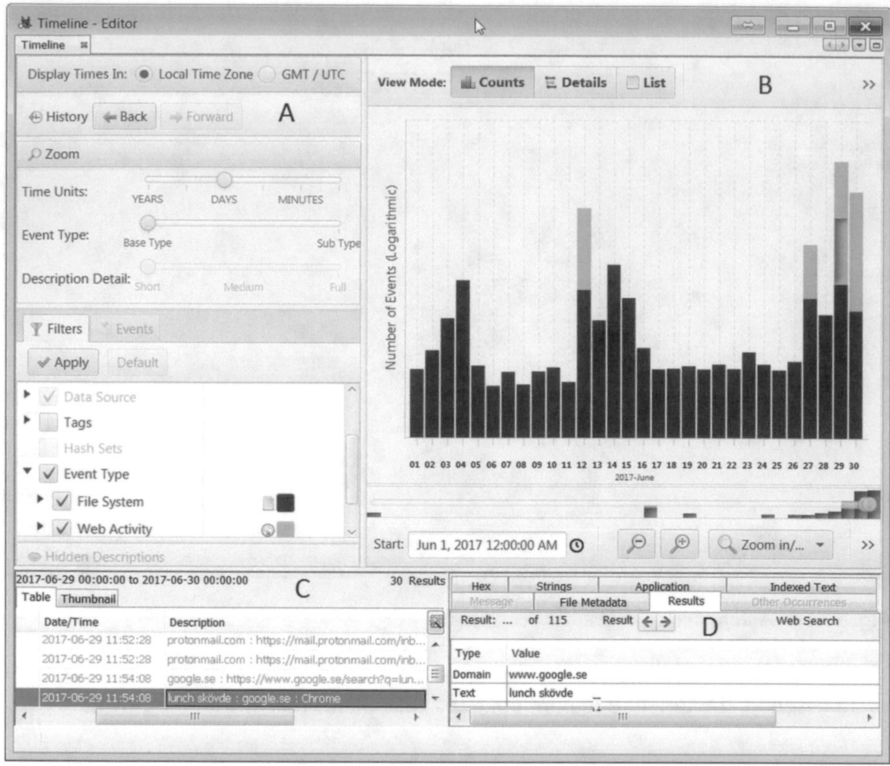

Fig. 17.17 Autopsy timeline feature

AccessData Registry Viewer, the most apparent differences appear to be the following:

- You may load several hives into Registry Explorer for simultaneous analysis. You may also save your work as a project and continue later, and that is a huge benefit over Registry Viewer's one hive at the time approach.
- Registry Explorer does not provide any very good way of reporting. You may export any data that you see, but in the mind of the author, you have to compile your own reports.

Well then, not that is out of the way, let us get going with Registry Explorer. An overview of the interface is shown in Fig. 17.18.

The interface is straightforward and similar to the interface of AccessData Registry Viewer. The right pane displays the registry hive you are examining as a browse tree structure where every node is a key or a sub-key. There is also a tab in this pane that allows you to switch to bookmark view; the bookmarks are registry keys that are defined as bookmarks by default or by the user to allow for quick access.

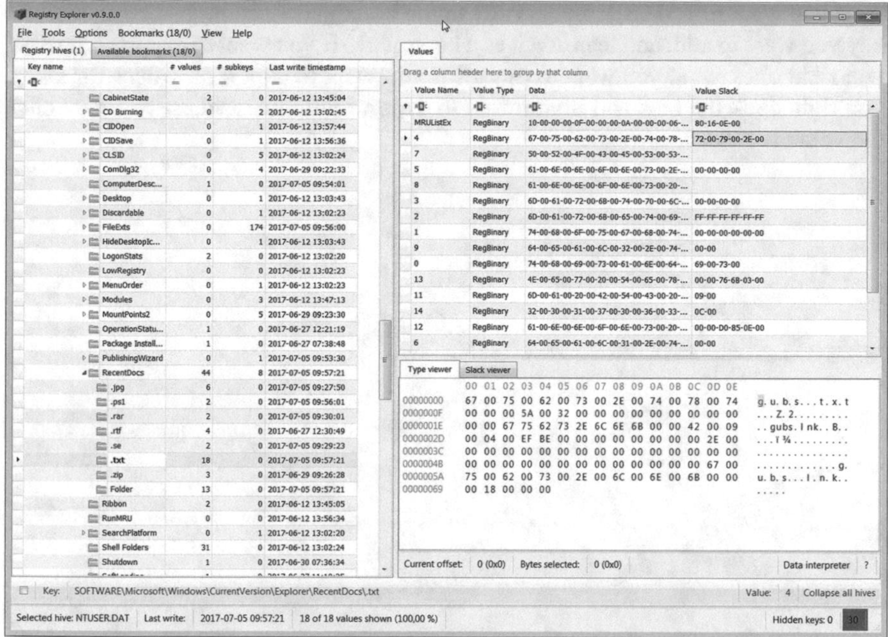

Fig. 17.18 Registry Explorer overview

The top right pane contains the values that belong to a marked key, and the bottom right pane displays the data relating to that key in hex and ASCII. A quite useful feature of Registry Explorer is the data interpreter. If you mark a section of the hexadecimal data and press the data interpreter, Registry Explorer will interpret the data selection in a number of different ways allowing you to, for instance, convert time stamps in different formats on the fly.

Then, there is the top menu that provides some important and useful functions as follows:

- File is where you open and close registry hives as well as save the current project. You may also export the current listing in the left pane as a report. Note that this report will only report what is seen on screen in the left pane.
- Tools includes the search function where you can search for keys and values using strings and regular expressions. You can also limit a search to keys within a certain time range.
- Options includes options that controls the behavior of Registry Explorer. This includes whether or not to attempt to recover deleted values and settings for how time stamps should be displayed.
- Bookmarks contains shortcuts to the bookmarked keys.
- View and help dictates the layout of Registry Explorer and contains a help section, respectively.

If you want to add an additional key to the bookmark section, just right click the key you want to add, and then add it as a bookmark. If you want to export some data, you right click what you want to export. If you want to export all values for a key, you right click the key, and if you want to export individual values, you right click the value you need.

Part IV
Memory Forensics

In previous parts, memory has been discussed as an unorganized data blob. This is not really true; the memory does have a structure and can be analyzed in a structured way. As has been previously presented, whatever files or processes that a computer is working on are stored in memory. That implies that there is also a structure of how to store data in memory. This part is devoted to describing the foundations of how data is stored and managed in memory and a practical introduction to how different graphical and command line tools can be used for forensic analysis of memory in a criminal or corporate setting. For those that are interested, a very deep discussion on memory forensics using the tool Volatility is given in the book *The Art of Memory Forensics* by Ligh et al. (2014).

Reference

Ligh MH, Case A, Levy J, Walters A (2014) The art of memory forensics: detecting malware and threats in Windows, Linux, and Mac memory. Wiley, Indianapolis

Memory Analysis 18

As we know by now, the memory or RAM or whatever you want to call it will hold what the computer is currently working on. Further, it is a common truth that whatever is used by the computer must be in its "real" form in memory. While this is not necessarily always true due to memory encryption techniques and other anti-forensic approaches, there is still a very good chance that what is lingering in memory will be in its true form. That means that malware that is obfuscated when stored on a hard drive will assume its true form in memory, encrypted data will be in its decrypted state, and so on. Moreover, as the data in memory is volatile and removed every time the computer is turned off, you can be sure that whatever is found in memory has been put there during the current runtime of the computer. This makes the information current and that is good from a forensic standpoint. While the computer memory has been treated as an unorganized blob of data throughout this book, it is actually stored in a structured way. The final chapters will discuss how memory is managed and how a structured approach to memory analysis can be used in law enforcement as well as in incident response. This part begins with a theoretical background to some selected memory management topics and forensic techniques.

18.1 Data Storage

Before moving on, there are some fundamental topics to discuss regarding how data is stored in memory. At a glance, the memory can be compared to a hard drive in that it is a storage device that has several pages. The pages are contiguous blocks of the memory and are used to store data. As such, memory pages can be compared to sectors on a hard drive. It should also be noted that it is possible for the computer to swap a memory page out of memory and store it on disk to leave room for another process to be stored in memory. This process is called paging, and the pages that are swapped out will be stored in pagefile.sys that makes pagefile.sys a forensic artifact that can hold the same information as memory with the difference that it will survive a reboot.

J. Kävrestad, *Fundamentals of Digital Forensics*,
https://doi.org/10.1007/978-3-030-38954-3_18

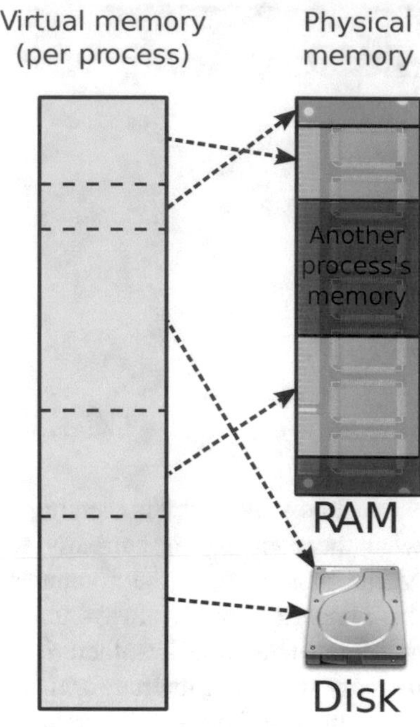

Fig. 18.1 Virtual to physical memory mapping by Ehamberg (2009). (CC BY-SA 3.0 (https://creativecommons.org/licenses/by-sa/3.0), from Wikimedia Commons)

Digging deeper into how data is stored in memory, it can be described as a linear supply of pages. The addressing of the pages is expressed as the offset from the first page and commonly written in hexadecimal. As we will soon discover, in the practical part of this section, a memory address can be expressed as "0xFFFFAAAA" and is then pointing to a page that begins at offset FFFFAAAA in physical memory. This would describe how memory allocation and addressing would work if modern computers worked only with one physical address space. However, modern computers employ a technique called virtual memory. In essence, every running process is given its own virtual address space. Within this virtual memory space, the process can allocate contiguous memory pages that are then mapped to physical memory by the computer. The benefits of applying virtual memory are that it is possible for a process to be allocated more memory than is physically available, and pages used by that process can be swapped between the actual memory and secondary storage, transparently to the process. Further, the process can allocate contiguous memory pages within its virtual memory even if the pages are not contiguous in the actual physical memory.

A consequence of using virtual memory is that the operating system must map the virtual memory pages of a process to the physical memory page where the data is actually stored. Note that pages in the virtual address space may be paged out from the physical memory and stored on disk. This process is visualized in Fig. 18.1.

As shown in Fig. 18.1, every process has its own virtual memory space that is then mapped to pages in physical memory or, if paged out, to a secondary storage device. This creates a situation where the processes will handle its memory pages as contiguous even if they can be fragmented in physical memory. Thus, to do a structured analysis of a memory dump, you need a software that is capable of doing this mapping. If you analyze a dump of physical memory as a big blob of data, there is a good chance that data stored in a contiguous manner in the virtual memory of a process is, in fact, scattered all over the dump of the physical memory.

That is, for how storage space is allocated and addressed in memory, of equal importance is how data is structured. With a simplistic explanation, data can be stored using basic or abstract data types. The basic data types commonly encountered during a memory analysis are those defined in the C programming language and do, for instance, include integers, chars, and floats. The abstract data types are rather aggregations or collections of basic data types. As one example, a list of running processes would be stored in a doubly linked list. Every entry in the list would contain one process that could be stored as an array that in turn can hold strings that are made up from chars. While this book does not make claim on fully describing every possible data type, the remainder of this sub-chapter will highlight some of the data types that are of importance for the understanding of the remainder of this section on memory forensics.

An array is essentially a fixed-length list of data types of the same type. Every entry into an array is called an element, and it is addressed using an index. As such, the first element in the array will be given index number 0, the next element index number 1, and so on. A plain array may only contain elements of the same type, like chars or ints or floats. The array is fixed size by nature and would be stored contiguously in memory.

Records and strings can be seen as special cases of arrays where a record is an array that can hold different types of data, even other arrays. Strings, however, can only hold character codes from predetermined character sets, such as ASCII.

Linked lists are somewhat similar to arrays but more flexible by nature. What differs a linked list from an array is that it can contain data of different types and that the elements are not indexed using numbers. Rather, the order of the elements will be organized using links that can be updated as needed by a process to add or remove elements or to rearrange the order of the elements. Notable for this book are two different ways of implementing linked lists, called singly or doubly linked lists. A singly linked list is implemented by letting every element in the list include a link to the next element. In a doubly linked list, every element will also include a link to the element before. A singly linked list can only be traversed in one direction, from start to end, while a doubly linked list can be traversed in both directions. There is also a special case of the singly linked list called circular linked list; this list contains a link from the last element to the first and can, thus, be traversed in full no matter what element you begin with. The first element in a linked list is called the head, and the last is called the tail. The different linked lists are visualized in Fig. 18.2.

Before moving, it should be noted that different operating systems and operating system versions handle memory allocation and management in different ways. A structured memory analysis is dependent on a tool that is able to read the memory in the same way as the operating system that managed the memory. As such, the remainder of this section will discuss memory analysis in criminal and corporate

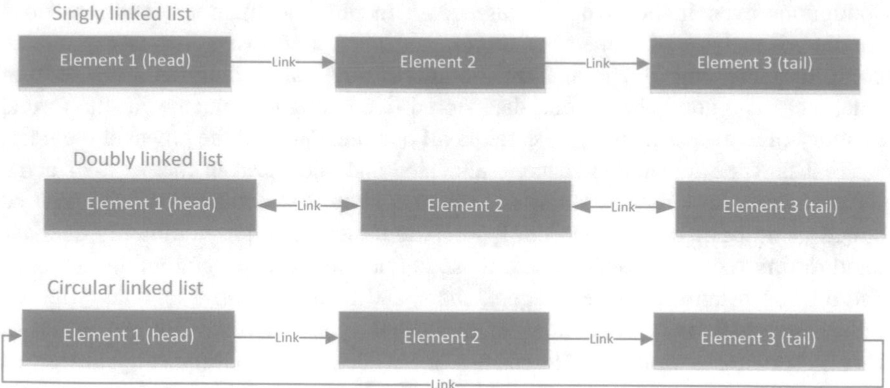

Fig. 18.2 Linked lists

settings beginning with a discussion on a tool called Volatility that can be used for the purpose of memory analysis.

18.2 Processes

A very common place to look for information of forensic value is among the running processes. The list of running processes will tell you what processes that are running at the moment and can be viewed from a running Windows computer using the Powershell command *ps*. Likewise, it is possible to extract a list of processes that was running when a memory dump was acquired. Examining active processes will give you an idea of what programs were running on the examined machine and can be a first step in finding malware or signs of intrusions.

Processes are identified using Process ID numbers (PID) and every process is spawned by some other process, called its parent. There is always a parent process ID (PPID) that identifies the parent of a process, except for the SYSTEM process whose parent is PPID 0, the system idle process. The processes are stored using a specific data structure, and the process list is stored as a doubly linked list. It is common for processes to create sockets to enable network communication, and examining those sockets is a very important part of memory forensics.

While looking for malware and intrusions one would look at processes, those will either hijack some existing process or create their own processes to do whatever they plan to do. In law enforcement, looking at processes is commonly more of an enumeration task carried out to get an idea of what software that is running on the examined device. Anyhow, hunting malware and intrusions is a tricky task—there is no standard definition how malware should be created. However, there is a common denominator. Processes spawned of hijacked as a part of intrusion or malware will behave differently then what is normal. Thus, looking for compromised processes would typically be about looking for process behaviors that is not normal. This can include looking for attempts to hide from listings. For instance, malware may hide from process listings by modifying pointers in the doubly linked list to go undetected by normal processes. Also, it is important to look for sockets created by processes to see if processes are trying to communicate in ways that they should not communicate. While experience and knowledge are important, some common forensic techniques include whitelisting and using indicators of compromise, as will be discussed later in this chapter.

18.3 Forensic Techniques

While the ending two chapters of this book will discuss some practical ways to find interesting artifacts in memory, this ending section to this chapter will discuss some general more automatic approaches to memory analysis, geared toward incident response. In essence, they involve defining normal operation and then detect and mark what is normal or what is abnormal. A reasonable part of incident response preparation would be to get a good understanding of what you should expect to find during an analysis session of a clean machine under normal working condition. That insight will tell you what you can disregard if you analyze a machine that is thought to be compromised. For instance, knowing that it is common and reasonable for the SYSTEM process to be associated with sockets that enable communication on ports 137, 138, and 139, you do not have to focus on those connections. However, if the same process is communicating on port 20,000, you might have a problem. In essence, a good practice is to assemble a list of processes and sockets that are common in your environment and match against running processes and active sockets on a machine that you are examining. A common way to automate this analysis is by the use of whitelisting.

Whitelisting has been described previously and involves creating and downloading sets of hash values for processes and data that is known to be good. Then hash values for the data in the memory dump that you are analyzing are also calculated and matched against the hash values in the hash sets. This way, you may filter out data that is known to be good. Since processes that are modified due to intrusion or malware will generate other hash values than the ones that have not been altered, whitelisting is a good way to filter out data that is known to be good and highlight data that could indicate an incident.

An opposite approach is to use *indicators of compromise (IoC)* to automatically identify traces of known incidents. Indicators of compromise are essentially definitions of incidents that can be downloaded and included in analysis software. IoC definitions will hold information about how certain incidents manifest themselves and are used to automatically find indications of those incidents. To exemplify, consider some malware that is hijacking the SYSTEM process and makes it communicate on port 20,000, a nonstandard behavior. An IoC for this malware would look for that specific behaviors and report if it is found. There are two big ways in which IoCs can be used in incident response. First, much like whitelisting a computer incident response team (CIRT) can prepare by downloading or creating

IoCs for difference incidents and evaluate memory dumps using those. If analyzed machines are compromised using any of the incidents covered by the set of IoCs, there is a good chance that the incident can be identified swiftly. Further, as the IoCs describe incidents, they do describe unwanted behaviors, meaning that they can, if luck is present, identify unknown incidents with similar behavior as well-known incidents. The IoC approach can also be used to analyze the extent of an incident even if it is new. In this case, a CIRT that identified a new incident can create an IoC and use that in analysis of other devices that may be compromised.

That will conclude this theoretical introduction to memory forensics. The remainder of the book will introduce some software that can be used in memory analysis and provide a practical introduction to the area.

18.4 Questions and Tasks

Here are the questions and tasks for this chapter.

1. What is paging?
2. How is storage space in memory allocated?
3. What is virtual and physical memory mapping?
4. Name and briefly describe the different types of linked lists.

Reference

Ehamberg (2009) Virtual memory.svg. Available online: https://commons.wikimedia.org/wiki/File:Virtual_memory.svg. Fetched 1 June 2018

Memory Analysis Tools 19

Just as good tools are essential for forensic analysis of secondary storage devices, they are essential to good memory analysis as well. Also, while a forensic expert needs tools that are good, easy to use, and good at producing material, it is still vital that the tools are reliant to produce quality data. Two well-used tools, which will be introduced in this chapter, are Volatility and Redline. Volatility is an open-source command line tool for memory analysis that is extremely versatile and flexible. Redline is a free tool developed and maintained by FireEye. Redline provides a graphical user interface and can do memory analysis as well as analyze volatile data from other sources and seems to be a tool more geared toward incident response. In an attempt to distinguish the tools, one could say that Volatility allows for more in-depth analysis, while Redline is more automated.

19.1 Volatility

A well-known and well-used tool for memory analysis is Volatility. It also happens to be an open source and free to use (Volatility Foundation 2017). In essence, it is actually a framework more than a single tool and can be seen as a collection of modules that can be utilized for memory analysis. It is written in Python and that in combination with the modular design allows for quite simple development of new modules as needed. As it is the opinion of the author that Volatility is somewhat of a tool that is well-known by a small society but hard to grasp if you never seen it before, this chapter will in turn describe the core of the tool and introduce how to get hold of it and the basics of how to use it. The upcoming chapters will show and discuss examples of how it can be used. Also, being a demonstrating chapter, this is the final chapter that does not contain any end-of-chapter questions.

J. Kävrestad, *Fundamentals of Digital Forensics*,
https://doi.org/10.1007/978-3-030-38954-3_19

```
root@volabox:/home/analyzer/Desktop/vola2_6/volatility# python vol.py -f memdump.mem --profile="Win10x64_16299" p
slist
Volatility Foundation Volatility Framework 2.6
Offset(V)          Name                    PID   PPID   Thds     Hnds   Sess  Wow64 Start
  Exit
------------------ -------------------- ------ ------ ------ -------- ------ ------ ------------------------------
- ------------------------------
0xffff9d032ce92440 System                    4      0     94        0 ------      0 2018-03-27 11:55:06 UTC+0000

0xffff9d032e546580 smss.exe                320      4      2        0 ------      0 2018-03-27 11:55:06 UTC+0000

0xffff9d032e4b7580 csrss.exe               404    396      9        0      0      0 2018-03-27 11:55:10 UTC+0000

0xffff9d032eb73080 smss.exe                476    320      0 --------      1      0 2018-03-27 11:55:11 UTC+0000
  2018-03-27 11:55:11 UTC+0000
0xffff9d032eb76080 wininit.exe             484    396      1        0      0      0 2018-03-27 11:55:11 UTC+0000
```

Fig. 19.1 Process listing with correct profile

```
/□??ctfmon.e        2468     216 79...2        0 ------        0 6236-07-21 07:00:39 UTC+0000
0xffff9d032f3e2578 --------------------   2728     256 79...4        0 ------        0 -
0xffff9d032f3943f8 ??o/□??explorer        2760     232 76...2        0 ------        0 6236-07-21 07:00:43 UTC+0000
0xffff9d032f84d578 --------------------   3120     292 79...4        0 ------        0
0xffff9d032f5b4578 05?.□??SearchUI        3292     256 80...2        0 ------        0
0xffff9d032f76e578 PF?/□??RuntimeB        3372     272 77...6        0 ------        0 6236-07-21 07:00:39 UTC+0000
0xffff9d032f9ec578 P??/□??RuntimeB        3540     272 80...0        0 ------        0 6236-07-21 07:00:39 UTC+0000
0xffff9d032fa7e578 0?D.□??SearchIn        3588     272 75...6        0 ------        0 6236-07-21 07:00:39 UTC+0000
0xffff9d032fbf3578 0>?/□??smartscr        3952     292 76...0        0 ------        0 6236-12-31 04:23:08 UTC+0000
0xffff9d032fcb4578 ?`?/□??SettingS        3264     408 76...8        0 ------        0 4409-10-27 08:20:09 UTC+0000
0xffff9d032faee578 `?Q/□??RuntimeB        4472     272 76...2        0 ------        0 6236-07-21 07:00:39 UTC+0000
0xffff9d032faf6578 ???/□??MSASCuiL        4572     232 80...6        0 ------        0 6236-07-21 07:00:39 UTC+0000
0xffff9d032fe72578 `??/□??VBoxTray        4660     252 80...0        0 ------        0 6236-07-21 07:00:39 UTC+0000
0xffff9d032fed5578 ?□/□??OneDrive         4764     312 78...8        0 ------        0 6236-07-21 07:00:39 UTC+0000
0xffff9d032f9ff078 ?nq/□??svchost.         952     364 80...0        0 ------        0 6236-07-21 14:38:47 UTC+0000
```

Fig. 19.2 Process listing with incorrect profile

19.1.1 What Is Volatility Made Up from?

From the viewpoint of a forensic examiner, Volatility is essentially made up of two things, profiles and plugins. The easiest way to describe them would be to say that profiles are used to make Volatility able to interpret a memory dump from a specific operating system and version, while plugins are the modules that actually do the analysis.

Starting with the profiles, they are used to make Volatility able to read a memory dump as it was seen by the computer that it was taken from. Given the previous discussion on data structures, paging, and virtual memory, it is evident that different operating system's versions may implement different methods in terms of how the data in memory is represented and used. Emulating this as perfect as possible is essential in order to get readable data from a memory dump. How profiles are created and what they are made up from is well beyond the scope of this book, but working with memory analysis, you should know that using a correct profile is essential for successful analysis. Luckily, Volatility includes a wealth of profiles for the most common operating systems, and whenever a new version comes along, a new profile is (commonly) released close thereafter. To visualize the need for a correct profile, look at Figs. 19.1 and 19.2 both showing a use case of Volatility used to look as the running processes of a computer at the time of a memory dump. Figure 19.1 shows a case where the correct profile is being used, and Fig. 19.2 shows a case where a slightly incorrect profile is being used.

Finding out what profile to use and how to get it is, as you surely understand, a very important part of a successful memory analysis endeavor. Luckily, as we will soon discover, Volatility can provide you with some assistance on that matter. If you try to use a profile that is totally incorrect, you will get an error message, but if you try to use a profile that is close to the correct one, Volatility will run and provide you with output. As the sample above demonstrates, it is important to make note of small errors in the output and try different profiles until a good one is identified.

The second part of Volatility that we need to know about is the plugins. While the profiles tell Volatility how to read a memory dump, the plugins will tell Volatility what to look for in the memory dump. In that regard, they are basically collections of code that decide what to search for in the memory data; one example was already presented in the example above where the plugin *pslist* was used to search for processes that were running at the time of the memory dump.

19.1.2 How to Get Volatility

One could argue that install instructions for a software have no place in a book such as this one. However, it has been noted by the author that the way you choose to install Volatility actually impacts its behavior and the forensics expert's ability to make a good analysis. So, to ensure that nothing gets lost because of how Volatility itself is acquired, a walkthrough of the different install options is hereby provided.

Being open source and free for use, Volatility is available on *GitHub*, and the easiest way to get hold of an updated version is to clone it from GitHub.[1] In this case, you would have to run Volatility on a Linux box. However, based on the author's personal experience, this is the most convenient way to go. An added bonus of cloning Volatility from GitHub is that you get the most updated profiles that are available. Using any of the other install options would leave you with the profiles that were packed into the install packet at the time when you downloaded it. For the practical parts of this section, Volatility was cloned from GitHub.

As an alternative to getting Volatility from GitHub, it is possible to download executables for Windows, Mac OS, and Linux as well as the source code from the Volatility Web page.[2] This alternative may be better suited in some cases, but keep in mind that with this option, you are stuck with the profiles that come packed into the executable at the time of download; also, the executables are updated less frequently than the GitHub repository.

[1]https://github.com/volatilityfoundation/volatility

[2]http://www.volatilityfoundation.org/releases

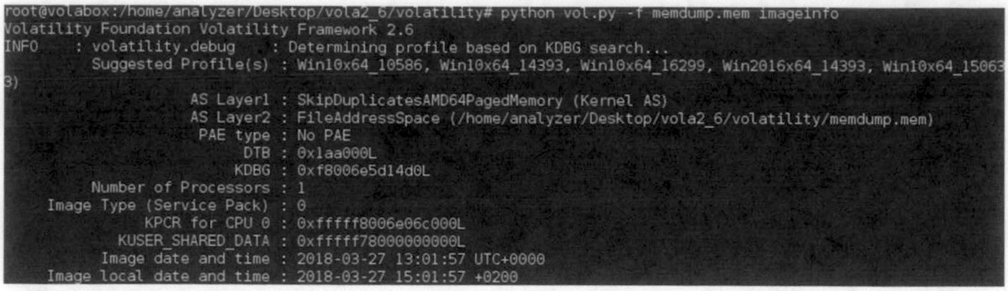

```
root@volabox:/home/analyzer/Desktop/vola2_6/volatility# python vol.py -f memdump.mem imageinfo
Volatility Foundation Volatility Framework 2.6
INFO    : volatility.debug    : Determining profile based on KDBG search...
          Suggested Profile(s) : Win10x64_10586, Win10x64_14393, Win10x64_16299, Win2016x64_14393, Win10x64_15063
3)
                     AS Layer1 : SkipDuplicatesAMD64PagedMemory (Kernel AS)
                     AS Layer2 : FileAddressSpace (/home/analyzer/Desktop/vola2_6/volatility/memdump.mem)
                      PAE type : No PAE
                           DTB : 0x1aa000L
                          KDBG : 0xf8006e5d14d0L
          Number of Processors : 1
     Image Type (Service Pack) : 0
                KPCR for CPU 0 : 0xfffff8006e06c000L
             KUSER_SHARED_DATA : 0xfffff78000000000L
           Image date and time : 2018-03-27 13:01:57 UTC+0000
     Image local date and time : 2018-03-27 15:01:57 +0200
```

Fig. 19.3 Volatility—imageinfo

19.1.3 Basic Usage

Getting to work with Volatility, the first thing to notice is that it is a command line tool. As such, it is built around using a CLI interface and passing commands and arguments to Volatility. If Volatility is acquired by cloning it from GitHub, simply go to the folder where it is stored and look for the Python script *vol.py* that is used to run Volatility. The basic syntax is as follows:

```
Python vol.py -f memoryimage --profile=selectedmemoryprofile module
```

Memory image is the path to the memory dump that you need to analyze. Selected memory profile is the memory profile you need Volatility to use. Finally, module is the task you want Volatility to run. Before moving further, you need to figure out the memory profile to use. You can make Volatility analyze the memory sample using the *imageinfo* module, as shown in Fig. 19.3.

Looking Fig. 19.3, you can see that Volatility suggests different profiles that can be used. Any will commonly work, to some extent, but otherwise it is a trial-and-error approach among the suggested profiles; you may notice differences in the output data, and testing to find the best working profile is encouraged. Note that the profile name must be spelled with exact casing. *Imageinfo* will also report the time when the memory dump was created, expressed in UTC and local time.

Once the profile is determined, you may start using the different plugins that are available for memory analysis. Some of the plugins will be described in the upcoming chapters. For a complete documentation of the available plugins, there is a wealth of information available in the online documentation.[3] You may also view available plugins through the help that is built into Volatility by issuing the following command:

- Python vol.py –h

[3] https://github.com/volatilityfoundation/volatility/wiki/Command-Reference

19.1.4 Volshell

As a final point before moving onto the practical demonstrations on memory analysis, volshell will be briefly introduced. Volshell is basically an interface that you can invoke that lets you explore a memory dump interactively. In essence, it allows you to print data at a specific address of the memory relating to a process. You may also walk linked lists and disassemble instructions at a certain address. As such, volshell allows you to view the data or a process in an address of you choosing and allows you to see the exact instructions of a process in memory; during malware analysis, this can be extremely valuable. However, this is a level of memory analysis that is well beyond the scope of this book. If you are interested, there are several sources that can provide you with further knowledge, including "The art of memory forensics" by Ligh et al. (2014).

The remainder of this section will introduce memory forensics in a more practical manner. Since there are some distinct differences in how one would carry out different tasks in different scenarios, the upcoming chapter will discuss memory analysis from a crime investigation scenario, and the section will end with a discussion on memory analysis with the target of detecting malware.

19.2 Redline

While Redline is not an open source, it is free to use and can be downloaded from the website of its creator, FireEye.[4] Redline can be used as a memory analysis tool, but is also able to analyze data from other sources to provide a more comprehensive analysis of volatile data. In contrast to Volatility, Redline is a graphical tool that lists information in different views, much like Autopsy and FTK. While this approach removes the ability to actually read memory data, an ability of Volatility, it may be easier for the novice taking her first steps into memory forensics. The remainder of this section will discuss the fundamentals of Redline. Usage examples, in the context of incident response, are provided in the ending chapter of this book.

19.2.1 Components of Redline

Redline is essentially made up from two components that can be used separately, a collector and an analyzer. The collector part is essentially a script creator that allows the examiner to create an agent used to collect data from an examined host. This makes the redline collector an acquisition tool that can be used to gather information from a device, and the gathered information is tailored to be analyzed with the analyzer part of Redline. When creating a collector, the forensic expert can choose what data to collect, and the options include browsing history, owner information,

[4] https://www.fireeye.com/

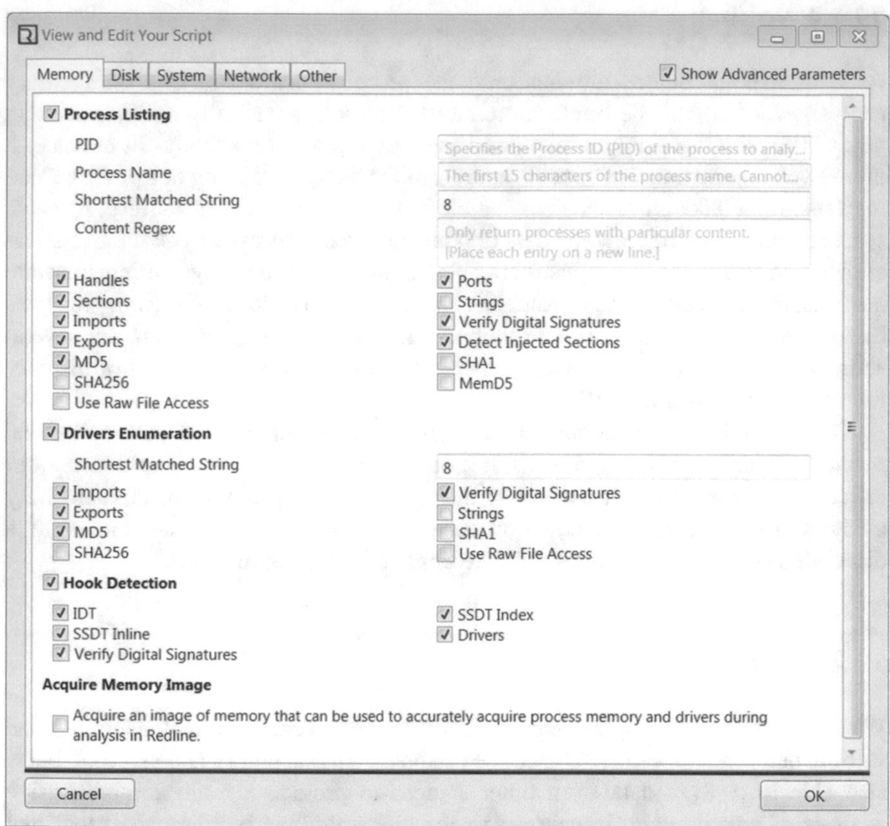

Fig. 19.4 Redline collector configuration

memory dump, and more. The actual collector can be executed on the target device, from a USB storage device without installation. The windows used to select option for a collector is presented in Fig. 19.4.

The analysis part of Redline is essentially an interface that allows you to browse the data from whatever you put into Redline, a memory dump, or data gathered with a collector. The Redline interface is displayed in Fig. 19.5.

As shown in Fig. 19.5, the Redline interface contains a navigation panc (lcft) and a data pane (right). The sample in Fig. 19.5 shows a case where the collector was used to gather data; you may also import a raw memory dump into Redline, but the options in the navigation pane will be mush fever. Also, a nice aspect if Redline is that it includes points of what to look for in the different areas. For instance, the port view under the process listing will include a tip about looking for processes with suspicious network connections.

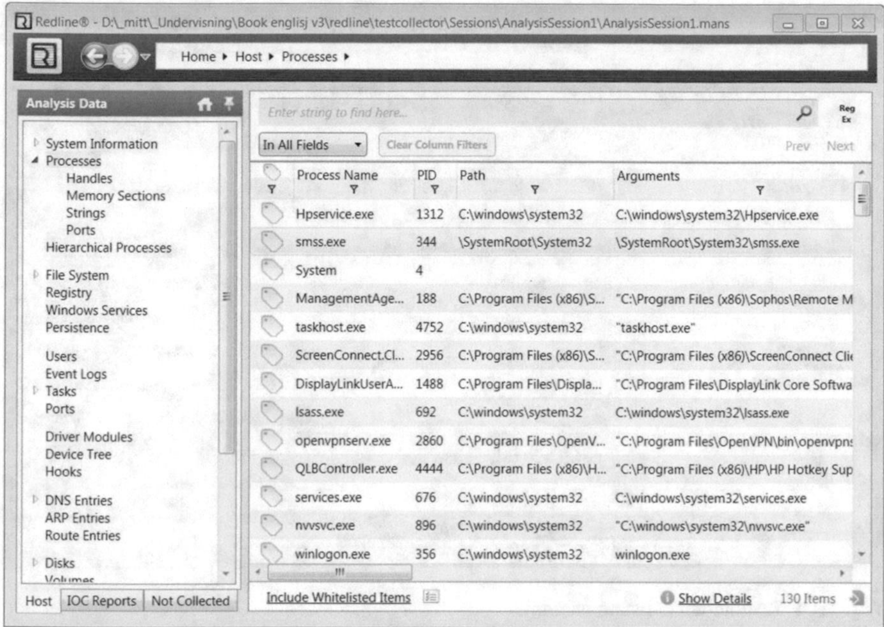

Fig. 19.5 Redline interface

19.2.2 Redline Usage

Apart from using Redline as a good acquisition tool and a nice interface, Redline supports white listing and the use of indicators of compromise. In using white listing, Redline calculates MD5 hash values for processes, Windows Services, and more. Those are then compared to a list of hash values from known good files that can then be filtered out from the analysis. Files that are identified to be good are marked with a green checkmark next to the MD5 hash values in the MD5 hash column of the data pane, as seen in Fig. 19.6.

While Redline includes a small hash set from installation, you can create your own hash set that is customized for your environment of download large hash sets from various sources on the Internet.

Indicators of compromise (IoC) specify illicit behaviors and can be used to automatically find traces of various incidents. Redline provides the ability of checking a case against IoC specified according to the Open IoC format.[5] Indicators of compromise are not included by default but can be downloaded online from various sources. Further, IoC analysis has to be actively chosen, and when doing so the case data will be analyzed against the specified IoC. This will be further discussed in the ending chapter of the book.

[5]https://www.symantec.com/connect/blogs/open-ioc

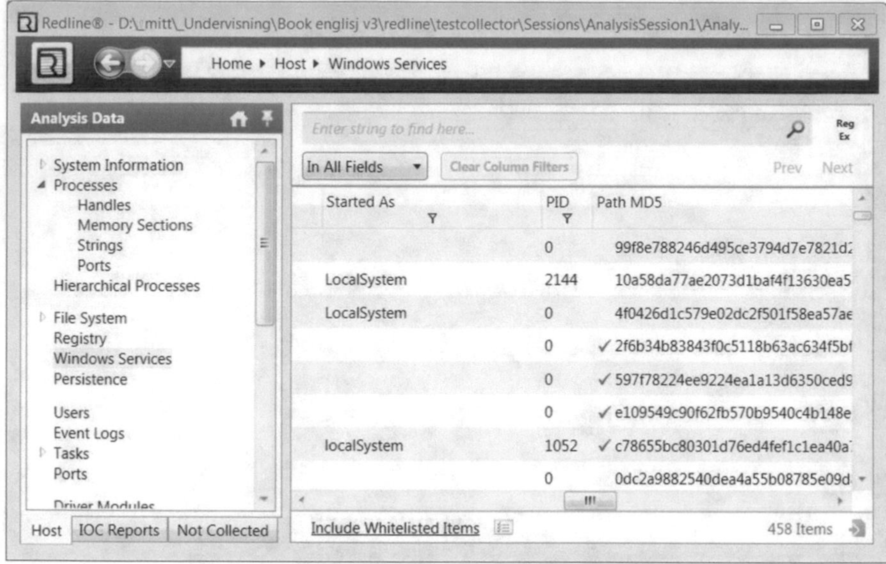

Fig. 19.6 Redline white listing example

References

Ligh MH, Case A, Levy J, Walters A (2014) The art of memory forensics: detecting malware and threats in windows, linux, and Mac memory. Wiley, New York

Volatility Foundation (2017) Volatility Foundation. Available Online: http://www.volatilityfoundation.org/. Fetched 6 July 2017

Memory Analysis in Criminal Investigations 20

Memory analysis during a forensic examination in a crime scenario is usually about looking for information that can be used in court. As been previously discussed, the possible targets of such an examination can range from finding e-mails to detecting malware. What is of actual interest will differ, and the intent of this chapter is to introduce and describe some of the Volatility modules that the author found to be useful during a forensic examination.

As a start, it is commonly interesting to view the processes that were running on the computer at the time of the memory dump. This can provide insight into what software was running on the computer and, thus, give valuable hints on where the continued analysis should focus. The module to use for this purpose is *pslist.* As shown in Fig. 20.1, *pslist* will provide a listing of processes that were running at the time of the memory dump.

Continuing along the same line is *netscan* that will report networking information. As shown in Fig. 20.2, *netscan* can also reveal running programs and what remote computers the examined computer is connected to and so on. From a forensic standpoint, finding information about network connections can help reveal if there should be other computers of relevance for the case.

Another module that can be neat for criminal forensics is *envars* that will display the environmental variables for one or all process. This can assist in figuring out where to look for artifacts relating to an application and decipher what users have been active on a system. Figure 20.3 shows an output sample from the AxCrypt.exe process that shows that it appears to belong to the username "joaki." This will tell us that the user is, most likely, present on the system and that the user has started the application AxCrypt.exe.

As previously discussed, one of the great powers of memory analysis is the ability to find open files that are stored encrypted. One way to begin the quest for open files is by using the module *filescan* that scans the memory dump for open files. *Filescan* will return a list of open files including the physical offset to where in memory the file is located, as shown in Fig. 20.4. Note that it is very helpful to filter the output

J. Kävrestad, *Fundamentals of Digital Forensics*,
https://doi.org/10.1007/978-3-030-38954-3_20

```
root@volabox:/home/analyzer/Desktop/vola2_6/volatility# python vol.py -f memdump.mem --profile="Win10x64_16299" pslist
Volatility Foundation Volatility Framework 2.6
Offset(V)          Name                    PID   PPID   Thds     Hnds   Sess  Wow64 Start                          Exit
------------------ -------------------- ------ ------ ------ -------- ------ ------ ------------------------------ ------
0xffff9d032ce92440 System                    4      0     94        0 ------      0 2018-03-27 11:55:06 UTC+0000
0xffff9d032e546580 smss.exe                320      4      2        0 ------      0 2018-03-27 11:55:06 UTC+0000
0xffff9d032e4b7580 csrss.exe               404    396      9        0      0      0 2018-03-27 11:55:10 UTC+0000
0xffff9d032eb73080 smss.exe                476    320      0 --------      1      0 2018-03-27 11:55:11 UTC+0000   2018-03
0xffff9d032eb76080 wininit.exe             484    396      1        0      0      0 2018-03-27 11:55:11 UTC+0000
0xffff9d032eb7c580 csrss.exe               496    476     11        0      1      0 2018-03-27 11:55:11 UTC+0000
0xffff9d032ebc6080 winlogon.exe            556    476      5        0      1      0 2018-03-27 11:55:11 UTC+0000
0xffff9d032ebc2080 services.exe            580    484      7        0      0      0 2018-03-27 11:55:11 UTC+0000
0xffff9d032e94a080 lsass.exe               616    484     11        0      0      0 2018-03-27 11:55:11 UTC+0000
0xffff9d032ea6b580 svchost.exe             704    580     21        0      0      0 2018-03-27 11:55:11 UTC+0000
0xffff9d032ead2080 fontdrvhost.ex          712    556      5        0      1      0 2018-03-27 11:55:11 UTC+0000
0xffff9d032ead1080 fontdrvhost.ex          720    484      5        0      0      0 2018-03-27 11:55:11 UTC+0000
0xffff9d032ee68400 svchost.exe             804    580     16        0      0      0 2018-03-27 11:55:12 UTC+0000
```

Fig. 20.1 Volatility—pslist

```
root@volabox:/home/analyzer/Desktop/vola2_6/volatility# python vol.py -f memdump.mem --profile="Win10x64_16299" netscan
Volatility Foundation Volatility Framework 2.6
Offset(P)          Proto    Local Address                  Foreign Address      State            Pid      Owner          Created
0x9d032d3376e0     UDPv4    0.0.0.0:3702                   *:*                                   800      svchost.exe    2018-03-27 13:01:43 UTC+0
000
0x9d032d466ec0     UDPv4    0.0.0.0:0                      *:*                                   272      AxCrypt.exe    2018-03-27 12:57:14 UTC+0
000
0x9d032d46b010     UDPv4    0.0.0.0:0                      *:*                                   272      AxCrypt.exe    2018-03-27 12:57:14 UTC+0
000
0x9d032d46b010     UDPv6    :::0                           *:*                                   272      AxCrypt.exe    2018-03-27 12:57:14 UTC+0
000
0x9d032d46c010     UDPv4    0.0.0.0:0                      *:*                                   272      AxCrypt.exe    2018-03-27 12:57:14 UTC+0
000
```

Fig. 20.2 Volatility netscan

```
root@volabox:/home/analyzer/Desktop/vola2_6/volatility# python vol.py -f memdump.mem --profile="Win10x64_16299" envars --pid="272"| grep joaki
Volatility Foundation Volatility Framework 2.6
     272 AxCrypt.exe          0x0000019d4f175a00 APPDATA                        C:\Users\joaki\AppData\Roaming
     272 AxCrypt.exe          0x0000019d4f175a00 HOMEPATH                       \Users\joaki
     272 AxCrypt.exe          0x0000019d4f175a00 LOCALAPPDATA                   C:\Users\joaki\AppData\Local
     272 AxCrypt.exe          0x0000019d4f175a00 OneDrive                       C:\Users\joaki\OneDrive
     272 AxCrypt.exe          0x0000019d4f175a00 Path                           C:\Windows\system32;C:\Windows;C:\Windows\System32\Wbem;C:\Windows
\System32\WindowsPowerShell\v1.0\;C:\Users\joaki\AppData\Local\Microsoft\WindowsApps
     272 AxCrypt.exe          0x0000019d4f175a00 TEMP                           C:\Users\joaki\AppData\Local\Temp
     272 AxCrypt.exe          0x0000019d4f175a00 TMP                            C:\Users\joaki\AppData\Local\Temp
     272 AxCrypt.exe          0x0000019d4f175a00 USERNAME                       joaki
     272 AxCrypt.exe          0x0000019d4f175a00 USERPROFILE                    C:\Users\joaki
```

Fig. 20.3 Volatility—envars

```
root@volabox:/home/analyzer/Desktop/vola2_6/volatility# python vol.py -f memdump.mem --profile="Win10x64_16299" filescan | grep txt
Volatility Foundation Volatility Framework 2.6
0x00009d032d271d60     16      0 R--rwd \Device\HarddiskVolume2\Users\joaki\AppData\Local\Packages\Microsoft.Windows.Cortana_cw5n1h2txyewy\LocalSt
ate\DeviceSearchCache\SettingsCache.txt
0x00009d032d6f8e30  32257      1 RW-r-d \Device\HarddiskVolume2\ProgramData\Microsoft\Windows Defender\Network Inspection System\Support\NisLog.tx
t
0x00009d032d803a40     15      0 R--rwd \Device\HarddiskVolume2\ProgramData\Microsoft\Windows Defender\Network Inspection System\Support\NisLog.tx
t
0x00009d032e3fce50     16      0 RW---- \Device\HarddiskVolume2\Users\joaki\AppData\Local\AxCrypt\rqamnxpo\encrypted.txt
0x00009d032f076740  32762      1 RW-rw- \Device\HarddiskVolume2\Users\joaki\AppData\Local\Microsoft\OneDrive\settings\Personal\downloads3.txt
```

Fig. 20.4 Volatility filescan

using *grep* as a computer normally has loads of open files. Make note of the file called *encrypted.txt,* and locating that file will now be our target.

Continuing the hunt for interesting files, there is the module called *mftparser.* What this module will do is look for Master File Table entries and, if specified, dump any resident files that can be found. Remember from Chap. 3 that files of about 600 bytes and smaller are completely stored in the Master File Table (MFT) and should be contained in a dump of the MFT. In this case, the module was used by issuing the command Volatility *–f memoryimage –profile = selectedmemoryprofile mftparser > > outfile.txt.* This stores the output to the file *outfile.txt* for further analysis. Parsing the output further with the Linux command *cat outfile.txt |grep –context = 15 encrypted* allowed for a search for the keyword *encrypted* in the output

```
$FILE_NAME
Creation                     Modified                     MFT Altered                  Access Date                  Name/Path
---------------------------- ---------------------------- ---------------------------- ---------------------------- ---------
2018-03-27 13:00:38 UTC+0000 2018-03-27 13:00:38 UTC+0000 2018-03-27 13:00:38 UTC+0000 2018-03-27 13:00:38 UTC+0000 Users\joaki\AppData\Local\AxCrypt\rqamnxpo\encrypted.txt

$DATA
0000000000: 54 45 58 54 54 4f 46 49 4e 44 49 4e 4d 45 4d      TEXTTOFINDINMEM
```

Fig. 20.5 Filtered output from mftparser

```
root@volabox:/home/analyzer/Desktop/volatility# python vol.py -f memdump.mem --profile="Win10x64_17134" yarascan --yara-rules="TEXTTOFINDINMEM"
Volatility Foundation Volatility Framework 2.6
Rule: r1
Owner: Process explorer.exe Pid 2760
0x1098a640  54 45 58 54 54 4f 46 49 4e 44 49 4e 4d 45 4d 00   TEXTTOFINDINMEM.
0x1098a650  10 41 ce e8 ff 7f 00 00 00 00 00 00 00 00 00 00   .A..............
0x1098a660  00 00 00 00 00 00 00 00 00 00 00 00 00 00 00 00   ................
0x1098a670  00 00 00 00 00 00 00 00 00 00 00 00 00 00 00 00   ................
0x1098a680  00 00 00 00 00 00 00 00 30 05 ce e8 ff 7f 00 00   ........0.......
0x1098a690  80 05 ce e8 ff 7f 00 00 38 06 ce e8 ff 7f 00 00   ........8.......
0x1098a6a0  18 06 ce e8 ff 7f 00 00 e0 04 ce e8 ff 7f 00 00   ................
0x1098a6b0  c8 05 ce e8 ff 7f 00 00 00 00 00 00 00 00 00 00   ................
0x1098a6c0  00 00 00 00 00 00 00 00 24 c3 dd 6f 03 4e fe 4b   ........$..o.N.K
0x1098a6d0  b1 85 3d 77 76 8d c9 0c 24 c3 dd 6f 03 4e fe 4b   ..=wv...$..o.N.K
0x1098a6e0  b1 85 3d 77 76 8d c9 0e 24 c3 dd 6f 03 4e fe 4b   ..=wv...$..o.N.K
0x1098a6f0  b1 85 3d 77 76 8d c9 00 24 c3 dd 6f 03 4e fe 4b   ..=wv...$..o.N.K
0x1098a700  b1 85 3d 77 76 8d c9 00 00 0a 00 00 52 05 00 00   ..=wv.......R...
0x1098a710  00 00 00 00 00 00 10 11 00 00 00 00 00 00 00 00   ................
0x1098a720  00 00 00 00 00 00 00 00 00 00 00 00 00 00 00 00   ................
0x1098a730  00 00 00 00 00 00 00 00 00 00 00 00 00 00 00 00   ................
```

Fig. 20.6 Yarascan using a string search

```
root@volabox:/home/analyzer/Desktop/volatility# python vol.py -f memdump.mem --profile="Win10x64_17134" yarascan --yara-rules="{54 45 58 54 54}"
Volatility Foundation Volatility Framework 2.6
Rule: r1
Owner: Process explorer.exe Pid 2760
0x09576030  54 45 58 54 54 4f 46 49 fc 55 ea f8 00 38 00 80   TEXTTOFI.U...8..
0x09576040  70 b0 a2 10 00 00 00 00 fb 55 eb f8 00 39 00 88   p........U...9..
0x09576050  20 80 98 10 00 00 00 00 fa 55 e8 f8 00 3a 00 80   .........U...:..
0x09576060  70 b0 a2 10 00 00 00 00 00 00 00 00 00 00 00 00   p...............
0x09576070  00 00 00 00 00 00 00 00 3c 9f 99 7a f1 27 20 00   ........<..z.'..
0x09576080  b0 4c 9f 10 00 00 00 00 90 05 bf 10 00 00 00 00   .L..............
0x09576090  00 00 00 00 00 00 00 00 00 00 00 00 00 00 00 00   ................
```

Fig. 20.7 Yarascan using a byte pattern

data. This sequence resulted in the output as shown in Fig. 20.5, displaying what appears to be a plain text version of the file we first saw by using the *filescan* module.

Continuing the list of commands useful for memory analysis in criminal investigations is one of the more useful modules, *yarascan*. *Yarascan* is a module that allows for text searches in an entire memory dump. While you could do the same using almost any forensic toolkit, it should be mentioned that doing searches in the context of Volatility allows for better results as Volatility is using specific memory profiles that enable it to view memory just as the computer did, while it is likely that a forensic toolkit will view memory as an unstructured blob of data. *Yarascan* is a powerful and flexible tool that allows you to specify search strings as plain text, as shown in Fig. 20.6, or as a byte pattern represented in hex, as shown in Fig. 20.7.

Note that the result will be presented as the data from the beginning of the hit and then subsequent addresses in memory. As shown in Fig. 20.7, every hit contains information about the process the hit is found in and the memory address of that hit, located in the left column. If further analysis of the surrounding data is interesting, *volshell* can be used for that purpose.

The examples so far have been created using a memory dump from a computer running Windows 10 build 1709. There are some more modules that should be of great interest for a forensic examiner, mostly pertaining to the registry. Unfortunately, at the time of writing this book, it appears as if Volatility is not able to read registry data from the memory dump used. For that reason, the remainder of this

```
root@volabox:/home/analyzer/Desktop/volatility# python vol.py -f memsample --profile="WinXPSP2x86" hivelist
Volatility Foundation Volatility Framework 2.6
Virtual    Physical   Name
---------- ---------- ----
0xe1bce008 0x0bf23008 \Device\HarddiskVolume1\Documents and Settings\Mal Ware\Local Settings\Application Data\Microsoft\Windows\UsrClass.dat
0xe1982758 0x0bc12758 \Device\HarddiskVolume1\Documents and Settings\Mal Ware\NTUSER.DAT
0xe1855b60 0x0a1beb60 \Device\HarddiskVolume1\Documents and Settings\LocalService\Local Settings\Application Data\Microsoft\Windows\UsrClass.dat
0xe17da748 0x09f00748 \Device\HarddiskVolume1\Documents and Settings\LocalService\NTUSER.DAT
0xe1861008 0x0a241008 \Device\HarddiskVolume1\Documents and Settings\NetworkService\Local Settings\Application Data\Microsoft\Windows\UsrClass.dat
0xe1862418 0x0a242418 \Device\HarddiskVolume1\Documents and Settings\NetworkService\NTUSER.DAT
0xe1674988 0x0795d988 \Device\HarddiskVolume1\WINDOWS\system32\config\software
0xe1477b60 0x07de0b60 \Device\HarddiskVolume1\WINDOWS\system32\config\default
0xe1485008 0x07df1008 \Device\HarddiskVolume1\WINDOWS\system32\config\SAM
0xe16a6b60 0x07cecb60 \Device\HarddiskVolume1\WINDOWS\system32\config\SECURITY
0xe1395b60 0x02e41b60 [no name]
0xe1035b60 0x02a9eb60 \Device\HarddiskVolume1\WINDOWS\system32\config\system
0xe102e008 0x02a98008 [no name]
```

Fig. 20.8 Volatility hivelist

```
root@volabox:/home/analyzer/Desktop/volatility# python vol.py -f memsample --profile="WinXPSP2x86" hashdump
Volatility Foundation Volatility Framework 2.6
Administrator:500:e52cac67419a9a224a3b108f3fa6cb6d:8846f7eaee8fb117ad06bdd830b7586c:::
Guest:501:aad3b435b51404eeaad3b435b51404ee:31d6cfe0d16ae931b73c59d7e0c089c0:::
HelpAssistant:1000:7bfaff5c79b08048be435a392e87f9b9:40426b2608532aecce96a876826f4e1b:::
SUPPORT_388945a0:1002:aad3b435b51404eeaad3b435b51404ee:760fa725e1249aa2d6da281ae6be6fc1:::
Mal Ware:1003:aad3b435b51404eeaad3b435b51404ee:31d6cfe0d16ae931b73c59d7e0c089c0:::
```

Fig. 20.9 Volatility hashdump

chapter is written using a memory dump supplied at the Web site belonging to the book *The Art of Memory Forensics* and is called sample009.bin.[1] The first registry module of interest is called *hivelist.* This module simply lists the registry hives that are present in memory, as shown in Fig. 20.8.

Continuing the journey into registry, another useful module is called *hashdump*. As shown in Fig. 20.9, it will provide you with two interesting pieces of information; first, it will give you the usernames of the users present on the computer, and second, it will provide you with their password hashes.

Knowing what registry hives are present in memory, you may also use the module *printkey* to print the values and sub-keys present in a sub-key. Figure 20.10 shows compressed output from the module *printkey* invoked by the following command:

Python vol.py –f memsample –profile = "WinXPSP2x86" printkey –K"Microsoft \Windows NT\CurrentVersion"

The value supplied after –*K* should be a path to a key in registry. As per default, Volatility will scan all registry hives for the supplied key and report any found sub-keys and values. As seen in the sample memory, the name of the registered owner could be determined to be "Mal."

Moving away from registry artifacts in memory, a module that deserves to be mentioned is *screenshot.* What it does is that it attempts to create a mock-up screenshot showing how the screen looked for every active user session found in memory. At times, this can provide insight into what the user could actually see on his or her screen. There are two things to notice about this module. First, every active session, including noninteractive sessions, will get a screenshot generated. This means that several empty pictures will be generated. Second, the screenshot will

[1] www.memoryanalysis.net/amf

```
egend: (S) = Stable   (V) = Volatile

----------------------------
egistry: \Device\HarddiskVolume1\WINDOWS\system32\config\software
ey name: CurrentVersion (S)
ast updated: 2008-09-18 05:33:00 UTC+0000

ubkeys:
  (S) Accessibility
  (S) AeDebug
  (S) Asr
  (S) Classes
  (S) Compatibility
  (S) Compatibility32
  (S) Console
  (S) Drivers
  (S) drivers.desc

UTPUT OMITTED.....

alues:
REG_SZ        SubVersionNumber : (S) ^@
REG_SZ        CurrentBuild     : (S) 1.511.1 () (Obsolete data - do not use)^@
REG_DWORD     InstallDate      : (S) 1208455061
REG_SZ        ProductName      : (S) Microsoft Windows XP^@
REG_SZ        RegDone          : (S) ^@
REG_SZ        RegisteredOrganization : (S) ^@
REG_SZ        RegisteredOwner : (S) Mal^@
REG_SZ        SoftwareType     : (S) SYSTEM^@
REG_SZ        CurrentVersion   : (S) 5.1^@
```

Fig. 20.10 Volatility printkey

not look just as a screenshot from a running desktop; it is more of a mock-up that can tell you some things about what Windows the user had open.

The final part to notice in this chapter is three modules that are used to detect information relating to a popular encryption software called TrueCrypt. While not demonstrated in this book, it is good to know about their existence and try them yourself whenever there is any suspicion of the software TrueCrypt being used. Those modules are:

- *Truecryptsummary* that returns a summary of information about TrueCrypt
- *Truecryptpassphrase* that looks for cached TrueCrypt passphrases
- *Truecryptmaster* that looks for TrueCrypt master keys

As an end to this chapter, there is a GUI to Volatility that is called Volatility Workbench and deserves a quick mention.[2] It is a GUI for Volatility that allows you to do most tasks you can do with Volatility in a graphical environment. It is demonstrated in Fig. 20.11.

[2]https://www.osforensics.com/tools/volatility-workbench.html

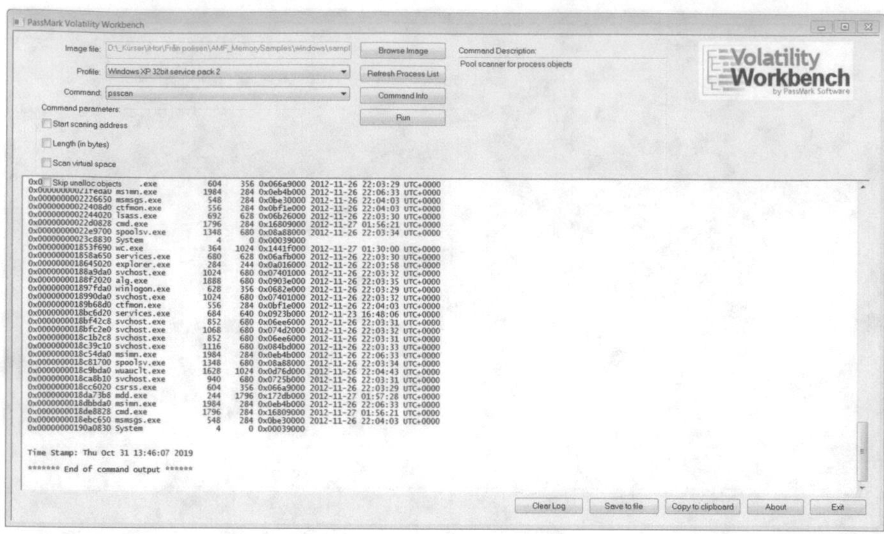

Fig. 20.11 Volatility Workbench

Some things to notice about using Volatility Workbench is that it come packed with a version of Volatility, meaning that you may not get the latest version with the latest profiles included. Further, it does not provide a way to figure out what profile to use, meaning that you still need to know what memory profile to apply. That I mind it does provide benefit and ease of use.

20.1 Questions and Tasks

Download the memory dump called sample009.bin from www.memoryanalysis.net/amf, and use Volatility to answer the following questions (create a memory dump of your own computer and finish the tasks if you cannot get hold of the suggested one; FTK imager can be used to create the dump):

1. When was the memory dump created?
2. What process has the PID of 1320?
3. What is the username of the user with RID 1003?
4. Are there any open network connections for PID 1320?

Malware Analysis 21

Changing the topic from criminal forensics to malware analysis, the first thing to know about using memory analysis to detect malware is to understand that it is, to a great extent, about understanding how a computer would normally operate and to find what differs from that. To benefit from this chapter, you should have a fair understanding of what malware includes, and at its essence it is fair to describe malware as code that does something that is not intended to happen on the computer. Depending on what the person that created the malware wanted to achieve, this can be about almost anything.

However, as a beginning to this demonstration on malware analysis, it appears reasonable to discuss a few different concrete things that a malware may do. The first is one that is rather obvious; a malware will usually attempt to disguise itself. This could include using different approaches in order to hide itself from process listings and similar. Further, a malware will commonly try to access stuff that is not supposed to be accessed. What this means is that a malware may infect a process and try to make that process do something it is not supposed to. Another identifier for a malware is that it sometimes tries to create network connections. This can, for instance, be in order to collect information from the infected host and send it to somewhere else. All in all, malware analysis is about looking for processes that should not be present in memory at all or that behaves in a way that does not follow the norm.

For the practical demonstration, this chapter will first describe the basics of using the Volatility command line for malware detection and then present the graphical tool Redline that can be used for the same purpose.

21.1 Malware Analysis with Volatility

During this demonstration we will look into a memory sample that is infected with a Trojan horse called SpyEye. The memory sample was taken from a computer running Windows XP, but the steps taken for analysis of a more modern computer

J. Kävrestad, *Fundamentals of Digital Forensics*,
https://doi.org/10.1007/978-3-030-38954-3_21

```
root@volabox:/home/analyzer/Desktop/volatility# python vol.py -f spyeye.vmem imageinfo
Volatility Foundation Volatility Framework 2.6
INFO    : volatility.debug    : Determining profile based on KDBG search...
          Suggested Profile(s) : WinXPSP2x86, WinXPSP3x86 (Instantiated with WinXPSP2x86)
                     AS Layer1 : IA32PagedMemoryPae (Kernel AS)
                     AS Layer2 : FileAddressSpace (/home/analyzer/Desktop/volatility/spyeye.vmem)
                      PAE type : PAE
                           DTB : 0x319000L
                          KDBG : 0x80545b60L
          Number of Processors : 1
     Image Type (Service Pack) : 3
                KPCR for CPU 0 : 0xffdff000L
             KUSER_SHARED_DATA : 0xffdf0000L
           Image date and time : 2011-01-06 14:50:19 UTC+0000
     Image local date and time : 2011-01-06 09:50:19 -0500
```

Fig. 21.1 Volatility imageinfo

```
analyzer@volabox:~/Desktop/volatility$ python vol.py -f spyeye.vmem --profile=WinXPSP2x86 pslist
Volatility Foundation Volatility Framework 2.6
Offset(V)  Name                    PID   PPID   Thds     Hnds   Sess  Wow64 Start                          Exit
---------- -------------------- ------ ------ ------ -------- ------ ------ ------------------------------ ------------------------------
0x825c8830 System                    4      0     58      387 ------      0
0x823fe020 smss.exe                572      4      3       19 ------      0 2010-11-11 22:02:08 UTC+0000
0x82503220 csrss.exe               636    572     13      399      0      0 2010-11-11 22:02:13 UTC+0000
0x81f4c550 winlogon.exe            660    572     21      596      0      0 2010-11-11 22:02:14 UTC+0000
0x8207d5f0 services.exe            704    660     17      285      0      0 2010-11-11 22:02:15 UTC+0000
0x824264c0 lsass.exe               716    660     20      356      0      0 2010-11-11 22:02:15 UTC+0000
0x8230c5f8 vmacthlp.exe            872    704      2       26      0      0 2010-11-11 22:02:16 UTC+0000
0x8226cda0 svchost.exe             904    704     16      191      0      0 2010-11-11 22:02:16 UTC+0000
0x823f2020 svchost.exe             972    704      9      264      0      0 2010-11-11 22:02:17 UTC+0000
0x822a0758 svchost.exe            1068    704     58     1256      0      0 2010-11-11 22:02:17 UTC+0000
0x81f4b020 svchost.exe            1108    704      7       82      0      0 2010-11-11 22:02:17 UTC+0000
0x82406da0 svchost.exe            1232    704     13      169      0      0 2010-11-11 22:02:18 UTC+0000
0x82436a48 spoolsv.exe            1456    704     12      121      0      0 2010-11-11 22:02:19 UTC+0000
0x82067858 svchost.exe            1540    704      6       95      0      0 2010-11-11 22:02:26 UTC+0000
0x82072660 jqs.exe                1612    704      6      149      0      0 2010-11-11 22:02:27 UTC+0000
0x82284b80 vmtoolsd.exe           1816    704      6      268      0      0 2010-11-11 22:02:30 UTC+0000
0x822e69f8 VMUpgradeHelper        1872    704      4      100      0      0 2010-11-11 22:02:30 UTC+0000
0x823e32f8 explorer.exe           1008    680     15      468      0      0 2010-11-11 22:02:55 UTC+0000
0x81ec2020 TSVNCache.exe          1252   1008      9       58      0      0 2010-11-11 22:02:58 UTC+0000
0x81ebd300 VMwareTray.exe         1484   1008      2       51      0      0 2010-11-11 22:03:00 UTC+0000
0x82159958 VMwareUser.exe         1588   1008      7      230      0      0 2010-11-11 22:03:00 UTC+0000
0x8214ba18 jusched.exe            1672   1008      2       97      0      0 2010-11-11 22:03:00 UTC+0000
0x8236d7a0 wuauclt.exe             536   1068      4      107      0      0 2010-11-11 22:03:33 UTC+0000
0x824578b0 imapi.exe              1040    704      5      114      0      0 2010-11-11 22:03:54 UTC+0000
0x82458020 alg.exe                2108    704      7      107      0      0 2010-11-11 22:03:54 UTC+0000
0x82389020 wscntfy.exe            2772   1068      2       29      0      0 2010-11-11 22:03:56 UTC+0000
0x81f7a708 WPFFontCache_v0        3084    704      7       70      0      0 2010-11-11 22:05:04 UTC+0000
0x81f5e020 jucheck.exe            3892   1672      3      105      0      0 2010-11-11 22:08:01 UTC+0000
0x82226b48 cleansweep.exe         2268   1008      0 --------      0      0 2011-01-06 14:36:52 UTC+0000   2011-01-06 14:36:52 UTC+0000
0x820bd760 gmer.exe               2728   1008      2       33      0      0 2011-01-06 14:37:41 UTC+0000
analyzer@volabox:~/Desktop/volatility$
```

Fig. 21.2 Volatility pslist

would be the same. To begin the examination, the *imageinfo* module is used to determine what memory profile to use, as depicted in Fig. 21.1. An introduction to Volatility can be found in Chap. 19.

As shown in Fig. 21.1, you can see that Volatility suggests different profiles that can be used. In this case, the WinXPSP2x86 profile is fine and that will be used throughout the rest of this example. Getting started with our examination, a quick way to get some low-hanging fruit would be to start looking at what processes were running at the computer at the time of the memory dump; just as in the previous example, we will use the *pslist* for this purpose, and you may also use *pstree* that will provide output that makes parent/child relationships more visual. The output will be a listing of processes found by walking the doubly linked list that contains the processes. The output for our case is presented in Fig. 21.2.

The list of processes in memory is stored in a doubly linked list, and the *pslist* module will walk that list and output the processes found therein. Whenever a process is terminated, it is removed from the list, making it uncommon to discover terminated processes using *pslist*. Also, a technique that is sometimes used by

```
analyzer@volabox:~/Desktop/volatility$ python vol.py -f spyeye.vmem --profile=WinXPSP2x86 psscan
Volatility Foundation Volatility Framework 2.6
Offset(P)          Name                PID   PPID PDB        Time created                   Time exited
------------------ ---------------- ------ ------ ---------- ------------------------------ ------------------------------
0x0000000001ebd300 VMwareTray.exe     1484   1008 0x0a940180 2010-11-11 22:03:00 UTC+0000
0x0000000001ec2020 TSVNCache.exe      1252   1008 0x0a940340 2010-11-11 22:02:58 UTC+0000
0x0000000001ed9b50 wmiprvse.exe       2912    888 0x0a3004c0 2010-11-11 21:57:43 UTC+0000
0x0000000001f4b020 svchost.exe        1108    704 0x0a940140 2010-11-11 22:02:17 UTC+0000
0x0000000001f4c550 winlogon.exe        660    572 0x0a940060 2010-11-11 22:02:14 UTC+0000
0x0000000001f5e020 jucheck.exe        3892   1672 0x0a9402a0 2010-11-11 22:08:01 UTC+0000
0x0000000001f7a708 WPFFontCache_v0    3084    704 0x0a940400 2010-11-11 22:05:04 UTC+0000
0x0000000002067858 svchost.exe        1540    704 0x0a9401c0 2010-11-11 22:02:26 UTC+0000
0x0000000002072660 jqs.exe            1612    704 0x0a940200 2010-11-11 22:02:27 UTC+0000
0x000000000207d5f0 services.exe        704    660 0x0a940080 2010-11-11 22:02:15 UTC+0000
0x00000000020bd760 gmer.exe           2728   1008 0x0a9403a0 2011-01-06 14:37:41 UTC+0000
0x000000000214ba18 jusched.exe        1672   1008 0x0a940300 2010-11-11 22:03:00 UTC+0000
0x0000000002159958 VMwareUser.exe     1588   1008 0x0a9402e0 2010-11-11 22:03:00 UTC+0000
0x0000000002226b48 cleansweep.exe     2268   1008 0x0a940460 2011-01-06 14:36:52 UTC+0000   2011-01-06 14:36:52 UTC+0000
0x000000000226cda0 svchost.exe         904    704 0x0a9400e0 2010-11-11 22:02:16 UTC+0000
0x0000000002284b80 vmtoolsd.exe       1816    704 0x0a940240 2010-11-11 22:02:30 UTC+0000
0x00000000022a0758 svchost.exe        1068    704 0x0a940120 2010-11-11 22:02:17 UTC+0000
0x00000000022e69f8 VMUpgradeHelper    1872    704 0x0a940260 2010-11-11 22:02:30 UTC+0000
0x000000000230c5f8 vmacthlp.exe        872    704 0x0a9400c0 2010-11-11 22:02:16 UTC+0000
0x000000000236d7a0 wuauclt.exe         536   1068 0x0a9402c0 2010-11-11 22:03:33 UTC+0000
0x0000000002389020 wscntfy.exe        2772   1068 0x0a940380 2010-11-11 22:03:56 UTC+0000
0x00000000023e32f8 explorer.exe       1008    680 0x0a940320 2010-11-11 22:02:55 UTC+0000
0x00000000023f2020 svchost.exe         972    704 0x0a940100 2010-11-11 22:02:17 UTC+0000
0x00000000023fe020 smss.exe            572      4 0x0a940020 2010-11-11 22:02:08 UTC+0000
0x0000000002406da0 svchost.exe        1232    704 0x0a940160 2010-11-11 22:02:18 UTC+0000
0x00000000024264c0 lsass.exe           716    660 0x0a9400a0 2010-11-11 22:02:15 UTC+0000
0x0000000002436a48 spoolsv.exe        1456    704 0x0a9401a0 2010-11-11 22:02:19 UTC+0000
0x00000000024578b0 imapi.exe          1040    704 0x0a940220 2010-11-11 22:03:54 UTC+0000
0x0000000002458020 alg.exe            2108    704 0x0a940360 2010-11-11 22:03:54 UTC+0000
0x0000000002503220 csrss.exe           636    572 0x0a940040 2010-11-11 22:02:13 UTC+0000
0x00000000025c8830 System                4      0 0x00319000
```

Fig. 21.3 Volatility psscan

malware to avoid detection is to remove them from the process list even if they are not terminated. Thus, a running process that is not presented using *pslist* would be suspicious. The module *psscan* also looks for processes but does not rely on the linked list; instead, it scans the memory for the objects that are the actual processes and presents a process listing based on that. Thus, a next step would be to use *psscan*; the output from *psscan* is presented in Fig. 21.3.

At this time, it would be time for some analysis of the output. First, it is reasonable to see if *psscan* found any running processes that was not detected by *pslist*. If any such profile is found, it can be a process that is trying to hide itself and is therefore a target for continued examination. The discrepancy found in our case is the process *wmiprvse.exe*. This process would belong to the Windows management instrumentation that is part of the operating system. However, the fact that it is not found using *pslist* and that its parent process, with id 888, is nowhere to be found is odd. In this case, one could dump the memory of the process and run in through a virus scanner; let us do that before we continue with our examination. The easiest way to dump the memory of a process would be to use *procdump*; in this case Volatility outputs that it is not possible to get the executable for the process and, using *memmap* to see if the process has any pages in memory, it returns nothing. The conclusion at this stage would be that *wmiprvse.exe* does not have any data that we can work on, and thus we have to move on. Of course, now one could use volshell to manually explore the data at the offset, but for now we are out for low-hanging fruit.

The final step in looking for suspicious processes would be to just look at the active processes and see if there are any that we do not expect. This approach requires you to know a bit about what processes to expect and that comes with experience. The game is basically to look up any process that you do not know to be safe, using Google. But before we do that, we should look for more suspicious data.

```
root@volabox:/home/analyzer/Desktop/volatility# python vol.py -f spyeye.vmem --profile=WinXPSP2x86 connscan
Volatility Foundation Volatility Framework 2.6
Offset(P)  Local Address             Remote Address            Pid
---------- ------------------------- ------------------------- ---
0x01eacc00 192.168.16.129:1039       65.55.185.26:443          1068
0x01fd3170 192.168.16.129:1040       207.46.21.58:80           1068
```

Fig. 21.4 Volatility connscan

```
root@volabox:/home/analyzer/Desktop/volatility# python vol.py -f spyeye.vmem --profile=WinXPSP2x86 sockets
Volatility Foundation Volatility Framework 2.6
Offset(V)       PID   Port  Proto Protocol        Address         Create Time
---------- -------- ------ ------ --------------- --------------- -----------
0x822ea7c0     3892   1026      6 TCP             0.0.0.0         2010-11-11 22:08:01 UTC+0000
0x81f73e98      716    500     17 UDP             0.0.0.0         2010-11-11 22:02:27 UTC+0000
0x822453b8        4    445      6 TCP             0.0.0.0         2010-11-11 22:02:08 UTC+0000
0x81f497e0      972    135      6 TCP             0.0.0.0         2010-11-11 22:02:17 UTC+0000
0x8236c510     2108   1025      6 TCP             127.0.0.1       2010-11-11 22:03:54 UTC+0000
0x81f61ad8     1068    123     17 UDP             127.0.0.1       2011-01-06 14:36:59 UTC+0000
0x824b13d8      716      0    255 Reserved        0.0.0.0         2010-11-11 22:02:27 UTC+0000
0x81fd8d58     1232   1900     17 UDP             127.0.0.1       2011-01-06 14:36:59 UTC+0000
0x822557f0      716   4500     17 UDP             0.0.0.0         2010-11-11 22:02:27 UTC+0000
0x81f483b8        4    445     17 UDP             0.0.0.0         2010-11-11 22:02:08 UTC+0000
0x81f49008     1612   5152      6 TCP             127.0.0.1       2010-11-11 22:02:27 UTC+0000
root@volabox:/home/analyzer/Desktop/volatility#
```

Fig. 21.5 Volatility sockets

In this case, there is one process, *cleansweep.exe*, which should attract our attention. This is because it appears to have been terminated at exactly the same time as it was started. In my experience, this is not a common behavior. Also, it spent a long time in the doubly linked list for active processes, after it was terminated. This is shown by *pslist*. Again, the way to go would be to use procdump to extract it from memory; in this case it also failed because some page was paged out. Instead, one can use memdump to dump the memory pages still in memory using the following command:

Python vol.py –f spyeye.vmem –profile = “WinXPSP2x86” memdump –D dump/ -p 2268

At this stage, one would scan the output data using a virus scanner, and in this case there were no hits forcing the examination to continue. A reasonable next step could be to look for network activity. Beginning this effort one can use *connscan* to find TCP connections. The output for our case is shown in Fig. 21.4.

A quick lookup shows that those IP addresses are belonging to Microsoft, meaning a dead end and that our efforts have to continue. Continuing the network lane, we can use sockets, as shown in Fig. 21.5.

The *sockets* plugin will tell us what processes have active listening sockets. Thus, we can reference the list to see if there are any processes that are listening to network connections when they should not. Looking at our list of processes with sockets, we can determine the following:

- PID 3892 is jucheck.exe and has to do with updating Java.
- PID 716 is lsass.exe that handles logins to the Windows computer. One should consider that having open sockets is indeed a suspicious behavior, but looking at

the Microsoft official documentation, it is actually supposed to have sockets open on port 500 and 4500, as in this case.

- PID 4 is a system, and the port that the socket is listening (445) to is related to SMB, the default Windows file sharing protocol.
- PID 972 is svchost.exe and handles services. Port 135 is for remote management.
- PID 2108 is alg.exe that helps programs get access to the Internet. As such, having open sockets is normal.
- PID 1068 is another instance of svchost.exe and so is PID 1232.

The data from *sockets* appears to be another dead end, so let us go back to the initial process listing where cleansweep.exe appeared to be a suspicious process. It has a parent PID of 1008 that belongs to explorer.exe. This is normal for a user-activated process; they will commonly have explorer.exe as their parent. Anyhow, let us continue exploring cleansweep.exe using the plugin *malfind.* While that did not provide any hits, it would be interesting to do *malfind* on the parent process, 1008, as well. At this stage, there were some hits indicating that there are suspicious instructions within the explorer.exe process. At this stage, we can supply –D to *malfind* to output the suspicious code as files that we can run through a virus scanner. The command used is

Python vol.py –f spyeye.vmem –profile = "WinXPSP2x86" malfind –D dump/ -p 1008</Emphasis>

Analyzing the output files using the website VirusTotal[1] generates loads of hits for the Trojan horse SpyEye. Thus, we used memory analysis to conclude that the host we are analyzing was infected with SpyEye.

Backing the tape just a little bit, one should understand what *malfind* actually does. At a glance, it looks for malicious executables and shellcode within processes. In our sample, it was directed at a single process, but it can also be used to search the entire memory dump. When doing its analysis, *malfind* will look at two different things, the data and the disassembly of the data. This is visualized in Fig. 21.6 where the top portion of the output is data in hex and the bottom part is the assembly code of that data.

Looking at the code section, *malfind* will look for executables; in our case the data section begins with *MZ* that identifies the start of an executable. Further, *malfind* will also look at the disassembly to find actual instructions that are suspicious. Note that *malfind* will often generate lot of false positives since all executables are not evil and all suspicious instructions are not actually malicious. As such, the output of *malfind* should be further examined. One way to do that is to run the output of *malfind* through some antivirus for scanning.

While this demonstration does not, by far, cover the steps that need to be taken to detect any malware, it does demonstrate what malware analysis is about, namely,

[1]https://www.virustotal.com/

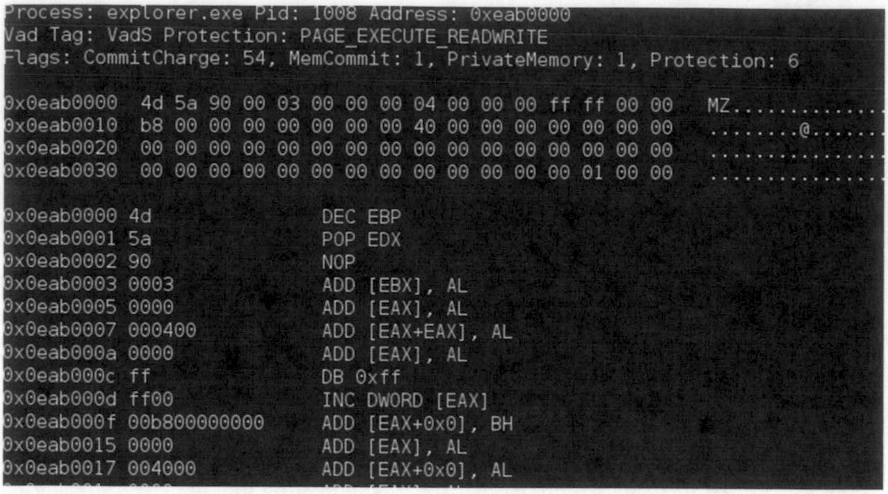

```
Process: explorer.exe Pid: 1008 Address: 0xeab0000
Vad Tag: VadS Protection: PAGE_EXECUTE_READWRITE
Flags: CommitCharge: 54, MemCommit: 1, PrivateMemory: 1, Protection: 6

0x0eab0000  4d 5a 90 00 03 00 00 00 04 00 00 00 ff ff 00 00   MZ..............
0x0eab0010  b8 00 00 00 00 00 00 00 40 00 00 00 00 00 00 00   ........@.......
0x0eab0020  00 00 00 00 00 00 00 00 00 00 00 00 00 00 00 00   ................
0x0eab0030  00 00 00 00 00 00 00 00 00 00 00 00 00 01 00 00   ................

0x0eab0000 4d               DEC EBP
0x0eab0001 5a               POP EDX
0x0eab0002 90               NOP
0x0eab0003 0003             ADD [EBX], AL
0x0eab0005 0000             ADD [EAX], AL
0x0eab0007 000400           ADD [EAX+EAX], AL
0x0eab000a 0000             ADD [EAX], AL
0x0eab000c ff               DB 0xff
0x0eab000d ff00             INC DWORD [EAX]
0x0eab000f 00b800000000     ADD [EAX+0x0], BH
0x0eab0015 0000             ADD [EAX], AL
0x0eab0017 004000           ADD [EAX+0x0], AL
```

Fig. 21.6 Volatility malfind

using different ways of looking at the data in the memory dump in order to find something suspicious and move on. In this case, the cleansweep.exe process was immediately suspicious just from the process listing and googling, for it would reveal that it was probably a cause of the infection. Also, it is important to notice that malware usually wants to infect legitimate processes, that is, a method that will make the malicious instructions look legitimate and provide them with permissions needed to do badly. As such, it is a good practice to focus not only on the actual process that is suspicious but also processes that it has some relationship with.

21.2 Malware Analysis with Redline

Redline is a graphical memory analysis tool that is maintained by FireEye.[2] In brief, it has three major functions:

- Data collection
- Data analysis
- Indicator of compromise (IOC) analysis

It is possible to analyze a memory dump taken with, for instance, FTK imager, but to use all functions in Redline, it is recommended to capture data using the data collection tool in Redline. That is essential in doing an IOC analysis since it will capture more volatile data that is included in a memory dump. Let's go through the

[2]https://www.fireeye.com/services/freeware/redline.html

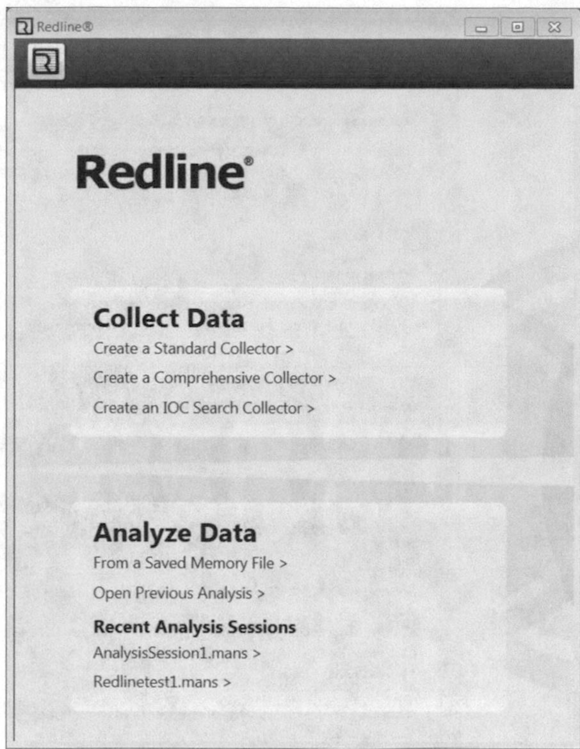

Fig. 21.7 Redline front

process of working with Redline starting with data collection. Opening Redline, you are presented with the screen as shown in Fig. 21.7.

To collect data with Redline, you need to create a collector. The collector is a script that you can customize to collect the data you want. To create a collector, you click one of the options in the "Collect data" box and will then be presented with the dialogue demonstrated in Fig. 21.8.

The main options are to decide where to save the collector and to decide if you want the collector to acquire a memory dump. You can also specify what other data the collector should gather by clicking "Edit your script." As demonstrated in Fig. 21.9, you can fine-tune what data the script will collect and the possible collection point range from event logs and system information to files and process listings.

Once your collector is created, it is stored as a file called "RunRedlineAudit.bat" and can be executed on the machine that you want to collect data from. Remember to execute it from a removable device to minimize the impact it has on the target system. The instructions and end dialogue from the collector creation are presented in Fig. 21.10.

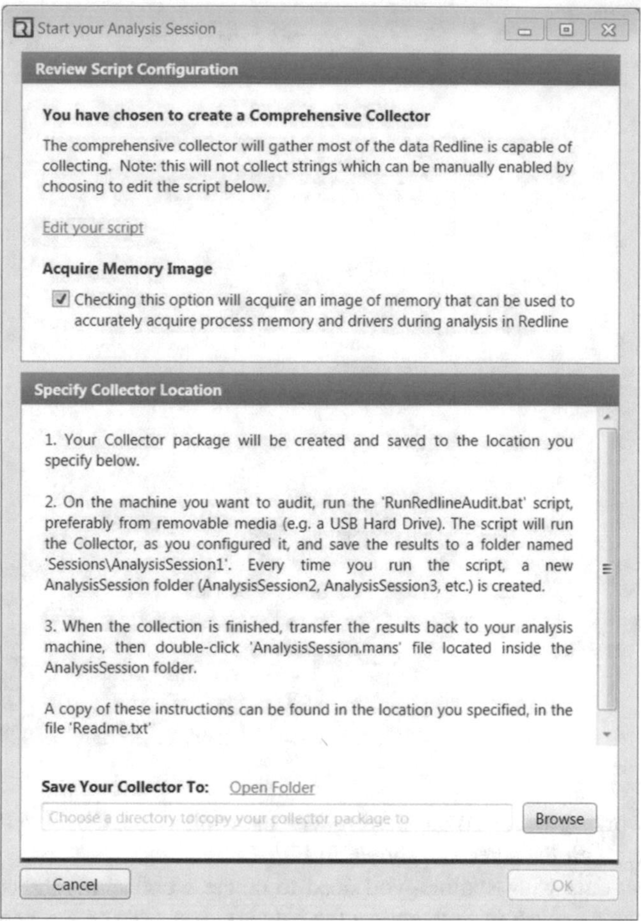

Fig. 21.8 Redline collector configuration

Following the collection of data, it is time to do the actual analysis. You start the analysis from the Redline front page using one of the following options:

- "From a Saved Memory File" is the option to use if you want to analyze a memory dump acquired with a tool other than a Redline collector.
- "Open Previous Analysis" can be used to open an analysis performed by a Redline collector or a previous saved analysis. When analyzing data gathered with a Redline collector, some processing has already been taken care of during collection.

Once the analysis is ready, you will see the window presented in Fig. 21.11. In this case, a Redline collector was used to gather data.

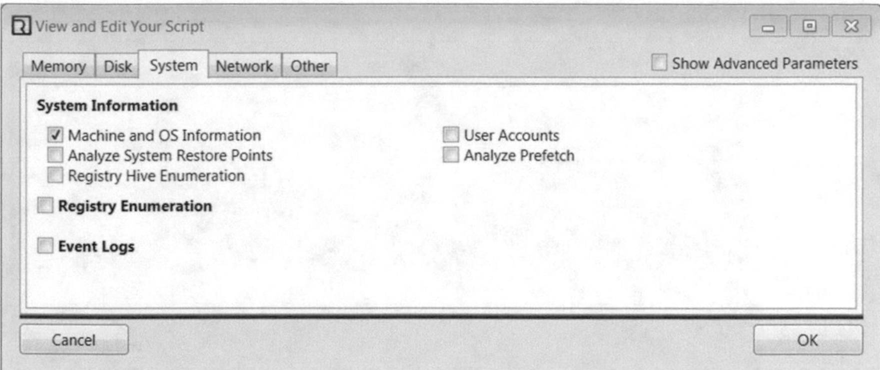

Fig. 21.9 Redline script editor

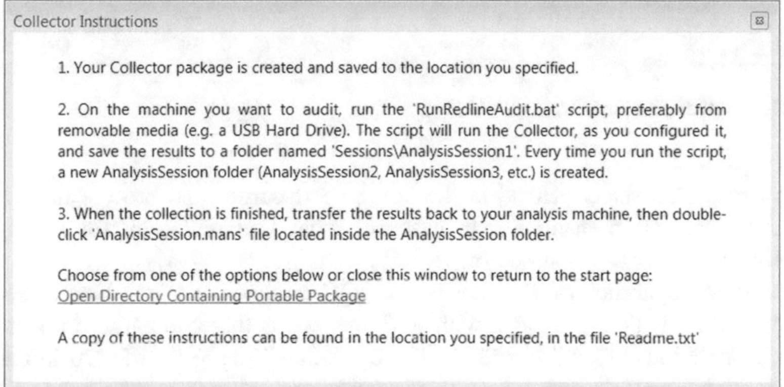

Fig. 21.10 Collector instructions

In essence, there are five different views you can use for analysis:

- "System Information" lets you review basic system information such as operating system, installed data, registered owner, and BIOS information.
- "I am reviewing a Triage Collection from HX" is designed for in-depth analysis of processes and their behavior.
- "I am investigating a Host Based or an External Investigative Lead" is another view where you can analyze events and organize them in a timeline.
- "I am Reviewing Web History Data" is a view that allows you to review browser history.
- "I want to search my search my data with a set of Indicators of Compromise" allows you to import IOC for malicious activity and search for those indicators in the host you are examining.

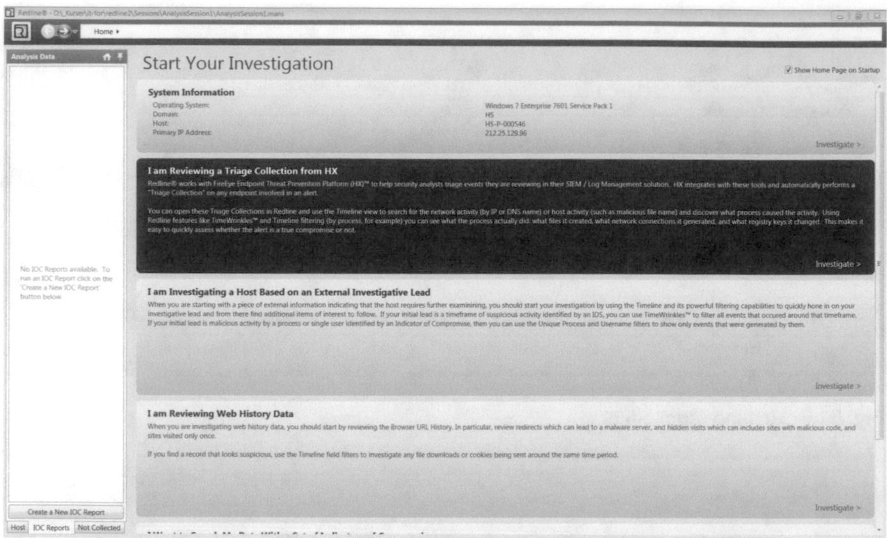

Fig. 21.11 Redline analysis front

You may also select "Host" in the bottom left corner and browse through the acquired information manually. In essence, what you will look for is signs of malicious behavior as discussed previously.

The final capability of Redline is the IOC analysis. As has been discussed previously in this book, the idea with IOC analysis is that you gather indicators of different malicious behaviors and see if those behaviors are manifested in the host you are analyzing. In a case where you identify one infected host in your network, you may create an IOC profile for that infection and use it to analyze other hosts in your network. This approach can reduce the time needed to contain and fully recover from an incident.

To perform an IOC analysis, click the option "I want to search my search my data with a set of Indicators of Compromise" from the analysis home page. This action will take you to the dialogue shown in Fig. 21.12.

In this view, you select a folder where you store IOC specifications. The specifications are essentially XML files. You can then select what specifications to apply to this particular case. In this particular case, the IOC for SpyEye generated hits, as seen in Fig. 21.13. This is not very surprising since the memory dump known to be infected with SpyEye was used for the demonstration in this step.

As seen in Fig. 21.13, Redline suggests that the memory dump is infected with SpyEye and points to the part of the IOC that matches.

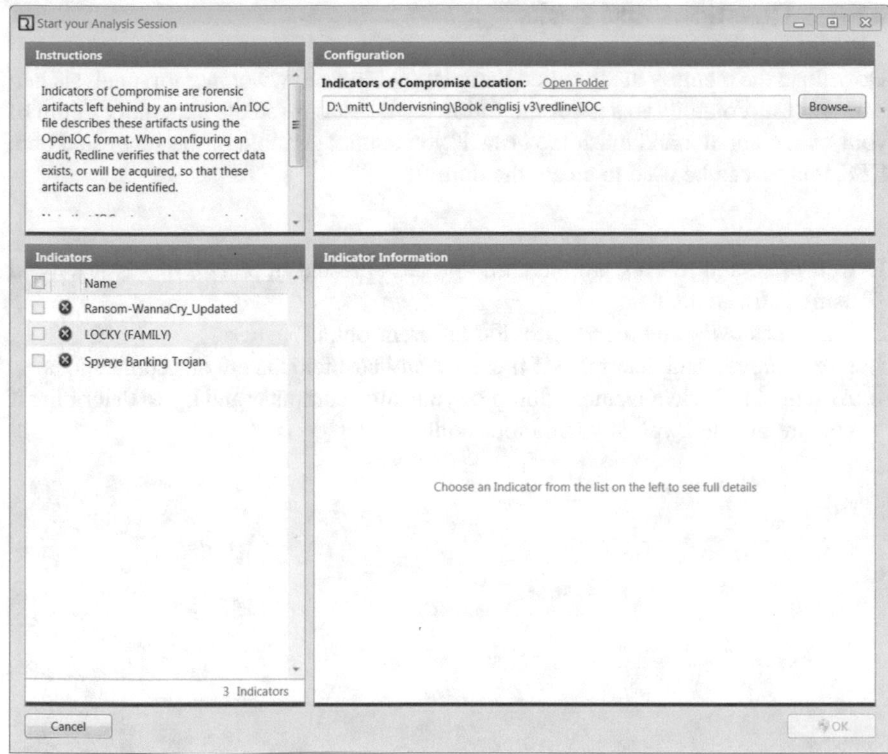

Fig. 21.12 Reline IOC analysis

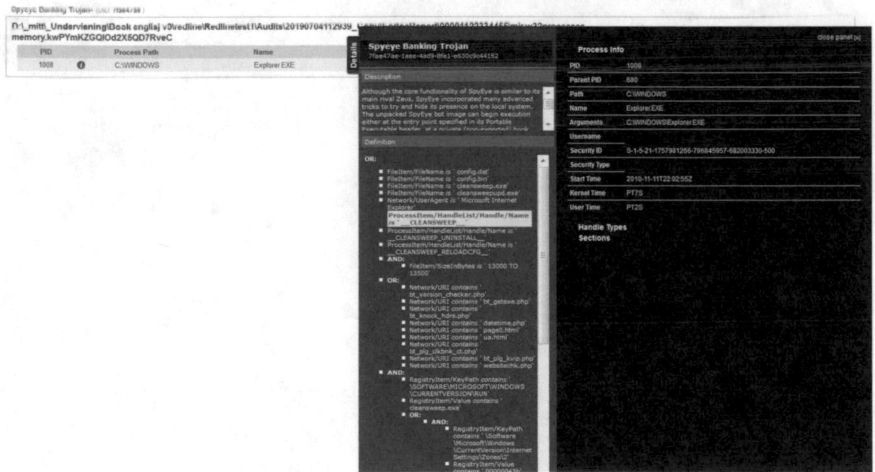

Fig. 21.13 IOC analysis results

21.3 Questions and Tasks

Download the memory dump called Sample009.bin from www.memoryanalysis.net/amf and use Volatility to answer the following questions (create a memory dump of your own computer and finish the tasks if you cannot get hold of the suggested one; FTK imager can be used to create the dump):

1. Run *pslist* and *psscan*; are there any process present in *psscan* that is not listed using *pslist*, if so, name it?
2. Why does *pslist* and *psscan* provide different output?
3. Use connscan and determine if there are any suspicious network connections.
4. As a final task, do a memory dump of your own computer and try to determine if you are infected with any malicious code.

Appendices

Appendix A

Solutions

This appendix presents answers to the questions and tasks for each chapter. Where it is not possible to provide an answer, a discussion is presented instead.

Chapter 1

1. Forensic experts are involved in almost every kind of case. It is very common for digital evidence to be present in any kind of investigation ranging from theft to fraud to murder. The forensic expert's main duty is to examine digital evidence. The forensic expert may also assist during house searches and participate as a consultant on technical questions. IT is quite common that the forensic expert is called to court as a witness, and it happens that the forensic expert assists during interrogations.
2. In example to investigate if someone broke company regulation. Forensic experts are commonly hired to analyze what happened during an intrusion or similar attack or to recover data using forensic techniques.
3. All devices able to carry digital information.
4. The person who ordered the examination, the person owning or using the equipment that is being examined, and the justice system.

Chapter 2

The answers to the questions are best discussed and answered in your class.

Chapter 3

1. Secondary storage devices are every type of device that can store digital information for long-term preservation. While this excludes RAM and cache memory, it includes all types of hard drives, USB sticks, flash cards, CDs, DVDs, and tapes.

J. Kävrestad, *Fundamentals of Digital Forensics*,
https://doi.org/10.1007/978-3-030-38954-3

2. The file is removed from the MFT, and thus, the drive space can be allocated to another file. Until the file is overwritten, it can easily be recovered by searching for file signatures.
3. Resident files are completely located in MFT and nonresident files are not.
4. Because different applications store data in different ways.
5. Use regedit to find out what time zone your computer is set to use.
6. A one-way function that takes some data as input and produces a digest that is unique for that input. For a hash algorithm to be secure, it must be collision resistant and cannot be reversible.

Chapter 4

1. File metadata is information that is maintained by the file system and provides information about a file. In the NTFS file system, the file owner, created date, modified date, accessed date, and more are tracked. EXIF information is also metadata but additional metadata for pictures. This information is generated by the device taking a picture and can include whatever the camera manufacturer chooses but commonly includes camera make and model, time stamps, device serial number, and GPS coordinates describing where the picture was taken.
2. Because they describe how files folders and executables have been used. This information can help in deciding the origin of a file, how often a program has been used, and so forth. Further, these artifacts can show if the computer accessed files and folder or even executables located on a remote storage or a USB device. As such, they can provide clues about what other devices that should be examined.
3. Whenever a folder containing pictures is listed in a mode where miniatures are displayed, a thumbcache database is created for that folder. This database is commonly not removed, and thus, the thumbcache will contain miniatures of pictures that have been deleted from the computer.
4. Examining log files will provide insight into how the computer or a specific program has been used. Many important events that happen in the operating system or a program leave a log entry, and further logs are used by programs to keep track of statistic, connections, messages, and more. As such, analyzing log files can tell you about the circumstances of how a program or the system was used. As one example, analyzing current time settings will tell you if the computer clock is correct or not. Analyzing the log files can tell you if the settings have ever been changed, and this provides information about how reliable time stamps in the computer are.
5. The simple answer is whenever it is of importance to the case. As one example, it could be when a computer was analyzed as part of a crime about illicit images, but no such material was found on the computer. However, a USB device was found in a location that the suspect and several others have access to. The USB device contained illicit images, but the suspect claimed that it was not his; however, analyzing the computer revealed that the USB device has been connected to the computer and used to view the images on the USB device. This was the case in an investigation that the author of this book conducted.

Chapter 5

1. It is an attack where the algorithm used in encryption is attacked and cracked or the implementation of that algorithm. The idea is to find a weakness that allows you to decrypt data without having to figure out the correct password.
2. A brute force attack will try every possible password until the correct one is found, making it an attack that will eventually find the correct password. The downside is that it is very slow and will never find longer password because the time required will be insane. A dictionary attack uses a predefined list of potential passwords and tests them in turn. Thus, it can be much quicker but will only work if the password is present in the dictionary.
3. Creating a good dictionary required the use of several sources of information including:
   (a) Language-specific dictionaries
   (b) Leaked databases
   (c) Compilation of biographical information
   (d) Text indexes

Chapter 6

What you should learn from this task is that digital evidence is common in almost all types of criminal cases. Digital traces are left at many occasions in our lives and can tell much about what a person did, when, and where. Discuss the results of this task with some of your peers and/or teacher!

Chapter 7

Discuss the results of this task with some of your peers and/or teacher.

Chapter 8

1. Because memory holds information that shows what the computer has done since the last reboot. The memory can also hold valuable data such as passwords and encrypted versions of decrypted data.
2. It is a bit-by-bit copy or a storage device. It is considered best practice to create a disk image and analyze the disk image instead of the actual storage device during a forensic examination. This is to ensure that the storage device is not compromised.
3. Volatile data is data that is stored for short-term usage. The contents of the RAM are an example of volatile data.

4. Preparation enhances the ability to perform a live examination with good results. One way to prepare is to have a prepacked bag of tools, and another way is to read up on the suspect that is targeted. This allows you to get an idea of what to expect on the scene. Another part of the preparation step is to synchronize with police officers and others that are taking part in the house search so that you have a good idea about what to expect at the scene.
5. It ensures that the computer that you are examining is not compromised and usually enhances performance. As such, it is often enforced by laws and regulations.

Chapter 9

Discuss the results of this task with some of your peers and/or teacher.

Chapter 10

1. Unbiased means that the results are produced and presented in an objective manner, and reproducible means that the way that the results were achieved is presented good enough for someone else to conduct the same examination with the same results. In a criminal context, this is important to ensure a fair investigation and trial of the suspect of the crime. Further, it means that whenever producing a forensic report that contains conclusions drawn by the forensic expert, those have to be clearly separated from the objective findings.
2. (a) Understand the case: Read up on the case to get an understanding of it.

   (b) Analyze questions/purpose: Understand what the investigators want from the forensic examination.

   (c) Find basic information: Get basic information from the examined devices, such as users and registered owner.

   (d) Find information relating to objectives: Find data relating to what was established in (b).

   (e) Analyze found information: Analyze the findings and draw conclusions.

   (f) Report: Present the findings to the investigators.
3. So that a reader can easily understand and interpret the conclusions drawn during the examination.
4. The simple answer is no in most legislation. This is because Dropbox is a cloud storage service. Analyzing data in the cloud will commonly require additional warrants. When you have a search warrant for a computer or a location that covers what you can find in that location or computer. This means that everything actually stored on the computer is up for grabs, but data stored in other locations is not. In the extreme, a file stored on Dropbox that is open would be stored in RAM and is as such not up for grabs. You may see that the computer is viewing Dropbox in a Web browser and that there are files of interest; you may take a picture of the file listing but not open the actual files as that would require a file

download from a remote location. Note that this topic is up for legal discussion in several legislations and that local law varies, and you should contact an expert on your local law to get a definitive answer to this dilemma.

Chapter 11

1. The images will likely differ in size since they were compressed in different ways.
2. You can use FTK imager, and it is available for free from the AccessData Web page.
3. You can use FTK imager, and it is available for free from the AccessData Web page.
4. As has been clear throughout the book, what steps to take and in what order is case dependent. As such, there are cases where imaging would be done before collection of volatile data and such. In some jurisdictions, the decision can be premade by law since it may only allow for collection of secondary storage. However, more common would be a case where you believe that what is stored in secondary media is of most importance and there are reasons to believe that the computer cannot be accessible long enough for more tasks than imaging. One could also argue that if you believe that the most important evidence will be located in the Pagefile, you do not want to risk compromising that by running unnecessary processes that can cause the Pagefile to be modified due to paging.
5. The process is described by Halderman et al. (2009).

Chapter 12

1. Do it during preprocessing or as additional analysis in FTK, or apply the keyword search ingest module in Autopsy.
2. Happy searching!
3. The regular expressions will mean the following:
   (a) This is a quite evil example as it will match any string of numbers of any size.
   (b) This will match any occurrence or the string .docx.
   (c) This will match any occurrence or an alphanumerical string followed by a space followed by another string of alphanumerical characters. One could use this to match names; however, the purpose of this example is to show that some regular expressions will produce a lot of false positives.
   (d) This will match the string .exe or the string .bin.
4. The differences that appear are due to the fact that the index search is limited by settings for noise words, delimiters, and characters to include in the index. The live search will search all data in the case "as-is."

Chapter 13

1. A mask is a way to express the pattern of a password and can be used to build brute force attacks or combined with. For one, you can have a dictionary attack and append a mask to make Hashcat try every word in the dictionary followed by a year or number.

2. A decryption attack is an attack when a weakness in a the encryption algorithm or implementation of it is exploited in order to crack whatever needs to be cracked without having to guess the password.
3. Allows a hash as input and nothing else; as such you cannot give a compete file to Hashcat. Instead, you need to extract the password hash and pass that to Hashcat.
4. Inception is used by connecting a computer with Inception installer to the target computer over FireWire. If you cannot break your log-in screen, it can be due to one of the following reasons:
   (a) Your computer is set to disable FireWire when the computer is logged off.
   (b) Inception can only access 4 GB of RAM; if it cannot find the log-in process in that area, the attack will not work.
5. Several free tools are available if you search for rar cracking. Using a dictionary with the password included should do the trick, and a brute force is hard against a rar file as it uses a very slow encryption algorithm making the attack time-consuming. If you are using it, you can simply add the file to PRTK and follow the instructions. In Hashcat, you need to extract the password hash from the file and pass the hash to Hashcat.

Chapter 14

1. Found in Windows registry.
2. Found in Windows registry.
3. Found in Windows registry.
4. You can find this data by examining the MBR in FTK imager.
5. Because the file itself is often not deleted. What is deleted is the entry in the MFT.
6. A ZIP archive is a compound file that needs to be expanded before it can be fully analyzed.
7. EXIF data is metadata stored in pictures. Since it can include information such as GPS coordinates, model of the device taking the picture, and name of the device taking the picture, it is very interesting for a forensic examiner.
8. Analyze the MBR to see if there are any gaps between the listed partitions. If gaps are found, the data in the gaps should be further examined to look for signatures of partitions.

Chapter 15

1. There are several factors for why this is hard. The most obvious is that any data can be changed at any time and as such; a forensic examination can describe what is accurate at the time of examination, but saying that something never happened is cumbersome. Further, stating that a computer was not remote controlled implies that the forensic expert analyzed every possible way to remote control a computer. That is near impossible since it requires extreme amounts of time, and it is hard to expect the forensic expert to know about every possible way to remote control a computer.

2. Timelining is an approach where you point out activities that you want to tie to a person and activities that identify that person. The idea is that if someone is evidently using the computer at a time when some interesting action is performed, it is very likely that the identified someone performed the interesting actions. Because of the anonymous nature of data, it is hard to say that a computer was always used by some person, but using timelining, it can be possible to tie certain events to a person.
3. Scenario testing is analyzing a computer to see if a scenario holds true. In the case with remote controlling, a computer scenario testing could be analyzing if the computer was remote controlled using TeamViewer. This makes the scope of the analysis far smaller than if you set out to test if a computer was ever remote controlled. Using a suspect's claim as a scenario can prove or disprove the suspect's statement and act as convicting or freeing evidence.
4. Discuss the results of this task with some of your peers and/or teacher!

Chapter 18

1. Paging is used to temporarily store data allocated in memory on a secondary storage device. The idea is that whenever memory resident data belonging to a process seems to be unused, it can be moved to secondary storage so that another process can use the memory area. If the data is needed again, it can be paged in.
2. The memory is divided into sections called pages, and pages are allocated to processes.
3. The pages allocated to a process in physical memory are often fragmented. To enable the processes to view their memory as a contiguous block, they are each given a virtual memory of their own. The virtual memory can be seen as a sandbox that is private to the process. The virtual memory of a process is mapped to the physical pages assigned to the process.
4. (a) Linked lists: List of elements where the end of every element is a pointer to the next.

   (b) Doubly linked list, same as above but the beginning of every element is also a pointer to the element before.

   (c) Circularly linked list: as a, but the final element contains a backlink to the first element.

Chapter 20

1. UTC: 2009-02-11 20:31, UTC -8: 2009-02-11 12:31
2. alg.exe
3. Malware
4. No.

Note: If you used another memory dump than the suggested, discuss the results with your peers!

Chapter 21

1. Yes, bash.exe with PID1604.
2. In memory, processes are arranged in a linked list. *pslist* will rely on that list to identify processes. *psscan* will instead do a scan of process data structures and can therefore detect processes that attempt to hide from listing or that are terminated.
3. The output would be as follows:

Volatility Foundation Volatility Framework 2.6

Offset (P)	Local address	Remote address	Pid
______	__________	__________	_____
0x01e72590	192:168:128:128 : 1126	66:235:138:2 : 80	292
0x020ba510	192:168:128:128 : 1251	141:209:168:57 : 80	388
0x023c9448	192:168:128:128 : 1135	199:93:33:124 : 80	292
0x023f8008	192:168:128:128 : 1134	12:130:60:3 : 80	292
0x044c671a	115:37:0:0 : 28526	78:101:120:116 : 67	1952671086
0x0c36491e	116:101:73:112 : 25714	82:101:109:111 : 16740	1953723237
0x1b0fef80	9:0:0:0 : 25441	80:105:100:116 : 19567	1919897708

All three bottom connections look highly suspicious. First, the local IP addresses are weird and different. Not knowing much about the computer being examined, we cannot draw more conclusions than that. However, looking to the PID field, the PIDs are extremely high and not present in the process listing. Also, the remote addresses are using port numbers that should raise concerns. The two bottoms are unregistered, the top of the three connections is registered to BOOTP and DHCP, and it makes no sense for the computer to have an open connection to a DHCP server.

1. Discuss the results of this task with some of your peers and/or teacher!

Appendix B

Useful Scripts

This appendix lists a couple of scripts that can be useful for computer forensic experts. Feel free to use, modify, and redistribute as you want and need.

Capturing Basic Computer Information on Mac and Linux

```
#!/usr/bin/perl
use warnings;
use strict;
```

```
#Script that gathers computer time setting and IP-configuration from
running MAC/Linux system
#NOTE: Designed and tested for MAC OS X
print "NOTE! Run the script with elevated permissions if possible
(i.e as root of with sudo)\n";

print "chose name of output file (Will be stored in the location the
script is ran from)\n";
my $outputname=<>;
chomp($outputname);
open(OUT, ">>" ,"$outputname\.txt") or die "Cant open output file";

print "do you want to add case data to outputfile? (yes/no)\n";
my $i=<>;
chomp ($i);
if($i=~/yes/){
        print OUT "----Case data----\n\n";
        print "submit case number:";
        my $casenumber=<>;
        print OUT "CASE: $casenumber";

        print "\nsubmit evidence number:";
        my $evidence=<>;
        print OUT "EVIDENCE: $evidence";

        print "\nsubmit examiner name:";
        my $name=<>;
        print OUT "EXAMINER: $name";

        print "\nsubmit current date and time (Fröken UR):";
        my $realtime=<>;
        print OUT "Time of examination: $realtime";

        print OUT "\n\n----Gathered data presented below----\n";

}

print "\nGathering date and time.......\n";

use POSIX qw(strftime);
my $date = strftime "%Y%m%d_%H%M", localtime;
print OUT "####System date and time###\n $date\n\n";

print "Gathering system hostname......\n";
```

```
my $hostname=`hostname`;

print OUT "####System hostname (including domain information if present)####\n $hostname\n";

print "Gathering system IP-configuration......\n";
my $IPinfo=`ifconfig`;
print OUT "####System ip configuration####\n $IPinfo\n\n";

print "Gathering list of open connections (UDP/TCP)......\n";
my $OC=`netstat -ant`;
my @OC=split(/Active LOCAL/,$OC);

print OUT "####List of open connections####\n $OC[0]\n\n";

print "Gathering list of running processes......\n";
my $processes=`ps -ef`;
print OUT "####List of running processes####\n $processes\n\n";

print "Gathering list of mounted drives/shares......\n";
my $mounts=`mount`;
print OUT "####List of mounted drives/shares####\n $mounts\n\n";

print "Gathering list of system users......\n";
print OUT "####Information about system users####\n ";
my @users=`dscl \. list /Users | grep -v ^_\.\*`;
foreach (@users) {
        my $info=`id $_`;
        chomp($_);
        print OUT "\n---Information about the user $_ ---\n";
        print OUT $info;
}
close (OUT);
```

Capturing Basic Computer Information on Windows

```
#Script that gathers computer time setting and IP-configuration from running Windows
#Note that the script is designed for minimum memory usage

$outpath = Read-host -Prompt 'This script gather basic computer information. Input full path to the output file: '

[Datetime]::Now | Out-File -Append $outpath
Get-WmiObject Win32_Computersystem | Out-File -Append $outpath
```

```
get-wmiobject          win32_networkadapterconfiguration          -filter
"ipenabled=true" | Out-File -Append $outpath
netstat -aonp TCP| Out-File -Append $outpath
Get-Process| Out-File -Append $outpath
gwmi -Class Win32_LogicalDisk| Out-File -Append $outpath
Get-WmiObject        -Class        Win32_UserAccount        -Filter
"LocalAccount='True'"| Out-File -Append $outpath
```

Convert Autopsy Text Index to Useable Dictionary for Password Cracking

```
$filepath = Read-Host -Prompt "Enter full path to input file"
$outpath = Read-Host -Prompt "Enter full path to output file"

#Read input file and split it so that every METADATA entry get its
own array element

[string]$data = get-content -Path $filepath
[array]$new_data    =    $data.Split("--------------------------------
METADATA--------------------------------")

#FOREACH for parsing and extracting text

foreach ($element in $new_data){

     #Skip the parsing for the first element since it contains
unwanted data
     if($element -match "Lucene41PostingsWriter"){continue}

     #Slipt the datablob on whitespace and some special characters.
Hypens, dot etc, will be kept
     [array]$words = $element -split "[^\p{Ll}\p{Lu}\p{Lt}\p{Lo}\p
{Nd}\p{P}]+"

    #controlfulction to only extract words containing actual non-
whitepsace characters and that
    #are at least 4 characters long. Modify the three to change the
lenght treshhold
    foreach($word in $words){
            if($word -match "\w" -and $word.Length -gt 3) {

                #Append selected words to a file containing one word
per row
             Out-File -FilePath $outpath -InputObject $word -Append
                }
        }

    }
```

Parse Jitsi Chat Logs

```
#Script that parses jitsi chat logs and prints in a nice format.
#Note <msg> section needs to be cleaned to only include <msg> MES-
SAGE </msg> before using the script
#This can be done using search and replace in some text editor
#Prompt for input and output file paths and username of the local
and remote char accounts
$path = Read-Host "Enter path to source file: "
$outpath = Read-Host "Enter path, including filename, to output file:
"
$local = Read-Host "Enter the local username: "
$remote = Read-Host "Enter remote username: "

#Initiate arrays used later
$messages = @()
$messages_tidy = @()

#Import chat log content into a XML object, then select specific
objects of interest
[xml]$chatlog = Get-Content $path
$chatlog.history.record | %{$messages += $_.dir + ";" + $_.msg +
";" +  $_.timestamp}

#Replace in and out keywords width actual usernames
foreach($index in $messages){
    if($index -like "out*"){

        [regex]$pattern = "out"
        $messages_tidy += $pattern.replace($index,$local, 1)
        }
    elseif($index -like "in*"){
        [regex]$pattern = "in"
        $messages_tidy += $pattern.replace($index, $remote, 1)
        }
    }

#Ensure that no messages gets lost in the process...
if($messages.Length -ne $messages_tidy.Length){
    echo "Some message seems missing, exiting now......"
    break;
    }

#Write a headerrow and then output chat messaged to the outputfile.
```

```
$header = "Sender;Message;Timestamp"
Out-File -FilePath $outpath -InputObject $header

foreach($message in $messages_tidy){
    Out-File -FilePath $outpath -InputObject $message -Append

}
```

Appendix C

Sample Report (Template)

Protocol of Forensic Examination of Computer 1234567-32

Examination Data

Examination requested by:	Name of requesting officer
Lead forensic investigator:	Name of forensic expert in charge
Reason for examination:	Questions and objectives
Time of examination	Timespan of the examination
Additional information	Additional information such as what the suspect or some other person claimed

Summary

Provide a short summary of the examination and the results. It can be clever to include a vocabulary at the end of the report and mark all words explained in the vocabulary, for instance, using a "∗". Refer to the vocabulary in the summary. If the examination covers one piece of evidence, you can note the evidence identifier in the headline; otherwise, you need to list all evidence covered in the report, for instance, with a listing in the summary∗.

Findings

Your report should include a chapter with your objective findings. Whenever appropriate, include how you uncovered your findings and refer to exported material. A good line would be pictures that appear to be of pills were found on the desktop, and they were exported and delivered to the investigator on a USB drive. Further, GPS coordinates (1234, 1234) and model name (Canon D105) of the camera taking the picture were found in the Metadata of all pictures.

Conclusions

The conclusions section is where you can draw conclusion based on your findings. You may also include other sources of data such as information from interrogations or likewise. Based on the sample findings above, a proper line could be a visual inspection of the encountered pictures that tell that they seem to be of pills similar to the drugs seized during the house search. Further, the GPS coordinated matches the suspect's home address, and the camera used to take the pictures was the same as the one found in the suspect's home. In conclusion, the analysis strongly suggests that the pictures were taken at the suspect's home address and portrait the same or similar pills as the one found during the house search.

Word List

Summary—A summary is a short version of something.

Joakim Kävrestad
Forensic examiner at some police department.

Sample Report (Example Case in Chap. 7)

Protocol of Forensic Examination of Computer 1234567-32

Examination Data

Examination requested by:	Peregrin Took
Lead forensic investigator	Joakim Kävrestad
Reason for examination	Identify if pictures found in fraudulent ads can be tied to the computer and/or the suspect in the case
Time of examination	2018-05-14 to 2018-05-17
Additional information	Suspect claims that the pictures in the ads may be present on his computer due to him browsing said ads using the computer

Summary

The purpose of this examination was to identify if pictures used in online fraud ads were present on the computer that is the target of the examination. The pictures used in the ads were given to the examiner by the Officer Took. The examination should also attempt to determine how the pictures had been used on the computer and if they could be tied to the suspect. After the pictures had been discovered, it came of interest to analyze if the pictures had been taken with the suspect phone, an iPhone X with serial number 123456—analyzed and presented in a separate protocol.

Pictures that visually appeared to be the same as in the ads were found on the computer, and thus, the examination came to cover analysis of the pictures. Based on the EXIF∗ data in pictures, it could be determined that they were taken with an iPhone X at GPS coordinates that were in close proximity to the suspect's address.

Words marked with an asterisk (∗) are presented at the end of the protocol.

Findings

Hash lookup∗ was used to identify if the pictures used in the ads were present on the computer. A hash∗ database containing the pictures from the ads was created and matched with a hash database containing all files on the computer. Visual inspection of the matching pictures was performed to validate the results. The hash lookup identified that all pictures used in the ads were present on the computer in a folder called "C:\PICS." The names of the found pictures were:

- Jacket.jpg
- Shoes.jpg
- Merrys awesome sword.jpg

The pictures was extracted from the computers and delivered to Officer Took on a DVD.

EXIF data was extracted from the found pictures, and the EXIF data included name of the model of the camera and GPS coordinates. The EXIF information was the same for all pictures and included the following information:

- Camera model: iPhone X
- GPS coordinates:
  - Latitude 68.27211388888889
  - Longitude 23.715005555555555
  - Altitude 168.26573426573427

The ∗ was examined, and the key *Software\Microsoft\Windows\CurrentVersion \Explorer\RecentDocs\jpg* showed that the computer has been used to open the pictures.

Conclusions

The first aim of this was to identify if pictures used in fraudulent ads were present on the computer. Pictures that visually appeared to be the same as the pictures in the ads were found in the folder "C:\PICS"; further, hash lookup was used to identify the pictures and showed that the pictures in the ads matched the pictures stored on the computer exactly. In summary, the analysis shows that the pictures in the ads were present in the computer.

Further, the suspect claimed that the pictures could be stored in his computer due to him browsing the ads using a Web browser. When browsing the Internet, pictures may be downloaded to your computer and stored in predeterminable temporary folders. "C:\PICS" is not such a folder. Further, the analysis of the Windows registry shows that the pictures have been opened using the computer. In summary, the analysis strongly suggests that the suspects claim cannot explain how the pictures were placed on the computer.

Looking into how the pictures ended up on the computer and where they came from, the EXIF data was examined and showed that they were taken in close proximity to the suspect's home address and with a phone of the same make and model as the suspect's phone. This indicates that the pictures were taken using the suspect's phone.

Word List

EXIF—EXIF data is data stored in an image file that provides information about the image. The data can include what camera that took the picture, GPS coordinates, and more.

Hash—A hash is a function that can create a unique alphanumerical value from a data set. The data set can be anything from a picture to a word file, and the value can be compared to a fingerprint of the input value.

Hash lookup—The process of comparing hash values for different files to determine if they are identical.

Joakim Kävrestad
Forensic examiner at Awesome police station.

Appendix D

List of Time Zones

See Table 1.

Table 1 List of time zones (Microsoft. 2017-3)

Name of time zone	Time
Dateline Standard Time	(GMT−12:00) International Date Line West
Samoa Standard Time	(GMT−11:00) Midway Island, Samoa
Hawaiian Standard Time	(GMT−10:00) Hawaii
Alaskan Standard Time	(GMT−09:00) Alaska
Pacific Standard Time	(GMT−08:00) Pacific Time (USA and Canada); Tijuana
Mountain Standard Time	(GMT−07:00) Mountain Time (USA and Canada)
Mexico Standard Time 2	(GMT−07:00) Chihuahua, La Paz, Mazatlan
US Mountain Standard Time	(GMT−07:00) Arizona
Central Standard Time	(GMT−06:00) Central Time (USA and Canada)
Canada Central Standard Time	(GMT−06:00) Saskatchewan
Mexico Standard Time	(GMT−06:00) Guadalajara, Mexico City, Monterrey

(continued)

Table 1 (continued)

Name of time zone	Time
Central America Standard Time	(GMT−06:00) Central America
Eastern Standard Time	(GMT−05:00) Eastern Time (USA and Canada)
US Eastern Standard Time	(GMT−05:00) Indiana (East)
S.A. Pacific Standard Time	(GMT−05:00) Bogota, Lima, Quito
Atlantic Standard Time	(GMT−04:00) Atlantic Time (Canada)
S.A. Western Standard Time	(GMT−04:00) Caracas, La Paz
Pacific S.A. Standard Time	(GMT−04:00) Santiago
Newfoundland and Labrador Standard Time	(GMT−03:30) Newfoundland and Labrador
E. South America Standard Time	(GMT−03:00) Brasilia
S.A. Eastern Standard Time	(GMT−03:00) Buenos Aires, Georgetown
Greenland Standard Time	(GMT−03:00) Greenland
Mid-Atlantic Standard Time	(GMT−02:00) Mid-Atlantic
Azores Standard Time	(GMT−01:00) Azores
Cape Verde Standard Time	(GMT−01:00) Cape Verde Islands
GMT Standard Time	(GMT) Greenwich Mean Time: Dublin, Edinburgh, Lisbon, London
Greenwich Standard Time	(GMT) Casablanca, Monrovia
Central Europe Standard Time	(GMT+01:00) Belgrade, Bratislava, Budapest, Ljubljana, Prague
Central European Standard Time	(GMT+01:00) Sarajevo, Skopje, Warsaw, Zagreb
Romance Standard Time	(GMT+01:00) Brussels, Copenhagen, Madrid, Paris
W. Europe Standard Time	(GMT+01:00) Amsterdam, Berlin, Bern, Rome, Stockholm, Vienna
W. Central Africa Standard Time	(GMT+01:00) West Central Africa
E. Europe Standard Time	(GMT+02:00) Bucharest
Egypt Standard Time	(GMT+02:00) Cairo
FLE Standard Time	(GMT+02:00) Helsinki, Kiev, Riga, Sofia, Tallinn, Vilnius
GTB Standard Time	(GMT+02:00) Athens, Istanbul, Minsk
Israel Standard Time	(GMT+02:00) Jerusalem
South Africa Standard Time	(GMT+02:00) Harare, Pretoria
Russian Standard Time	(GMT+03:00) Moscow, St. Petersburg, Volgograd
Arab Standard Time	(GMT+03:00) Kuwait, Riyadh
E. Africa Standard Time	(GMT+03:00) Nairobi
Arabic Standard Time	(GMT+03:00) Baghdad
Iran Standard Time	(GMT+03:30) Tehran
Arabian Standard Time	(GMT+04:00) Abu Dhabi, Muscat
Caucasus Standard Time	(GMT+04:00) Baku, Tbilisi, Yerevan
Transitional Islamic State of Afghanistan Standard Time	(GMT+04:30) Kabul
Ekaterinburg Standard Time	(GMT+05:00) Ekaterinburg
West Asia Standard Time	(GMT+05:00) Islamabad, Karachi, Tashkent

(continued)

Table 1 (continued)

Name of time zone	Time
India Standard Time	(GMT+05:30) Chennai, Kolkata, Mumbai, New Delhi
Nepal Standard Time	(GMT+05:45) Kathmandu
Central Asia Standard Time	(GMT+06:00) Astana, Dhaka
Sri Lanka Standard Time	(GMT+06:00) Sri Jayawardenepura
N. Central Asia Standard Time	(GMT+06:00) Almaty, Novosibirsk
Myanmar Standard Time	(GMT+06:30) Yangon Rangoon
S.E. Asia Standard Time	(GMT+07:00) Bangkok, Hanoi, Jakarta
North Asia Standard Time	(GMT+07:00) Krasnoyarsk
China Standard Time	(GMT+08:00) Beijing, Chongqing, Hong Kong SAR, Urumqi
Singapore Standard Time	(GMT+08:00) Kuala Lumpur, Singapore
Taipei Standard Time	(GMT+08:00) Taipei
W. Australia Standard Time	(GMT+08:00) Perth
North Asia East Standard Time	(GMT+08:00) Irkutsk, Ulaanbaatar
Korea Standard Time	(GMT+09:00) Seoul
Tokyo Standard Time	(GMT+09:00) Osaka, Sapporo, Tokyo
Yakutsk Standard Time	(GMT+09:00) Yakutsk
A.U.S. Central Standard Time	(GMT+09:30) Darwin
Cen. Australia Standard Time	(GMT+09:30) Adelaide
A.U.S. Eastern Standard Time	(GMT+10:00) Canberra, Melbourne, Sydney
E. Australia Standard Time	(GMT+10:00) Brisbane
Tasmania Standard Time	(GMT+10:00) Hobart
Vladivostok Standard Time	(GMT+10:00) Vladivostok
West Pacific Standard Time	(GMT+10:00) Guam, Port Moresby
Central Pacific Standard Time	(GMT+11:00) Magadan, Solomon Islands, New Caledonia
Fiji Islands Standard Time	(GMT+12:00) Fiji Islands, Kamchatka, Marshall Islands
New Zealand Standard Time	(GMT+12:00) Auckland, Wellington
Tonga Standard Time	(GMT+13:00) Nuku'alofa

Reference

Microsoft (2017-3) Microsoft time zone index values. Available online: https://msdn.microsoft.com/en-us/library/ms912391(v=winembedded.11).aspx. Fetched July 1, 2017

Appendix E

Complete Jitsi Chat Log


```
<?xml version="1.0" encoding="UTF-8" standalone="no"?>
<history>
  <record timestamp="2017-06-27T13:16:07.826+0200">
    <dir>in</dir>
    <msg><![CDATA[zup_]]></msg>
    <msgTyp>text/plain</msgTyp>
    <enc>UTF-8</enc>
    <uid>1498562173704181378 90</uid>
                <receivedTimestamp>2017-06-27T13:16:07.260+0200</
receivedTimestamp>
  </record>
  <record timestamp="2017-06-27T13:16:21.179+0200">
    <dir>out</dir>
    <msg><![CDATA[kollar lite affärer....sj?]]></msg>
    <msgTyp>text/plain</msgTyp>
    <enc>UTF-8</enc>
    <uid>149856218114519064878</uid>
                <receivedTimestamp>2017-06-27T13:16:21.149+0200</
receivedTimestamp>
  </record>
  <record timestamp="2017-06-27T13:16:42.293+0200">
    <dir>in</dir>
    <msg><![CDATA[samma, lurar p[ vad som ar vart att salja..]]
></msg>
    <msgTyp>text/plain</msgTyp>
    <enc>UTF-8</enc>
    <uid>149856220870413141993</uid>
                <receivedTimestamp>2017-06-27T13:16:42.259+0200</
receivedTimestamp>
  </record>
  <record timestamp="2017-06-27T13:16:52.792+0200">
    <dir>out</dir>
    <msg><![CDATA[hur säkrar du?]]></msg>
    <msgTyp>text/plain</msgTyp>
    <enc>UTF-8</enc>

    <uid>149856221278425383895</uid>
                <receivedTimestamp>2017-06-27T13:16:52.785+0200</
receivedTimestamp>
  </record>
  <record timestamp="2017-06-27T13:17:20.785+0200">
```

```
      <dir>in</dir>
      <msg><![CDATA[kor engelsk dator, svart lista ut vart jag ar!]]></msg>
      <msgTyp>text/plain</msgTyp>
      <enc>UTF-8</enc>
      <uid>14985622472202168995</uid>
      <receivedTimestamp>2017-06-27T13:17:20.774+0200</receivedTimestamp>
   </record>
   <record timestamp="2017-06-27T13:17:30.963+0200">
      <dir>out</dir>
      <msg><![CDATA[tror inte det funkar, ,lira tor!]]></msg>
      <msgTyp>text/plain</msgTyp>
      <enc>UTF-8</enc>
      <uid>14985622509533149O715</uid>
      <receivedTimestamp>2017-06-27T13:17:30.955+0200</receivedTimestamp>
   </record>
   <record timestamp="2017-06-27T13:17:46.289+0200">
      <dir>in</dir>
      <msg><![CDATA[har kollat pa det, vet inte, krangligt!]]></msg>
      <msgTyp>text/plain</msgTyp>
      <enc>UTF-8</enc>
      <uid>14985622727203437744</uid>
      <receivedTimestamp>2017-06-27T13:17:46.272+0200</receivedTimestamp>
   </record>
   <record timestamp="2017-06-27T13:18:16.749+0200">
      <dir>out</dir>
      <msg><![CDATA[vi får se...., ska ut o köra nu]]></msg>
      <msgTyp>text/plain</msgTyp>
      <enc>UTF-8</enc>
      <uid>14985622967401999847</uid>
      <receivedTimestamp>2017-06-27T13:18:16.741+0200</receivedTimestamp>
   </record>
   <record timestamp="2017-06-27T13:18:22.691+0200">
      <dir>in</dir>
      <msg><![CDATA[k thx bye]]></msg>
      <msgTyp>text/plain</msgTyp>
      <enc>UTF-8</enc>
      <uid>14985623091289998450</uid>
      <receivedTimestamp>2017-06-27T13:18:22.680+0200</receivedTimestamp>
```

```
    </record>
    <record timestamp="2017-06-29T09:25:10.619+0200">
        <dir>in</dir>
        <msg><![CDATA[hade din konakt winky eller?]]></msg>
        <msgTyp>text/plain</msgTyp>

        <enc>UTF-8</enc>
        <uid>14987211118332315 7419</uid>
        <receivedTimestamp>2017-06-29T09:25:10.584+0200</receivedTimestamp>
    </record>
    <record timestamp="2017-06-29T09:25:16.007+0200">
        <dir>out</dir>
        <msg><![CDATA[ring]]></msg>
        <msgTyp>text/plain</msgTyp>
        <enc>UTF-8</enc>
        <uid>14987211160015132863</uid>
        <receivedTimestamp>2017-06-29T09:25:16.003+0200</receivedTimestamp>
    </record>
    <record timestamp="2017-06-29T11:28:56.442+0200">
        <dir>in</dir>
        <msg><![CDATA[lol, din gubbe ville att jag ska betala till polen, tror du detta funkar för att göra bakkoton?]]></msg>
        <msgTyp>text/plain</msgTyp>
        <enc>UTF-8</enc>
        <uid>14987285280463313 5586</uid>
        <receivedTimestamp>2017-06-29T11:29:00.000+0200</receivedTimestamp>
    </record>
    <record timestamp="2017-06-29T11:29:19.585+0200">
        <dir>out</dir>
        <msg><![CDATA[hallå SKICKA INTE SÅNT!]]></msg>
        <msgTyp>text/plain</msgTyp>
        <enc>UTF-8</enc>
        <uid>14987285595673328 9131</uid>
        <receivedTimestamp>2017-06-29T11:29:19.576+0200</receivedTimestamp>
    </record>
    <record timestamp="2017-06-29T11:29:28.633+0200">
        <dir>out</dir>
        <msg><![CDATA[men ja.....idiot!]]></msg>
        <msgTyp>text/plain</msgTyp>
        <enc>UTF-8</enc>
```

```
      <uid>149872856862214632876</uid>
                  <receivedTimestamp>2017-06-29T11:29:28.625+0200</
receivedTimestamp>
   </record>
   <record timestamp="2017-06-29T11:29:38.044+0200">
      <dir>out</dir>
      <msg><![CDATA[lugn, jag shreddar den]]></msg>
      <msgTyp>text/plain</msgTyp>
      <enc>UTF-8</enc>
      <uid>14987285780318102467</uid>
                  <receivedTimestamp>2017-06-29T11:29:38.034+0200</
receivedTimestamp>
   </record>

   <record timestamp="2017-06-29T11:30:13.642+0200">
      <dir>in</dir>
      <msg><![CDATA[rätt najs väder hos hemma!]]></msg>
      <msgTyp>text/plain</msgTyp>
      <enc>UTF-8</enc>
      <uid>149872861126430554666</uid>
                  <receivedTimestamp>2017-06-29T11:30:13.633+0200</
receivedTimestamp>
   </record>
   <record timestamp="2017-06-29T11:31:09.292+0200">
      <dir>out</dir>
      <msg><![CDATA[gött, ordning på saker?]]></msg>
      <msgTyp>text/plain</msgTyp>
      <enc>UTF-8</enc>
      <uid>14987286692808427856</uid>
                  <receivedTimestamp>2017-06-29T11:31:09.284+0200</
receivedTimestamp>
   </record>
   <record timestamp="2017-06-29T11:31:18.105+0200">
      <dir>in</dir>
      <msg><![CDATA[visst, rullar på karnekegränd!]]></msg>
      <msgTyp>text/plain</msgTyp>
      <enc>UTF-8</enc>
      <uid>149872867571729818420</uid>
                  <receivedTimestamp>2017-06-29T11:31:18.096+0200</
receivedTimestamp>
   </record>
   <record timestamp="2017-06-29T11:31:28.658+0200">
      <dir>out</dir>
```

```
      <msg><![CDATA[kasnke vi ska slå samman?]]></msg>
      <msgTyp>text/plain</msgTyp>
      <enc>UTF-8</enc>
      <uid>149872868864331461466</uid>
                  <receivedTimestamp>2017-06-29T11:31:28.648+0200</
receivedTimestamp>
   </record>
   <record timestamp="2017-06-29T11:31:40.794+0200">
      <dir>in</dir>
      <msg><![CDATA[får se, bra o ha ensam buisness]]></msg>
      <msgTyp>text/plain</msgTyp>
      <enc>UTF-8</enc>
      <uid>14987286984212875993</uid>
                  <receivedTimestamp>2017-06-29T11:31:40.786+0200</
receivedTimestamp>
   </record>
   <record timestamp="2017-06-29T11:43:25.330+0200">
      <dir>in</dir>
     <msg><![CDATA[lol på bilerna på dig me mina saker...ser ganster
ut]]></msg>
      <msgTyp>text/plain</msgTyp>
      <enc>UTF-8</enc>

      <uid>149872940290527785517</uid>
                  <receivedTimestamp>2017-06-29T11:43:25.322+0200</
receivedTimestamp>
   </record>
   <record timestamp="2017-06-29T11:43:45.855+0200">
      <dir>out</dir>
      <msg><![CDATA[haha idd, du hade av metadata på kameran va?]]
></msg>
      <msgTyp>text/plain</msgTyp>
      <enc>UTF-8</enc>
      <uid>149872942584328989997</uid>
                  <receivedTimestamp>2017-06-29T11:43:45.847+0200</
receivedTimestamp>
   </record>
   <record timestamp="2017-06-29T11:43:55.456+0200">
      <dir>in</dir>
      <msg><![CDATA[lol ja e la inte dum eller, altid AV1]]></msg>
      <msgTyp>text/plain</msgTyp>
      <enc>UTF-8</enc>
      <uid>149872943303024228041</uid>
                  <receivedTimestamp>2017-06-29T11:43:55.448+0200</
receivedTimestamp>
   </record>
```

```
   <record timestamp="2017-06-30T10:07:32.788+0200">
      <dir>in</dir>
      <msg><![CDATA[fixa mer winks]]></msg>
      <msgTyp>text/plain</msgTyp>
      <enc>UTF-8</enc>
      <uid>149881004661110933177</uid>
                 <receivedTimestamp>2017-06-30T10:07:32.777+0200</
receivedTimestamp>
      </record>
      <record timestamp="2017-06-30T10:07:38.409+0200">
      <dir>out</dir>
      <msg><![CDATA[kom fort]]></msg>
      <msgTyp>text/plain</msgTyp>
      <enc>UTF-8</enc>
      <uid>149881005839726360958</uid>
                 <receivedTimestamp>2017-06-30T10:07:38.398+0200</
receivedTimestamp>
   </record>
 </history>
```

Index

J. Kävrestad, *Fundamentals of Digital Forensics*,
https://doi.org/10.1007/978-3-030-38954-3

Printed in the United States
By Bookmasters